# The Unseen Archives

## A photographic history of

# Manchester United

First published in 1999 by Mustard

Mustard is an imprint of Parragon

Parragon
Queen Street House
4 Queen Street
Bath
BA1 1HE, UK

ISBN 1 84164 293 2

Produced by
International Publishing Associates
PO Box 8
Lydney
Gloucestershire
GL15 4YN
UK

Book design and research by Lance Bellers
Written by Steve Absalom and Simon Spinks
Image Quality and Scanning by John Symonds

With thanks to Hugh Gallagher, Paul O'Donnell, Michelle Gabbidon,
Allie Saunders, Paula Bellers and Ian Wylie.

# Contents

# The Agony And

They became the kings of Europe on May 26, 1999. One night in Barcelona clinched the treble, a place in football history and finally laid to rest the ghost of the 1968 team. The class of '99 at last surpassed the masters of yesteryear on what would have been Sir Matt Busby's 90th birthday, the man who started it all 45 years ago.

But the manner of United's astonishing victory over Bayern Munich was typical of the club – two goals in injury time won the game after an unbearable 90 minutes at 1-0 down. The history of Manchester United is one of the Agony and the Ecstasy. As Alex Ferguson has said: "This team tortures you, and then delights you like no other."

In this book you will see as never before how the history of Manchester United unfurled, thanks to the last great archive of photographs, recently discovered in the libraries of the newspapers in Mirror Group.

From United's beginnings as a railwayman's scratch team at Newton Heath in 1878 to the recent glorious assault on the bastions of European football, and its elevation to the realms of "the world's richest football club", every fan down the ages has experienced a rollercoaster of emotions.

Fathers and sons, mothers and daughters, have endured the agony of failure – unthinkable relegation in the seventies at the hands of Manchester City – and the unforgettable tragedy of February 6, 1958, when a team many regarded as the finest British club squad ever assembled was all but wiped out at Munich Airport during a bid for the elusive European Cup. The ghosts of Duncan Edwards, Tommy Taylor and their colleagues still hover over Old Trafford in the minds of millions around the world who have followed the club's fortunes.

But there have been so many high points which make Manchester United so special. The rebuilding of the club after the war by the man still seen as the Godfather of Old Trafford, Matt Busby, brought not only trophy success but a host of players who injected skill, glamour and yes, a certain controversy into English football which few genuine football fans can deny. The names of Bobby Charlton, George Best, Denis Law and Nobby Stiles are revered as much today among the faithful as when they took on Europe in the memorable 1968 European Cup Final at Wembley and destroyed Benfica 4-1 with a display of footballing passion and grace so often absent from English performances against foreign opposition.

Though the team's fortunes declined somewhat in the seventies, with the sting of relegation, brought on by Denis Law's infamous

# The Ecstasy

back heel for Manchester City to send United into Division Two, there were still great names brought into the fold. Stalwarts such as Martin Buchan, Steve Coppell, Stuart Pearson and Lou Macari provided the same verve that has always been United's trademark. Manager Tommy Docherty was an inspiration, taking The Reds to the Division 2 championship in 1975, and two successive Cup Finals, an achievement still talked about in Manchester pubs.

I t was the eighties which saw United regain their confidence to take on the big guns again. Although the Holy Grail of the championship would elude them for a decade, a strong team base was being built by manager Ron Atkinson – not in many fans' minds a typical United manager but appreciated nevertheless – with the likes of Robson, Ray "Butch" Wilkins, Gordon Strachan and the inimitable Mark "Sparky" Hughes. These were the players who would re-establish United as a major force in football and remain loyal to the club they adored as much as the fans.

But United also changed with the times as clubs started to look abroad for talent, and there is one name on every United fan's lips when the reign of the Foreign Legion started at Manchester United in the nineties under the managership of Alex Ferguson,

a chip off the Busby block if ever there was one. Eric Cantona, picked up for a snip from Leeds, transformed The Reds into a formidable force, leading the team with a swashbuckling style rarely seen since the days of Denis Law. His goals, his presence on the pitch, the upturned collar which so annoyed defenders as much as his consummate skill and his seeming dismissal of anything less than immaculate, brought a new dimension to United as they marched towards the double in 1994.

He was joined, of course, by the young talent United were nurturing. Beckham, Giggs, Scholes and Butt have taken the team to even greater achievement and given the club a youth base the envy of the world.

The magic and mystique of Manchester United are not difficult to pinpoint. It is simply that the mediocre will never do, only the best will get to wear the red and white and managers like Ferguson are continuing a tradition which goes back 50 years.

As United enter a new Millennium, the team's following has exploded. It has been estimated that, around the world, over four million support The Reds and follow their progress religiously.

As Alex Ferguson said after watching the team fight its way to the historic treble, the first team in Europe to do so:

"It doesn't get much better than this."

# In The Beginning

**W**hen Manchester United won their fifth Championship in seven seasons this year; a jubilant Alex Ferguson, never one to overstate his case, called his squad of superstars "The gods of the game". In today's high-octane, billion-pound business of football, that was high praise indeed, and justified after a season of astonishing success and glamour. But the real founding fathers of what is now the biggest club in the world were a group of Lancashire And Yorkshire Railway workers who got together over 120 years ago to create a football team. They were hard, no-nonsense men bred on the work ethic at the heart of industrial England who loved the game and took it seriously. Newton Heath LYR – The Heathens as they quickly became known locally – was born and with it a legend that has spanned the century and spread like a religion across the world. Initially, the team played other departments of the LYR or rival railway companies, though they eyed the giants of the then Football League, such as Preston North End and Blackburn Rovers, enviously. But they were good, so good in fact that they dominated the local opposition and quickly established a reputation as tough, yet skillful team. By 1890 they were confident enough to apply for membership of the Football League, but were rejected. Undaunted, the team applied three times and were finally accepted in 1892 as the League was restructured with Newton Heath joining the First Division. But it was a baptism of fire and disappointment. The club finished bottom in its first season, leaking 85 goals and gaining just 18 points as the team struggled on quagmire pitches to gain a foothold among the elite. The second season was even worse. Newton Heath were relegated to the Second Division where they stayed for two years and by 1898 suffered the agony of watching rivals Manchester City take their place in the First. The club was heading for big trouble. Disciplinary problems with players

didn't help team morale and as crowds deserted them the club faced the ignominy of bankruptcy. Even its then president, William Healey, wanted out and attempted to have the club wound up because of the money – almost £243 – he was owed. But as always in times of such adversity, a lifeline was thrown in the form of the team's captain and full-back Harry Stafford. He ran an amazing fundraising campaign to cover the team's expenses and then enlisted the help of local businessmen in injecting new funds into the club, the fore-runner of sponsorship which is so much an integral part of football today. Now that is what is called a defender!

But the experience of fighting for its life had changed Newton Heath beyond all recognition. It now had the financial muscle to progress with new players, and a new management under breweries boss John Henry Davies as president. The decision was taken to change the name. But to what? The name of Manchester had to be in there somewhere. Manchester Central? Manchester Celtic even? Both were rejected in favour of a title which one day would become famous in every corner of the world. In 1902, Newton Heath became officially – Manchester United.

**T**hese then were the crucial – if painful – birth pangs of the club we know and follow so avidly today. United could look forward at last and the arrival of its first real manager, Burnley secretary Ernest Mangnall, in 1903 signalled the start of the club as a thoroughly professional, up-to-date outfit. He brought in new players like goalkeeper Harry Moger, strikers Charlie Sagar and John Picken and by 1905 United were a force to be reckoned with, reaching the quarter-finals of the FA Cup and ending the season with the joy of promotion to Division One at last after 12 years in the doldrums. Mangnall was no slouch in the transfer business, snapping up now legendary names such as

---

IN THE BEGINNING

## 1899/00

On the face of it Newton Heath had quite a good season, but they had failed to gain promotion again and the money was running out fast. However, there were some good league results to cheer fans. The Heathens whipped Grimsby Town 7-0 away at Christmas and left both Luton Town and Walsall trailing 5-0 later in the season. They won 20 out of the 34 games they played, lost 10, drew four and finished fourth with 44 points. Sadly, it was downhill all the way from then on.

**League (Division 2)**

| | | | | |
|---|---|---|---|---|
| Sep 2 | Gainsborough T | H | D | 2-2 |
| Sep 9 | Bolton W | A | L | 1-2 |
| Sep 16 | Loughborough T | H | W | 4-0 |
| Sep 23 | Burton Swifts | A | D | 0-0 |
| Sep 30 | Sheffield Wed | A | L | 1-2 |
| Oct 7 | Lincoln C | H | W | 1-0 |
| Oct 14 | Small Heath | A | L | 0-1 |
| Oct 21 | New Brighton | H | W | 2-1 |
| Nov 4 | Arsenal | H | W | 2-0 |
| Nov 11 | Burton Swifts | H | W | 4-0 |
| Nov 25 | Luton T | A | W | 1-0 |
| Dec 2 | Port Vale | H | W | 3-0 |
| Dec 16 | Middlesbrough | A | W | 2-1 |
| Dec 23 | Chesterfield | A | L | 1-2 |
| Dec 26 | Grimsby T | A | W | 7-0 |
| Dec 30 | Gainsborough T | A | W | 1-0 |
| Jan 6 | Bolton W | H | L | 1-2 |
| Jan 13 | Loughborough T | A | W | 2-0 |
| Jan 20 | Burton Swifts | H | W | 4-0 |
| Feb 3 | Sheffield Wed | H | W | 1-0 |
| Feb 10 | Lincoln C | A | L | 0-1 |
| Feb 17 | Small Heath | H | W | 3-2 |
| Feb 24 | New Brighton | A | W | 4-1 |
| Mar 3 | Grimsby T | H | W | 1-0 |
| Mar 10 | Arsenal | A | L | 1-2 |
| Mar 17 | Barnsley | H | W | 3-0 |
| Mar 24 | Leicester Fosse | A | L | 0-2 |
| Mar 31 | Luton T | H | W | 5-0 |
| Apr 7 | Port Vale | A | L | 0-1 |
| Apr 13 | Leicester Fosse | H | W | 3-2 |
| Apr 14 | Walsall | H | W | 5-0 |
| Apr 21 | Middlesbrough | A | D | 0-0 |
| Apr 28 | Chesterfield | H | W | 2-1 |

Final League position: **4th**

| P | W | D | L | F/A | Pts |
|---|---|---|---|---|---|
| 34 | 20 | 4 | 10 | 63/27 | 44 |

**FA Cup**

| | | | | |
|---|---|---|---|---|
| Oct 28 | South Shore (Q1) | A | L | 1-3 |

## 1900/01

The turn of the century mean't a turn for the worse for struggling Newton Heath. Fans began to vote with their feet as they lost more games than they won and slumped to 10th place. By now the club was so

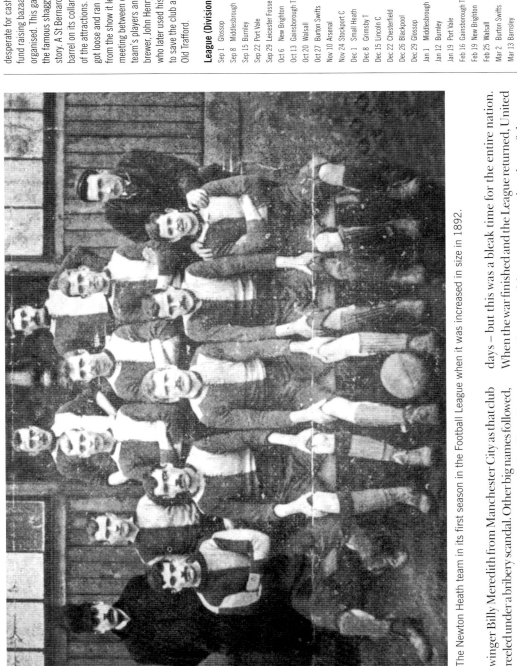

The Newton Heath team in its first season in the Football League when it was increased in size in 1892.

winger Billy Meredith from Manchester City as that club reeled under a bribery scandal. Other big names followed, Turnbull, Bannister, Burgess and Charlie Roberts were the stars of the day and by 1908 United were Champions again and FA Cup winners in 1909, beating Bristol City 1-0. These were good days to be a United supporter. Fans even had the pleasure of a new ground – the club began its new life in the original Theatre Of Dreams, Old Trafford (capacity 100,000!), in 1910, finishing fifth in the first season and winning the championship the following year. But as always seems to be the case with United, life was never dull. Drama follows delirium like night follows day. The club was rocked in 1912 by the resignation of Ernest Mangnall who quit to move across the divide to Manchester City. The departure of such an influential figure – akin to Fergie quitting for Liverpool or Leeds today – sent United into a spiral of decline. Up to the outbreak of the First World War, the team started to disintegrate and the crowds became disenchanted. The war only compounded the problems. Top flight football was suspended – the team played in a hastily put together "Lancashire Section" – and United's resources were severely stretched as the ground still had to be maintained.

Few fans today can imagine five years without Premiership football – we can barely last a week these days – but this was a bleak time for the entire nation. When the war finished and the League returned, United were in no position to recreate the glory of the pre-war years. In 1921 the agony was piled on when the team's undoubted top man, Billy Meredith, quit to rejoin his old club Manchester City. Many United followers today can remember what it felt like when "King" Denis Law left Old Trafford and joined City in the 1973-1974 season. Sheer disbelief. Gut-wrenching pain. Anywhere but City. It was no surprise therefore when United crashed out of Division One in 1922 having won only eight games to begin a period of three years in the wilderness. By 1927, despite returning to the elite, United supporters were growing increasingly frustrated. They wanted major success, not mediocrity, and the Supporters' Club took the initiative. They demanded big changes and threatened a boycott of the club, a rather futile gesture as the team was so bad the big crowds stayed at home anyway. The club struggled from one financial crisis to another during the thirties: the battles in the boardroom and the endless bank meetings were far more dramatic than anything on the pitch. The club very nearly lost Old Trafford when the banks pulled the plug on its credit. The perilous financial state of many of today's clubs is nothing new. It has been a part of the fabric of football for over a century and Manchester United was fighting

desperate for cash a grand fund raising bazaar was organised. This gave rise to the famous shaggy dog story. A St Bernard with a barrel on its collar was one of the attractions. When it got loose and ran away from the show it led to a meeting between one of the team's players and a rich brewer, John Henry Davies, who later used his money to save the club and build Old Trafford.

## League (Division 2)

| | | | | |
|---|---|---|---|---|
| Sep 1 | Glossop | A | L | 0-1 |
| Sep 8 | Middlesbrough | H | W | 4-0 |
| Sep 15 | Burnley | A | L | 0-1 |
| Sep 22 | Port Vale | H | W | 4-0 |
| Sep 29 | Leicester Fosse | A | L | 0-1 |
| Oct 6 | New Brighton | H | W | 1-0 |
| Oct 13 | Gainsborough T | A | W | 1-0 |
| Oct 20 | Walsall | H | D | 1-1 |
| Oct 27 | Burton Swifts | A | L | 1-3 |
| Nov 10 | Arsenal | A | L | 1-2 |
| Nov 24 | Stockport C | A | L | 0-1 |
| Dec 1 | Small Heath | H | L | 0-1 |
| Dec 8 | Grimsby T | A | L | 0-2 |
| Dec 15 | Lincoln C | H | W | 4-1 |
| Dec 22 | Chesterfield | A | L | 1-2 |
| Dec 26 | Blackpool | H | W | 4-0 |
| Dec 29 | Glossop | H | W | 3-0 |
| Jan 1 | Middlesbrough | A | W | 1-2 |
| Jan 12 | Burnley | H | L | 0-1 |
| Jan 19 | Port Vale | A | L | 0-2 |
| Feb 16 | Gainsborough T | H | D | 0-0 |
| Feb 19 | New Brighton | A | L | 0-2 |
| Feb 25 | Walsall | A | D | 1-1 |
| Mar 2 | Burton Swifts | H | D | 1-1 |
| Mar 13 | Barnsley | H | W | 1-0 |
| Mar 16 | Arsenal | H | W | 1-0 |
| Mar 20 | Leicester Fosse | H | L | 2-3 |
| Mar 23 | Blackpool | A | W | 2-1 |
| Mar 30 | Stockport C | H | W | 3-1 |
| Apr 5 | Lincoln C | A | L | 0-2 |
| Apr 6 | Small Heath | A | L | 0-1 |
| Apr 9 | Barnsley | A | L | 2-6 |
| Apr 13 | Grimsby T | H | W | 1-0 |
| Apr 27 | Chesterfield | H | W | 1-0 |

Final League position: 10th

| P | W | D | L | F/A | Pts |
|---|---|---|---|---|---|
| 34 | 14 | 4 | 16 | 42/38 | 32 |

## FA Cup

| | | | | |
|---|---|---|---|---|
| Jan 5 | Portsmouth (S) | H | W | 3-0 |
| Feb 9 | Burnley (1) | H | D | 0-0 |
| Feb 13 | Burnley (1R) | A | L | 1-7 |

# 1901/02

Newton Heath looked doomed as a club. It was £2,670 in debt and about to go bust. Bankruptcy would have meant being booted out of the league and the team being disbanded. The captain, Harry Stafford, came up with an 11th hour rescue plan at a crunch creditors' meeting. It involved a

## 1902/03

A milestone. Saved from oblivion by four wealthy businessmen, the club played its first season as Manchester United. The badly needed injection of cash, plus some new players, gave the flagging side the boost it needed. They won 15 league games, notched up 38 points and

takeover bid by four businessmen, including brewer John Henry Davies. They chipped in £500 each for a major say in the running of the club. At the end of April 1902, Newton Heath was ditched as a title, in favour of Manchester United. Other names suggested and rejected at the time were Manchester Central and Manchester Celtic. The cavalry arrived just in time as Newton Heath ended a disastrous season 15th with only 28 points.

### League (Division 2)

|  |  | |  |
|---|---|---|---|
| Sep 7 | Gainsborough T | H | W 3-0 |
| Sep 14 | Middlesbrough | A | L 0-5 |
| Sep 21 | Bristol C | H | W 1-0 |
| Sep 28 | Blackpool | A | W 4-2 |
| Oct 5 | Stockport C | H | D 3-3 |
| Oct 12 | Burton U | A | D 0-0 |
| Oct 19 | Glossop | A | D 0-0 |
| Oct 26 | Doncaster R | H | W 6-0 |
| Nov 9 | WBA | H | L 1-2 |
| Nov 16 | Arsenal | A | L 0-2 |
| Nov 23 | Barnsley | H | W 1-0 |
| Nov 30 | Leicester Fosse | A | L 2-3 |
| Dec 7 | Preston NE | A | L 1-5 |
| Dec 21 | Port Vale | H | W 1-0 |
| Dec 25 | Lincoln C | A | L 0-2 |
| Dec 26 | Glossop | H | W 1-0 |
| Feb 15 | Burnley | H | W 2-0 |
| Feb 22 | Doncaster R | A | L 0-4 |
| Jan 1 | Preston NE | H | L 0-2 |
| Jan 4 | Gainsborough T | A | D 1-1 |
| Jan 18 | Bristol C | A | L 0-4 |
| Jan 25 | Blackpool | H | L 0-1 |
| Feb 1 | Stockport C | A | L 0-1 |
| Feb 11 | Burnley | H | W 2-0 |
| Mar 1 | Lincoln C | H | D 0-0 |
| Mar 8 | WBA | A | L 0-4 |
| Mar 17 | Chesterfield | A | L 0-3 |
| Mar 22 | Barnsley | A | L 2-3 |
| Mar 28 | Burnley | A | L 0-1 |
| Mar 29 | Leicester Fosse | H | W 2-0 |
| Apr 7 | Middlesbrough | H | W 2-0 |
| Apr 19 | Port Vale | A | D 1-1 |
| Apr 21 | Burton U | H | L 1-2 |
| Apr 23 | Chesterfield | H | W 2-0 |

**Final League position: 15th**

| P | W | D | L | F/A | Pts |
|---|---|---|---|---|---|
| 34 | 11 | 6 | 17 | 38/53 | 28 |

### FA Cup

| | | | |
|---|---|---|---|
| Dec 14 | Lincoln C (1) | H | L 1-2 |

for its life. Salvation came in 1931 in the form of a £2,000 loan from Manchester businessman James Gibson who cleared the club's debts and took control in return. He then embarked on an ambitious reconstruction, bringing in a new manager Scott Duncan, a former Glasgow Rangers and Newcastle player, but though United had staggered back from the brink of extinction its fortunes on the pitch showed scant improvement. They were struggling in Division Two, playing badly, and by 1934 they were plunging towards the black hole of Division Three. The founders of Newton Heath way back in the previous century must have been turning in their graves. Backs against the wall, United faced Millwall on May 5 knowing they had to win – away. It didn't help that in the same week, Manchester City were on course for an FA Cup Final victory with a player United fans would come to idolise, Matt Busby. But United pulled through, beating Millwall 2-0 with a resilience that has rung down the decades and was seen even this season when The Reds beat Juventus 3-2 after going down 2-0 in Italy. The work ethic which is the hallmark of United sides has its roots way back in the history of this great club. That survival feat at Millwall galvanised the club again and they ended up Division Two Champions in the 1935-1936 season. But the euphoria was short-lived and the roller-coaster continued - United couldn't live with the First Division and were promptly relegated again, only to bounce back in 1937. Then one of the greatest names in United's history made his debut. United scout Louis Rocca spotted a young man by the name of Johnny Carey playing in Ireland and brought him to Old Trafford (25 years later another young Irishman would come to the rescue of The Reds). The full-back made his debut on September 25, 1937 against Southampton and gave heart to fans who could only hope for better things as City were flying high as Champions. But there were other names emerging who would play a big part in United's eventual revival, not least local-born Stan Pearson who played inside left in a team fast finding the right balance between youth and experience.

United progressed, winning promotion to Division One, but storm clouds of war were looming once again over Europe. In 1939, football was suspended as the country plunged into the biggest crisis in its history. Old Trafford was bombed and reduced to a shell, the glories and the disappointments of what had gone before still ringing through its skeletal, burnt-out structure. It was in need of a saviour, someone with vision and a tenacity to revive the club's dignity against all the odds. On February 15, 1945, a certain Scotsman arrived at the ground. Looking around the ruins, he felt the frisson of expectation and hope which has so pervaded the club known as Manchester United throughout its history. Little did he know then what glories he would bring to this ground and what joy – and heartache – its fans would suffer with him every inch of the way Matt Busby had arrived.

Proud day. The 1908-1909 United team and staff with The Englis

United players in lighthearted mood during a training session in 1909.

finished fifth. A far cry from the previous season, when they limped in 15th, just four places from the bottom of Divison 2. They enjoyed plenty of FA Cup action too, trouncing Accrington spectacularly 7-0 in their first match and winning five games, before losing to Everton 1-3. The only cloud was rivals Manchester City being promoted to Division 1.

## League (Division 2)

| | | | | |
|---|---|---|---|---|
| Sep 6 | Gainsborough T | A | W | 1-0 |
| Sep 13 | Burton U | H | W | 1-0 |
| Sep 20 | Bristol C | A | L | 1-3 |
| Sep 27 | Glossop | H | D | 1-1 |
| Oct 4 | Chesterfield | H | W | 2-1 |
| Oct 11 | Stockport C | A | L | 1-2 |
| Oct 25 | Arsenal | A | W | 1-0 |
| Nov 8 | Lincoln C | A | W | 3-1 |
| Nov 15 | Small Heath | H | L | 0-1 |
| Nov 22 | Leicester F | A | D | 1-1 |
| Dec 6 | Burnley | A | W | 2-0 |
| Dec 20 | Port Vale | A | D | 1-1 |
| Dec 25 | Manchester C | H | D | 1-1 |
| Dec 26 | Blackpool | H | D | 2-2 |
| Dec 27 | Barnsley | H | W | 2-1 |
| Jan 3 | Gainsborough T | A | W | 3-1 |
| Jan 10 | Burton U | A | L | 1-3 |
| Jan 17 | Bristol C | H | L | 1-2 |
| Jan 24 | Glossop | A | W | 3-1 |
| Jan 31 | Chesterfield | A | L | 0-2 |
| Feb 14 | Blackpool | A | L | 0-2 |
| Feb 24 | Doncaster R | A | D | 2-2 |
| Mar 7 | Lincoln C | H | L | 1-2 |
| Mar 9 | Arsenal | H | W | 3-0 |
| Mar 21 | Leicester F | H | W | 5-1 |
| Mar 23 | Stockport C | H | D | 0-0 |
| Mar 30 | Preston NE | H | L | 0-1 |
| Apr 4 | Burnley | H | W | 4-0 |
| Apr 10 | Manchester C | A | W | 2-0 |
| Apr 11 | Preston NE | A | L | 1-3 |
| Apr 13 | Doncaster R | H | W | 4-0 |
| Apr 18 | Port Vale | H | W | 2-1 |
| Apr 20 | Small Heath | A | L | 1-2 |
| Apr 25 | Barnsley | A | D | 0-0 |

**Final League position: 5th**

| P | W | D | L | F/A | Pts |
|---|---|---|---|---|---|
| 34 | 15 | 8 | 11 | 53/38 | 38 |

## FA Cup

| | | | | |
|---|---|---|---|---|
| Nov 1 | Accrington S (30) | H | W | 7-0 |
| Nov 13 | Oswaldtwistle R (40) | H | W | 3-2 |
| Nov 29 | Southport C (50) | H | W | 4-1 |
| Dec 13 | Burton U (INT) | H | D | 1-1 |
| Dec 17 | Burton U (INTR) | H | W | 3-1 |
| Feb 7 | Liverpool (1) | H | W | 2-1 |
| Feb 21 | Everton (2) | A | L | 1-3 |

**Final League position: 5th**

| P | W | D | L | F/A | Pts |
|---|---|---|---|---|---|
| 34 | 15 | 8 | 11 | 53/38 | 38 |

# 1903/04

When the season got off to a bad start, fans began to get restless. This led to the appointment of the club's first real manager, cycling nut Ernest Mangnall, in

September 1903. The former secretary at Burnley once rode from Land's End to John O'Groats and jumped into the saddle at United. His dynamic style forced the side to go up a gear. By the end of the season 28 players had figured in first team games. He believed the ball should be kept away from players during training to make them even keener to get hold of it on Saturdays. New additions to the side included influential half-back Charlie Roberts, who caused a sensation wearing short shorts. The team finished the season third, having won 20 games and lost only six.

### League (Division 2):

| | | | | |
|---|---|---|---|---|
| Sep 5 | Bristol C | H | D | 2-2 |
| Sep 7 | Burnley | A | L | 0-2 |
| Sep 12 | Port Vale | A | L | 0-1 |
| Sep 19 | Glossop | A | W | 5-0 |
| Sep 26 | Bradford C | H | W | 3-1 |
| Oct 3 | Arsenal | A | L | 0-4 |
| Oct 10 | Barnsley | H | W | 4-0 |
| Oct 17 | Lincoln C | A | D | 0-0 |
| Oct 24 | Stockport Co | H | W | 3-1 |
| Nov 7 | Bolton W | H | L | 0-2 |
| Nov 21 | Preston NE | H | W | 4-2 |
| Dec 19 | Gainsborough T | H | W | 3-1 |
| Dec 25 | Chesterfield | H | W | 3-1 |
| Dec 26 | Burton U | A | D | 2-2 |
| Jan 2 | Bristol C | A | D | 1-1 |
| Jan 9 | Port Vale | H | W | 2-0 |
| Jan 16 | Glossop | H | W | 3-1 |
| Jan 23 | Bradford C | A | D | 3-3 |
| Jan 30 | Arsenal | H | W | 1-0 |
| Feb 13 | Lincoln C | H | W | 2-0 |
| Mar 9 | Blackpool | A | L | 1-2 |
| Mar 12 | Burnley | H | W | 3-1 |
| Mar 19 | Preston NE | A | D | 1-1 |
| Mar 26 | Grimsby T | H | W | 2-0 |
| Mar 28 | Stockport C | A | W | 3-0 |
| Apr 1 | Chesterfield | A | W | 2-0 |
| Apr 2 | Leicester F | A | W | 1-0 |
| Apr 5 | Barnsley | A | W | 2-0 |
| Apr 9 | Blackpool | H | W | 3-1 |
| Apr 12 | Grimsby T | A | L | 1-3 |
| Apr 16 | Gainsborough T | H | W | 2-0 |
| Apr 23 | Burton U | H | W | 2-0 |
| Apr 25 | Bolton W | A | D | 0-0 |
| Apr 30 | Leicester | H | W | 5-2 |

### Final League position: 3rd

| P | W | D | L | F/A | Pts |
|---|---|---|---|---|---|
| 34 | 20 | 8 | 6 | 65/33 | 48 |

### FA Cup

| | | | | |
|---|---|---|---|---|
| Dec 12 | Small Heath (INT) | H | D | 1-1 |
| Dec 16 | Small Heath (INTR) | A | D | 1-1 |
| Dec 21 | Small Heath (INTR2) | N | D | 1-1 |
| | (at Bramall Lane) | | | |
| Jan 11 | Small Heath (INTR3) | N | W | 3-1 |
| | (at Hyde Road) | | | |
| Feb 6 | Notts Co (1) | A | D | 3-3 |
| Feb 10 | Notts Co (1R) | H | W | 2-1 |
| Feb 20 | Sheffield Wed (2) | A | L | 0-6 |

APRIL 26, 1909.

## Incidents in Saturday's English Cup Final at the Crystal Palace.

Page 9

Moger, Manchester's goalkeeper, kicking out.

The only goal of the match, which was scored by A. Turnbull (x).

The two—Roberts (4) (Manchester) and Wedlock 'n'...

...and Charles Beresford presenting the Cup to Roberts.

Clay (X), Bristol's goalkeeper, punching out.

A Bristol shot goes outside the post.

Moger, Manchester's goalkeeper, near the goal post, falls in bringing off a save.

Palace on Saturday in preventing Roberts, Manchester United's captain, with the English Cup after that team's victory over Bristol City by a goal to nothing.—(Daily Mirror and Russell and Sons.)

"It has been one of the finest games that has ever been played in the country. The game of football is a national game; it encourages the best characteristics of the British race. The more the game is encouraged the better." So spoke Lord Charles Beresford at the Crystal

Football mad. How The Daily Mirror covered the 1909 Final between United and Bristol City.

Rocca's Brigade! Louis Rocca's horse and carriage welcome for the victorious United team in 1909.

## 1904/05

Newly-appointed manager Ernest Mangnall's ideas began paying off. With players like keeper Harry Moger, strikers John Picken and Charlie Sagar and half-back Charlie Roberts in the squad they were on a winning streak. After losing to Bolton in September 1904, the side went 18 games without defeat. Up until February 1905 they won 16 matches and drew two. They finished 3rd with 53 points. Off the pitch the club suffered a financial setback when they were banned from selling booze inside the ground. Also United director Harry Stafford and former secretary James West were suspended by the FA for making illegal payments to players, a common practice in those days.

### League (Division 2)

Sep 3 Port Vale A D 2-2
Sep 10 Bristol C H W 4-1
Sep 17 Bolton W H L 1-2
Sep 24 Glossop A W 2-1
Oct 8 Bradford C A D 1-1
Oct 15 Lincoln C H W 2-0
Oct 22 Leicester F A W 3-0
Oct 29 Barnsley H W 4-0
Nov 5 WBA A W 2-0
Nov 12 Burnley H W 1-0
Nov 19 Grimsby T A W 1-0
Dec 3 Doncaster R H W 3-1
Dec 10 Gainsborough T H W 3-1
Dec 17 Burton U A W 3-2
Dec 24 Liverpool H W 3-1
Dec 26 Chesterfield H W 3-0
Dec 31 Port Vale H W 6-1
Jan 2 Bradford C H W 7-0
Jan 3 Bolton W A W 4-2
Jan 7 Bristol C H D 1-1
Jan 21 Glossop H W 4-1
Feb 11 Lincoln C A L 0-3
Feb 18 Leicester F H W 4-1
Feb 25 Barnsley A D 0-0
Mar 4 WBA H W 2-0
Mar 11 Burnley A L 0-2
Mar 18 Grimsby T H W 2-1
Mar 25 Blackpool H W 1-0
Apr 1 Doncaster R A W 6-0
Apr 8 Gainsborough T A D 0-0
Apr 15 Burton U H W 5-0
Apr 21 Chesterfield A L 0-2
Apr 22 Liverpool A L 0-4
Apr 24 Blackpool H W 3-1

### FA Cup

Jan 14 Fulham (INT) H D 2-2
Jan 18 Fulham (INTR) A D 0-0
Jan 23 Fulham (INTR2) N L 0-1
(at Villa Park)

Final League position: 3rd

| P | W | D | L | F/A | Pts |
|---|---|---|---|-----|-----|
| 34 | 24 | 5 | 5 | 81/30 | 53 |

## 1905/06

After a brilliant season, Ernest Mangnall's United were promoted to The First Division. They finished second overall, four points behind Bristol City and nine points ahead of third place Chelsea. The squad became FA Cup giant killers too. Having beaten Staple Hill 7-0 and Norwich City 3-0 they then thrashed five-time winners, current holders and four-time League champions, Aston Villa, 5-1. It was a fantastic result which catapulted United into the quarter-finals for the first time since 1897. Although they were then narrowly beaten by Arsenal 3-2, fans knew the team were on the road to greatness.

### League (Division 2)

Sep 2 Bristol C H W 5-1
Sep 4 Blackpool A W 1-0
Sep 9 Grimsby T A W 2-1
Sep 16 Glossop H W 5-0
Sep 23 Stockport C A W 3-1
Sep 30 Blackpool H W 1-0
Oct 7 Bradford C H D 0-0
Oct 14 WBA A L 0-1
Oct 21 Leicester H W 3-2
Oct 25 Gainsborough T A D 2-2
Oct 28 Hull C A W 1-0
Nov 4 Lincoln C H W 2-1
Nov 11 Chesterfield A L 0-1
Nov 18 Port Vale H W 3-0
Nov 25 Barnsley A W 3-0
Dec 2 Clapton O H W 4-0
Dec 9 Burnley A W 3-1
Dec 23 Burton U A W 3-0
Dec 25 Chelsea H D 0-0
Dec 30 Bristol C A D 1-1
Jan 6 Grimsby T H W 5-0
Jan 15 Leeds C A L 0-3
Jan 20 Glossop A W 5-2
Jan 27 Stockport C A W 5-1
Feb 10 Bradford C A W 5-1
Feb 17 WBA H D 0-0
Mar 3 Hull C H W 5-1
Mar 17 Chesterfield H W 4-1
Mar 24 Port Vale A L 0-1
Mar 29 Leicester C A W 5-2
Mar 31 Barnsley H W 5-1
Apr 7 Clapton A W 1-0
Apr 13 Chelsea A D 1-1
Apr 14 Glossop H W 1-0
Apr 16 Gainsborough T H W 2-0
Apr 21 Leeds C H W 3-1
Apr 25 Lincoln C A W 3-1
Apr 28 Burton U H W 6-0

### FA Cup

Jan 13 Staple Hill (1) H W 7-2
Feb 3 Norwich (2) H W 3-0
Feb 24 Aston Villa (3) H W 5-1
Mar 10 Arsenal (4) H L 2-3

Final League position: 2nd

| P | W | D | L | F/A | Pts |
|---|---|---|---|-----|-----|
| 38 | 28 | 6 | 4 | 90/28 | 62 |

## 1906/07

United were back in Division One. While the players dazzled fans with their skills on the pitch, manager Ernest Mangnall astounded the world of football with some fancy moves off it. When rivals Manchester City were shattered by a series of illegal payment scandals, he outwitted the opposition in May 1906 by signing up an early version of George Best, the Welsh wizard Billy Meredith, even though the king of cool, who played with a toothpick dangling from his mouth, had been banned from football until April 1908. Then, in another stunning display of cunning, he snatched Sandy Turnbull, Jimmy Bannister and Herbert Burgess from under the noses of other clubs, just before desperate City were due to put them up for auction. Mangnall had played a blinder. The team finished 8th overall and were stronger than ever.

### League (Division 1)

Sep 1 Bristol C A W 2-1
Sep 3 Derby C A W 2-1
Sep 8 Notts Co H D 0-0
Sep 15 Sheffield U A W 2-0
Sep 22 Bolton W H L 1-2
Sep 29 Derby Co H D 1-1
Oct 6 Stoke C H W 2-1
Oct 13 Blackburn R A W 4-1
Oct 20 Sunderland A L 1-4
Oct 27 Birmingham H W 2-1
Nov 3 Everton A L 0-3
Nov 10 Arsenal H L 2-5
Nov 17 Sheffield Wed A L 2-4
Nov 24 Bury H W 3-1
Dec 1 Manchester C A L 0-3
Dec 8 Middlesbrough H W 3-1
Dec 15 Preston NE A W 2-1
Dec 22 Newcastle U H L 1-3
Dec 25 Liverpool H D 0-0
Dec 26 Aston Villa A L 0-2
Dec 29 Bristol C H W 1-0
Jan 1 Aston Villa H W 1-0
Jan 5 Notts Co A L 0-3
Jan 19 Sheffield U H W 2-0
Jan 26 Bolton W A W 1-0
Feb 2 Newcastle U A L 0-5
Feb 9 Stoke C H W 4-1
Feb 16 Blackburn R H W 3-0
Feb 23 Preston NE H D 1-1
Mar 2 Birmingham A L 0-4
Mar 16 Arsenal H W 2-0
Mar 25 Sunderland H W 2-0
Mar 30 Bury A W 1-0
Apr 1 Liverpool A L 2-3
Apr 6 Manchester C H D 1-1
Apr 10 Sheffield Wed H W 5-0
Apr 13 Middlesbrough A L 0-2
Apr 22 Everton H W 3-0

Final League position: 8th

| P | W | D | L | F/A | Pts |
|---|---|---|---|-----|-----|
| 38 | 17 | 8 | 13 | 53/56 | 42 |

### FA Cup

Jan 12 Portsmouth (1) A D 2-2
Jan 16 Portsmouth (1R) H L 1-2

## 1907/08

Ernest Mangnall's magnificent men were on the march. His new team starred the cream of English soccer and they gave United fans a thrill after thrill. The hit squad included Billy Meredith, Sandy Turnbull, Herbert Burgess, Jimmy Bannister, George Wall, Alex Bell, Dick Duckworth and Charlie Roberts. With such a strong line-up it was almost certain they would triumph. Sure enough, The Reds won the League Championship for the first time, finishing nine points above Aston Villa and Manchester City. Mangnall's team put Divison 1 through the wringer. At one point they won 10 games on the trot. It was, without doubt, a classic season, marred only by the first signs of crowd trouble at Bradford and Sheffield.

### League (Division 1)

Sep 2 Aston Villa H W 4-1
Sep 7 Liverpool H W 4-0
Sep 9 Middlesbrough A W 2-1
Sep 14 Middlesbrough A L 1-2
Sep 21 Sheffield U H W 2-1
Sep 28 Chelsea A W 4-1
Oct 5 Nottingham F H W 4-0
Oct 12 Newcastle U A W 6-1
Oct 19 Blackburn R A W 5-1
Oct 26 Bolton W H W 2-1
Nov 2 Birmingham H W 4-3
Nov 9 Everton A W 4-3
Nov 16 Sunderland H W 4-2
Nov 23 Arsenal A W 4-2
Nov 30 Sheffield Wed H W 2-1
Dec 7 Bristol C H W 2-1
Dec 14 Notts Co A D 1-1
Dec 21 Manchester C H W 3-1
Dec 25 Bury A D 0-0
Dec 28 Preston NE H D 0-0
Jan 1 Bury H W 1-0
Jan 18 Sheffield U A L 0-2
Jan 25 Chelsea H W 1-0
Feb 8 Newcastle U H D 1-1
Feb 15 Blackburn R H L 1-2
Mar 14 Sunderland A L 0-1
Mar 21 Arsenal A L 0-4
Apr 4 Bristol C A L 0-2
Apr 8 Everton H W 2-0
Apr 11 Notts Co H W 1-0
Apr 17 Nottingham F A L 0-2
Apr 18 Manchester C H D 0-0
Apr 20 Aston Villa H L 1-1
Apr 22 Bolton W A D 2-2
Apr 25 Preston NE H W 2-1

Final League position: 1st

| P | W | D | L | F/A | Pts |
|---|---|---|---|-----|-----|
| 38 | 23 | 6 | 9 | 81/48 | 52 |

### FA Cup

Jan 11 Blackpool (1) H W 3-1
Feb 1 Chelsea (2) H W 1-0
Feb 22 Aston Villa (3) A W 2-0
Mar 7 Fulham (4) A L 1-2

## 1908/09

Having suffered hooliganism during the previous season, United were hoping to relax and enjoy their first outing to Europe in the summer of 1908. They certainly got a warm reception on a friendly tour of Hungary and Austria. When they crushed a local side 7-0 in Budapest the angry crowd turned on the team and pelted them with rocks. Back home safe, United set off on the FA Cup trail. Having beaten Brighton and Everton 1-0, they thrashed Blackburn 6-1. Once again Lady luck smiled on Mangnall's men. They were losing the next game against his old team Burnley 1-0 when it was called off because of a blinding blizzard. They won the replay 3-2 and got to the final against Bristol City by beating Newcastle 1-0. When the big game was held at Crystal Palace, a goal from Sandy Turnbull made sure the cup went back up north. A proud day for Manchester.

**League (Division 1)**

| | | | | |
|---|---|---|---|---|
| Sep 5 | Preston NE | A | W | 3-0 |
| Sep 7 | Bury | H | W | 2-1 |
| Sep 12 | Middlesbrough | H | W | 6-3 |
| Sep 19 | Manchester C | A | W | 2-1 |
| Sep 26 | Liverpool | H | W | 3-2 |
| Oct 3 | Bury | A | D | 2-2 |
| Oct 10 | Sheffield U | H | W | 2-1 |
| Oct 17 | Aston Villa | A | L | 1-3 |
| Oct 24 | Nottingham F | H | D | 2-2 |
| Oct 31 | Sunderland | A | L | 1-6 |
| Nov 7 | Chelsea | H | L | 0-1 |
| Nov 14 | Blackburn R | A | W | 3-1 |
| Nov 21 | Bradford C | H | W | 2-0 |
| Nov 28 | Sheffield Wed | H | W | 3-1 |
| Dec 5 | Everton | A | L | 2-3 |
| Dec 12 | Leicester F | H | W | 4-2 |
| Dec 19 | Arsenal | A | W | 1-0 |
| Dec 25 | Newcastle U | A | L | 1-2 |
| Dec 26 | Newcastle U | H | W | 1-0 |
| Jan 1 | Notts Co | H | W | 4-3 |
| Jan 2 | Preston NE | H | L | 0-2 |
| Jan 9 | Middlesbrough | A | L | 0-5 |
| Jan 23 | Manchester C | H | W | 3-1 |
| Jan 30 | Liverpool | A | L | 1-3 |
| Feb 13 | Sheffield U | A | D | 0-0 |
| Feb 27 | Nottingham F | A | L | 0-2 |
| Mar 13 | Chelsea | A | D | 1-1 |
| Mar 15 | Sunderland | H | D | 2-2 |
| Mar 20 | Blackburn R | H | L | 0-3 |
| Mar 31 | Aston Villa | H | L | 0-2 |
| Apr 3 | Sheffield Wed | A | L | 0-2 |
| Apr 9 | Bristol C | H | L | 0-1 |
| Apr 10 | Everton | H | D | 2-2 |
| Apr 12 | Bristol C | A | D | 0-0 |
| Apr 13 | Notts Co | A | W | 1-0 |
| Apr 17 | Leicester F | A | L | 2-3 |
| Apr 27 | Arsenal | H | L | 1-4 |
| Apr 29 | Bradford C | A | L | 0-1 |

Final League position: **13th**

| P | W | D | L | F/A | Pts |
|---|---|---|---|---|---|
| 38 | 15 | 7 | 16 | 58/68 | 37 |

**FA Cup**

| | | | | |
|---|---|---|---|---|
| Jan 16 | Brighton (1) | H | W | 1-0 |
| Feb 6 | Everton (2) | H | W | 1-0 |
| Feb 20 | Blackburn R (3) | H | W | 6-1 |
| Mar 5 | Burnley (4) | A | Aband | |
| Mar 10 | Burnley (4R) | A | W | 3-2 |
| Mar 27 | Newcastle U (SF) (at Brammal Lane) | N | W | 1-0 |
| Apr 24 | Bristol C (f) (at Crystal Palace) | N | W | 1-0 |

## 1909/10

The season nearly didn't happen at all. Just before kick-off League clubs tried to stop players being members of the Union Of Professional Footballers. It almost led to a strike and the United team started training independently under a new banner, The Outcasts. The bosses realised they couldn't win, caved in and recognised the union. With the threat of trouble lifted, United were free to move from Bank Street to their new ground at Old Trafford. It was financed by a loan of £60,000, worth millions today, from the club's big-hearted president, brewery tycoon John Henry Davies. Spookily, two days before the opening game against Liverpool on February 19, 1910, the abandoned wooden grandstand at Bank Street was smashed flat in a gale. Unfortunately United were dogged by injury problems, so the Merseysiders were able to take the shine off the occasion by winning 4-3.

**League (Division 1)**

| | | | | |
|---|---|---|---|---|
| Sep 1 | Bradford C | H | W | 1-0 |
| Sep 4 | Bury | H | W | 2-0 |
| Sep 6 | Notts Co | H | W | 2-1 |
| Sep 11 | Tottenham H | A | D | 2-2 |
| Sep 18 | Preston NE | H | D | 1-1 |
| Sep 25 | Notts Co | A | L | 2-3 |
| Oct 2 | Newcastle U | H | D | 1-1 |
| Oct 9 | Liverpool | A | L | 2-3 |
| Oct 16 | Aston Villa | H | W | 2-0 |
| Oct 23 | Sheffield U | A | W | 1-0 |
| Oct 30 | Arsenal | H | W | 1-0 |
| Nov 6 | Bolton W | A | W | 3-2 |
| Nov 13 | Chelsea | H | W | 2-0 |
| Nov 20 | Blackburn R | A | L | 2-3 |
| Nov 27 | Nottingham F | H | L | 2-6 |
| Dec 4 | Sunderland | A | L | 0-3 |
| Dec 18 | Middlesbrough | A | W | 2-1 |
| Dec 25 | Sheffield Wed | H | L | 0-3 |
| Dec 27 | Sheffield Wed | A | L | 1-4 |
| Jan 1 | Bradford C | A | W | 2-0 |
| Jan 8 | Bury | A | D | 1-1 |
| Jan 22 | Tottenham H | H | W | 5-0 |
| Feb 5 | Preston NE | A | L | 0-1 |
| Feb 12 | Newcastle U | A | W | 4-3 |
| Feb 19 | Liverpool | H | L | 3-4 |
| Feb 26 | Aston Villa | A | L | 1-7 |
| Mar 5 | Sheffield U | H | W | 1-0 |
| Mar 12 | Arsenal | A | D | 0-0 |
| Mar 19 | Bolton W | H | W | 5-0 |
| Mar 25 | Bristol C | H | W | 2-1 |
| Mar 26 | Chelsea | A | D | 1-1 |
| Mar 28 | Bristol C | A | L | 1-2 |
| Apr 2 | Blackburn R | H | W | 2-0 |
| Apr 6 | Everton | H | W | 3-2 |
| Apr 9 | Nottingham F | A | L | 0-2 |
| Apr 16 | Sunderland | H | W | 2-0 |
| Apr 23 | Everton | A | D | 3-3 |
| Apr 30 | Middlesbrough | H | W | 4-1 |

Final League position: **5th**

| P | W | D | L | F/A | Pts |
|---|---|---|---|---|---|
| 38 | 19 | 7 | 12 | 69/61 | 45 |

**FA Cup**

| | | | | |
|---|---|---|---|---|
| Jan 15 | Burnley (1) | A | L | 0-2 |

## 1910/11

This was the last triumphant season under Ernest Mangnall's leadership. United became League Champions by a whisker. It was tense, dramatic stuff. On the final Saturday Aston Villa were ahead by just one point and drawn away to struggling Liverpool. United, who had been beaten a week earlier 4-2 at Villa Park, were at home to Sunderland. Amazingly the Merseysiders managed to win 3-1 and The Reds 5-1. There were new faces in the line-up that carried off the sliverware. The team's strike force had been strengthened by the likes of former Nottingham Forest star Enoch "Knocker" West, who tucked away 19 goals during the season. United also won the FA Charity Shield in 1911, beating plucky Swindon Town 8-4.

**League (Division 1)**

| | | | | |
|---|---|---|---|---|
| Sep 1 | Arsenal | A | W | 2-1 |
| Sep 3 | Blackburn R | H | W | 3-2 |
| Sep 10 | Nottingham F | A | L | 1-2 |
| Sep 17 | Manchester C | H | W | 2-1 |
| Sep 24 | Everton | A | W | 1-0 |
| Oct 1 | Sheffield Wed | H | W | 3-2 |
| Oct 8 | Bristol C | A | W | 1-0 |
| Oct 15 | Newcastle U | H | W | 2-0 |
| Oct 22 | Tottenham H | A | D | 2-2 |
| Oct 29 | Middlesbrough | H | L | 1-2 |
| Nov 5 | Preston NE | A | W | 2-0 |
| Nov 12 | Notts Co | H | D | 0-0 |
| Nov 19 | Oldham | A | W | 3-1 |
| Nov 26 | Liverpool | A | L | 2-3 |
| Dec 3 | Bury | H | W | 3-2 |
| Dec 10 | Sheffield U | A | L | 0-2 |
| Dec 17 | Aston Villa | H | W | 2-0 |
| Dec 24 | Sunderland | A | W | 2-1 |
| Dec 26 | Arsenal | H | W | 5-0 |
| Dec 27 | Bradford C | A | L | 0-1 |
| Dec 31 | Blackburn R | A | L | 0-1 |
| Jan 2 | Bradford C | H | W | 1-0 |
| Jan 7 | Nottingham F | H | W | 4-2 |
| Jan 21 | Manchester C | A | D | 1-1 |
| Jan 28 | Everton | H | D | 2-2 |
| Feb 11 | Bristol C | H | W | 3-1 |
| Feb 18 | Newcastle U | A | W | 1-0 |
| Mar 4 | Middlesbrough | A | D | 2-2 |
| Mar 11 | Preston NE | H | W | 5-0 |
| Mar 15 | Tottenham H | H | W | 3-2 |
| Mar 18 | Notts Co | A | L | 0-1 |
| Mar 25 | Oldham | H | D | 0-0 |
| Apr 1 | Liverpool | H | W | 2-0 |
| Apr 8 | Bury | A | W | 3-0 |
| Apr 15 | Sheffield U | H | D | 1-1 |
| Apr 17 | Sheffield Wed | A | D | 0-0 |
| Apr 22 | Aston Villa | A | L | 2-4 |
| Apr 29 | Sunderland | H | W | 5-1 |

Final League position: **1st**

| P | W | D | L | F/A | Pts |
|---|---|---|---|---|---|
| 38 | 22 | 8 | 8 | 72/40 | 52 |

**FA Cup**

| | | | | |
|---|---|---|---|---|
| Jan 14 | Blackpool (1) | A | W | 2-1 |
| Feb 4 | Aston Villa (2) | H | W | 2-1 |
| Feb 25 | West Ham (3) | A | L | 1-2 |

## 1911-1912

The glory of the previous, title-winning season was a distant memory as United finished a miserable 13th in the league, suffering heavy losses at the hands of Sunderland 5-0, Aston Villa 6-0 and Sheffield United 6-0.To add insult to injury, the Reds were knocked out of the FA Cup in the fourth round by Blackburn – and then lost their Championship inspiration Ernest Mangnold to arch-rivals Manchester City. The coveted title would not return to Old Trafford for another 41 years.

**League (Division 1)**

| | | | | |
|---|---|---|---|---|
| Sep 2 | Manchester City | A | D | 0-0 |
| Sep 9 | Everton | H | W | 2-1 |
| Sep 16 | WBA | A | L | 0-1 |
| Sep 23 | Sunderland | H | D | 2-2 |
| Sep 30 | Blackburn | A | D | 2-2 |
| Oct 7 | Sheffield Wed | H | W | 3-1 |
| Oct 14 | Bury | A | W | 1-0 |
| Oct 21 | Middlesbrough | H | L | 3-4 |
| Oct 28 | Notts County | A | W | 1-0 |
| Nov 4 | Tottenham H | H | L | 1-2 |
| Nov 11 | Preston NE | H | D | 0-0 |
| Nov 18 | Liverpool | A | L | 2-3 |
| Nov 25 | Aston Villa | H | W | 3-1 |
| Dec 2 | Newcastle U | A | W | 3-2 |
| Dec 9 | Sheffield U | H | W | 1-0 |
| Dec 16 | Oldham | A | D | 2-2 |
| Dec 23 | Bolton W | H | W | 2-0 |
| Dec 25 | Bradford C | H | L | 0-1 |
| Dec 26 | Bradford C | A | W | 1-0 |
| Dec 30 | Manchester C | H | D | 0-0 |
| Jan 1 | Arsenal | H | W | 2-0 |
| Jan 6 | Everton | A | L | 0-4 |
| Jan 20 | WBA | H | L | 1-2 |
| Jan 27 | Sunderland | A | L | 5-0 |
| Feb 10 | Sheffield Wed | A | L | 0-3 |
| Feb 17 | Bury | H | D | 0-0 |
| Mar 2 | Notts Cty | H | W | 2-0 |
| Mar 16 | Preston NE | A | D | 0-0 |
| Mar 23 | Liverpool | H | D | 1-1 |
| Mar 30 | Aston Villa | A | L | 0-6 |
| April 5 | Arsenal | A | L | 1-2 |
| April 6 | Newcastle | H | L | 0-2 |
| April 9 | Tottenham H | A | D | 1-1 |
| April 13 | Sheffield U | A | L | 1-6 |
| April 17 | Middlesbrough | A | L | 0-3 |
| April 20 | Oldham | H | W | 3-1 |
| April 27 | Bolton W | A | D | 1-1 |
| April 29 | Blackburn | H | W | 3-1 |

Final League position: **13th**

| P | W | D | L | F/A | Pts |
|---|---|---|---|---|---|
| 38 | 13 | 11 | 14 | 45/60 | 37 |

**FA Cup**

| | | | | |
|---|---|---|---|---|
| Jan 13 | Huddersfield T (1) | H | W | 3-1 |
| Feb 3 | Coventry C (2) | A | W | 5-1 |
| Feb 24 | Reading (3) | A | D | 1-1 |
| Feb 29 | Reading (3R) | H | W | 3-0 |
| Mar 9 | Blackburn R (4) | H | D | 1-1 |
| Mar 14 | Blackburn R (4R) | A | L | 2-4 |

## 1912-1913

The team was now under the guidance of J.J Bentley after the defection of Ernest Mangnold to Manchester City, and he had a great deal more success, United finishing fourth in the league. But things were not looking bright as attendances slumped to 15,000 and the squad started to age. Meredith, Duckworth, Turnbull, Stacey and West still provided the backbone of the side, but it was clear that the team would not be the force it promised in earlier years. War was looming in Europe – and it would rob United of one of its biggest stars,Sandy Turnbull, killed on active duty in France. It was a gloomy time for the club and country.

**League (Division 1)**

| | | | | |
|---|---|---|---|---|
| Sep 2 | Arsenal | A | D | 0-0 |
| Sep 7 | Manchester C | H | L | 0-1 |
| Sep 14 | West Brom | A | W | 2-1 |
| Sep 21 | Everton | H | W | 2-0 |
| Sep 28 | Sheffield W | A | D | 3-3 |
| Oct 5 | Blackburn R | H | D | 1-1 |
| Oct 12 | Derby Cty | A | L | 1-2 |
| Oct 19 | Tottenham H | H | W | 2-0 |
| Oct 26 | Middlesbrough | A | L | 2-3 |
| Nov 2 | Notts County | H | W | 2-1 |
| Nov 9 | Sunderland | A | L | 1-3 |
| Nov 16 | Aston Villa | A | L | 2-4 |
| Nov 23 | Liverpool | H | W | 3-1 |
| Nov 30 | Bolton W | A | L | 1-2 |
| Dec 7 | Sheffield U | H | W | 4-0 |
| Dec 14 | Newcastle U | A | W | 3-1 |
| Dec 21 | Oldham | H | D | 0-0 |
| Dec 25 | Chelsea | A | W | 4-1 |
| Dec 26 | Chelsea | H | W | 4-2 |
| Dec 28 | Manchester C | A | W | 2-0 |
| Jan 1 | Bradford City | H | W | 2-0 |
| Jan 4 | West Brom | H | D | 1-1 |
| Jan 18 | Everton | A | L | 1-4 |
| Jan 25 | Sheffield W | H | W | 2-0 |
| Feb 8 | Blackburn R | A | D | 0-0 |
| Feb 15 | Derby Cty | H | W | 4-0 |
| Mar 1 | Middlesbrough | H | L | 2-3 |
| Mar 8 | Notts County | A | W | 2-1 |
| Mar 15 | Sunderland | H | L | 1-3 |
| Mar 21 | Arsenal | H | W | 2-0 |
| Mar 22 | Aston Villa | H | W | 4-0 |
| Mar 25 | Bradford C | A | L | 0-1 |
| Mar 29 | Liverpool | A | W | 2-0 |
| Mar 31 | Tottenham | A | D | 1-1 |
| April 5 | Bolton W | H | W | 2-1 |
| April 12 | Sheffield U | A | L | 1-2 |
| April 19 | Newcastle | H | W | 3-0 |
| April 26 | Oldham | A | D | 0-0 |

**FA Cup**

| | | | | |
|---|---|---|---|---|
| Jan 11 | Coventry C (1) | H | D | 1-1 |
| Jan 16 | Coventry C (1R) | A | W | 3-1 |
| Feb 1 | Plymouth A (2) | A | W | 2-0 |
| Feb 22 | Oldham (3) | A | D | 0-0 |
| Feb 26 | Oldham (3R) | H | L | 1-2 |

Final League position: **4th**

| P | W | D | L | F/A | Pts |
|---|---|---|---|---|---|
| 8 | 19 | 8 | 11 | 69/43 | 46 |

## 1913-14

As war loomed, United's fortunes declined. Crowds were falling away and the team was ageing. Of the championship-winning side, only Meredith, Stacey, Duckworth, Turnbull, West and Wall remained. Despite and bright start, notching nine wins with only one loss, between November and the end of the season the team would enjoy only six victories, finishing 14th in the league and avoiding relegation by one point. To increase the agony, Manchester City, now under the guidance of former United boss Ernest Mangnold, climbed to 5th place.

**League (Division 1)**

| | | | | |
|---|---|---|---|---|
| Sep 6 | Sheffield W | A | W | 3-1 |
| Sep 8 | Sunderland | H | W | 3-1 |
| Sep 13 | Bolton W | A | L | 0-1 |
| Sep 20 | Chelsea | A | W | 2-1 |
| Sep 27 | Oldham | H | W | 4-1 |
| Oct 4 | Tottenham | H | W | 3-1 |
| Oct 11 | Burnley | A | W | 2-1 |
| Oct 18 | Preston NE | H | W | 3-0 |
| Oct 25 | Newcastle Utd | A | W | 1-0 |
| Nov 1 | Liverpool | H | W | 3-0 |
| Nov 8 | Aston Villa | A | L | 1-3 |
| Nov 15 | Middlesbrough | H | L | 0-1 |
| Nov 22 | Sheffield Utd | A | L | 0-2 |
| Nov 29 | Derby Cty | H | D | 3-3 |
| Dec 6 | Manchester City | A | W | 2-0 |
| Dec 13 | Bradford City | H | D | 1-1 |
| Dec 20 | Blackburn R | A | W | 1-0 |
| Dec 25 | Everton | H | L | 0-1 |
| Dec 26 | Everton | A | L | 0-5 |
| Dec 27 | Sheffield W | H | W | 2-1 |
| Jan 1 | WBA | H | W | 1-0 |
| Jan 3 | Bolton W | A | L | 1-6 |
| Jan 17 | Chelsea | H | L | 0-1 |
| Jan 24 | Oldham | A | D | 2-2 |
| Feb 7 | Tottenham H | A | L | 1-2 |
| Feb 14 | Burnley | H | L | 0-1 |
| Feb 21 | Middlesbrough | A | L | 1-3 |
| Feb 28 | Newcastle Utd | H | D | 2-2 |
| Mar 5 | Preston NE | A | L | 2-4 |
| Mar 14 | Aston Villa | H | L | 0-6 |
| Apr 4 | Derby Cty | A | L | 2-4 |
| Apr 10 | Sunderland | A | L | 0-2 |
| Apr 11 | Manchester City | H | L | 0-1 |
| Apr 13 | WBA | A | L | 1-2 |
| Apr 15 | Liverpool | A | W | 2-1 |
| Apr 18 | Bradford City | A | D | 1-1 |
| Apr 22 | Sheffield Utd | H | W | 2-1 |
| Apr 25 | Blackburn R | H | D | 0-0 |

**FA Cup**

| | | | | |
|---|---|---|---|---|
| Jan 10 | Swindon T (1) | A | L | 0-1 |

Billy Meredith was the real star of United's early teams and won almost everything.

## 1914-15

Final League position: **14th**

| P | W | D | L | F/A | Pts |
|---|---|---|---|---|---|
| 38 | 15 | 6 | 17 | 52/62 | 36 |

The First World War broke out and United endured a truly dismal season. They only won nine out of 38 games and finished an inglorious 18th. The best victory they could manage was 4-1 at home to Bolton Wanderers in January and their worst defeat was away to Bradford in April, when they failed to score and conceded five goals. Despite the arrival, in December 1914, of the first man ever to hold the title of manager at United, John Robson from Brighton and Hove Albion, fans squirmed as their former supremo, ex-secretary Ernest Mangnall, took his new club, Manchester City, to greater heights.

**League (Divison 1)**

| Sep 2 | Oldham | H | L | 1-3 |
|---|---|---|---|---|
| Sep 5 | Manchester C | H | D | 0-0 |
| Sep 12 | Bolton W | A | L | 0-3 |
| Sep 19 | Blackburn R | H | W | 2-0 |
| Sep 26 | Notts Co | H | W | 3-0 |
| Oct 3 | Sunderland | H | W | 3-0 |
| Oct 10 | Sheffield Wed | A | L | 0-1 |
| Oct 17 | WBA | H | D | 0-0 |
| Oct 24 | Everton | A | L | 2-4 |
| Oct 31 | Chelsea | H | D | 2-2 |
| Nov 7 | Bradford C | A | L | 2-4 |
| Nov 14 | Burnley | H | L | 0-2 |
| Nov 21 | Tottenham H | A | L | 0-2 |
| Nov 28 | Newcastle U | H | W | 1-0 |
| Dec 5 | Middlesbrough | A | D | 1-1 |
| Dec 12 | Sheffield U | H | L | 1-2 |
| Dec 19 | Aston Villa | A | D | 3-3 |
| Dec 26 | Liverpool | A | D | 1-1 |
| Jan 1 | Bradford | H | L | 1-2 |
| Jan 2 | Manchester C | A | D | 1-1 |
| Jan 16 | Bolton W | H | W | 4-1 |
| Jan 23 | Blackburn R | A | D | 3-3 |
| Jan 30 | Notts Co | H | D | 2-2 |
| Feb 6 | Sunderland | A | L | 0-1 |
| Feb 13 | Sheffield Wed | H | W | 2-0 |
| Feb 20 | WBA | A | D | 0-0 |
| Feb 27 | Everton | H | L | 1-2 |
| Mar 13 | Tottenham H | H | W | 1-0 |
| Mar 20 | Burnley | A | L | 0-3 |
| Mar 27 | Tottenham H | H | D | 1-1 |
| Apr 2 | Liverpool | H | W | 2-0 |
| Apr 3 | Newcastle | A | L | 0-2 |
| Apr 5 | Bradford | A | L | 0-5 |
| Apr 6 | Oldham | A | L | 0-1 |
| Apr 10 | Middlesbrough | H | D | 2-2 |
| Apr 17 | Sheffield U | A | L | 1-3 |
| Apr 19 | Chelsea | A | W | 3-1 |
| Apr 26 | Aston Villa | H | W | 1-0 |

**FA Cup**

| Jan 9 | Sheffield W (1) | A | L | 0-1 |
|---|---|---|---|---|

Final League position: **18th**

| P | W | D | L | F/A | Pts |
|---|---|---|---|---|---|
| 38 | 9 | 12 | 17 | 46/62 | 30 |

## 1919-1920

This was a season when United had to bite the bullet. It was the end of the war and the fans started flocking back to football, but they seemed to be overshadowed by the rebuilding of Manchester City under the guidance of former Reds boss Ernest Mangnold. A new ground was opened at Maine Road but United were still suffering the effects of the war years, financially, and were slow to respond. It was a desultory season on the pitch – 13 wins all season left the team in 12th place at the close with no success in the FA Cup, going out 2-1 at home to Aston Villa on January 13. Despite this lacklustre performance, crowds of 40,000 plus were not unusual. Football was back, but not the Reds.

**League (Divison 1)**

| Aug 30 | Derby Cty | A | D | 1-1 |
|---|---|---|---|---|
| Sep 1 | Sheffield W | H | W | 1-0 |
| Sep 6 | Derby Cty | H | L | 0-2 |
| Sep 8 | Sheffield W | A | W | 3-1 |
| Sep 13 | Preston NE | H | W | 3-2 |
| Sep 20 | Preston NE | A | W | 5-1 |
| Sep 27 | Middlesbrough | H | D | 1-1 |
| Oct 4 | Middlesbrough | A | D | 1-1 |
| Oct 11 | Manchester C | H | D | 3-3 |
| Oct 18 | Manchester C | A | W | 1-0 |
| Oct 25 | Sheffield U | H | D | 0-0 |
| Nov 1 | Sheffield U | A | W | 3-0 |
| Nov 8 | Burnley | H | W | 1-2 |
| Nov 15 | Burnley | A | L | 0-1 |
| Nov 22 | Oldham | A | W | 3-0 |
| Feb 28 | Arsenal | H | L | 0-1 |
| Mar 6 | Everton | H | W | 1-0 |
| Mar 13 | Everton | A | D | 0-0 |
| Mar 20 | Bradford C | H | D | 0-0 |
| Mar 27 | Bradford C | A | L | 1-2 |
| Apr 2 | Bradford PA | A | L | 0-1 |
| Apr 3 | Bolton | H | D | 1-1 |
| Apr 6 | Bradford PA | A | W | 4-1 |
| Apr 10 | Bolton W | A | W | 5-3 |
| Apr 17 | Blackburn R | H | D | 1-1 |
| Apr 24 | Blackburn R | A | L | 0-5 |
| Apr 25 | Notts Cty | H | D | 0-0 |
| May 1 | Notts Cty | A | W | 2-0 |

**FA Cup**

| Jan 10 | Port Vale (1) | A | W | 1-0 |
|---|---|---|---|---|
| Jan 31 | Aston Villa (2) | H | L | 1-2 |

Final League position: **12th**

| P | W | D | L | F/A | Pts |
|---|---|---|---|---|---|
| 42 | 13 | 14 | 15 | 54/50 | 40 |

## 1920-1921

The gloom continued for the Old Trafford faithful this season as their hero Billy Meredith was transferred back to rivals Manchester City and performances on the pitch were less than sparkling. Ten draws and 17 losses saw the team end up 13th in the league with 40 points from 42 games.

Particularly galling were the 3-6 hammering by Newcastle at the start of the New Year and a 2-5 battering by Huddersfield Town as the season drew to a close.

There was no joy in the FA Cup either with a 1-2 defeat in a replay by Liverpool at Old Trafford in January.

**League (Division 1)**

| Aug 28 | Bolton W | H | L | 2-3 |
|---|---|---|---|---|
| Aug 30 | Arsenal | A | D | 1-1 |
| Sep 4 | Bolton W | A | D | 1-1 |
| Sep 6 | Arsenal | H | D | 1-1 |
| Sep 11 | Chelsea | H | W | 3-1 |
| Sep 18 | Chelsea | A | W | 2-1 |
| Sep 25 | Tottenham H | H | L | 0-1 |
| Oct 2 | Tottenham H | A | L | 1-4 |
| Oct 9 | Oldham | H | W | 4-1 |
| Oct 16 | Oldham | A | W | 2-2 |
| Oct 23 | Preston NE | H | W | 1-0 |
| Oct 30 | Preston NE | A | D | 0-0 |
| Nov 6 | Sheffield U | H | W | 2-1 |
| Nov 13 | Sheffield U | A | D | 1-1 |
| Nov 20 | Manchester C | H | L | 1-3 |
| Nov 27 | Manchester C | A | L | 0-3 |
| Dec 4 | Bradford | H | W | 5-1 |
| Dec 11 | Bradford | A | W | 4-2 |
| Dec 18 | Newcastle | H | W | 2-1 |
| Dec 25 | Aston Villa | A | W | 4-3 |
| Dec 27 | Aston Villa | H | L | 1-3 |
| Jan 1 | Newcastle U | A | L | 3-6 |
| Jan 15 | WBA | H | L | 1-4 |
| Jan 22 | WBA | A | W | 2-0 |
| Feb 5 | Liverpool | H | D | 1-1 |
| Feb 11 | Oldham | H | D | 1-1 |
| Feb 12 | Everton | A | W | 2-0 |
| Feb 20 | Sunderland | H | W | 3-0 |
| Feb 21 | Arsenal | H | W | 1-0 |
| Mar 5 | Sunderland | A | W | 3-2 |

# IN THE BEGINNING

## HEATHENS TO UNITED

### 1921-1922

United were about to enter a period in the football wilderness as a disastrous season saw the club relegated with only eight victories from 42 games and 73 goals conceded. The opening game set the tone of the rest of the season as Everton put five past a hapless defence. Sixteen years in the mainstream had come to an end and it would be another three years before United returned to the First Division. The Reds also suffered a 4-1 thrashing at home by Cardiff in the FA Cup in January. While Manchester City thrived under Ernest Mangnold, it was time to take stock and start rebuilding Old Trafford's fortunes.

**Final League position: 22nd**

| P | W | D | L | F/A | Pts |
| --- | --- | --- | --- | --- | --- |
| 42 | 8 | 12 | 22 | 41/73 | 28 |

**FA Cup**

| Date | Opponent | Venue | Result | Score |
| --- | --- | --- | --- | --- |
| Jan 7 | Cardiff C (1) | H | L | 1-4 |

**League (Division 1)**

| Date | Opponent | Venue | Result | Score |
| --- | --- | --- | --- | --- |
| Aug 27 | Everton | A | L | 0-5 |
| Aug 29 | WBA | H | L | 2-3 |
| Sep 3 | Everton | H | W | 2-1 |
| Sep 7 | WBA | A | D | 0-0 |
| Sep 10 | Chelsea | A | D | 0-0 |
| Sep 17 | Chelsea | H | D | 0-0 |
| Sep 24 | Preston NE | A | L | 1-4 |
| Oct 1 | Preston NE | H | D | 1-1 |
| Oct 8 | Tottenham H | A | D | 2-2 |
| Oct 15 | Tottenham H | H | W | 2-1 |
| Oct 22 | Manchester C | A | L | 1-4 |
| Oct 29 | Manchester C | H | W | 3-1 |
| Nov 5 | Middlesbrough | H | L | 3-5 |
| Nov 12 | Middlesbrough | A | L | 0-2 |
| Nov 19 | Aston Villa | A | L | 1-3 |
| Nov 26 | Aston Villa | H | W | 1-0 |
| Dec 3 | Bradford C | A | L | 1-2 |
| Dec 10 | Bradford C | H | D | 1-1 |
| Dec 17 | Liverpool | A | L | 1-2 |
| Dec 24 | Liverpool | H | D | 0-0 |
| Dec 26 | Burnley | H | L | 0-1 |
| Dec 27 | Burnley | A | L | 0-1 |
| Dec 31 | Newcastle U | A | L | 2-4 |
| Jan 2 | Newcastle U | H | L | 0-3 |
| Jan 14 | Sheffield U | A | L | 0-3 |
| Jan 21 | Sunderland | A | L | 1-2 |
| Jan 28 | Sunderland | H | L | 1-3 |
| Feb 11 | Huddersfield T | H | D | 1-1 |
| Feb 18 | Birmingham | A | W | 1-0 |
| Feb 25 | Birmingham | H | W | 1-0 |
| Feb 27 | Huddersfield T | A | L | 0-1 |
| Mar 3 | Southampton | H | L | 1-2 |
| Mar 9 | Everton | A | L | 0-2 |
| Mar 11 | Arsenal | H | W | 1-0 |
| Mar 12 | Bradford C | H | D | 1-1 |
| Mar 18 | Blackburn R | A | L | 0-3 |
| Mar 19 | Bradford C | A | D | 1-1 |
| Mar 25 | Burnley | A | L | 0-1 |
| Mar 26 | Huddersfield T | A | L | 2-5 |
| Mar 28 | Burnley | H | L | 0-3 |
| Apr 2 | Huddersfield T | H | W | 2-0 |
| Apr 9 | Middlesbrough | A | W | 4-2 |
| Apr 16 | Middlesbrough | H | W | 2-0 |
| Apr 23 | Blackburn R | H | L | 0-1 |
| Apr 30 | Blackburn R | A | L | 0-2 |
| May 2 | Derby Co | H | L | 0-1 |
| May 7 | Derby Co | H | W | 3-0 |

**Final League position: 13th**

| P | W | D | L | F/A | Pts |
| --- | --- | --- | --- | --- | --- |
| 42 | 15 | 10 | 17 | 64/86 | 40 |

**FA Cup**

| Date | Opponent | Venue | Result | Score |
| --- | --- | --- | --- | --- |
| Jan 9 | Liverpool (1) | A | D | 1-1 |
| Jan 12 | Liverpool (1R) | H | L | 1-2 |

### 1922-1923

Now demoted to Division 2, United were a mere shadow of the former team. None of the big names that had graced the team in the pre-war days remained at the club after the loss of Billy Meredith and the fans had to get used to seeing the likes of Clapton and South Shields visit Old Trafford. A better Cup run ended in February with a 4-0 defeat at the hands of Tottenham, but United's main priority was a return to the top flight. But the club was condemned to another year in the Second Division after defeats at Blackpool and Leicester late in the season effectively ended the promotion challenge, finishing fourth.

**Final League position: 4th**

| P | W | D | L | F/A | Pts |
| --- | --- | --- | --- | --- | --- |
| 42 | 17 | 14 | 11 | 51/36 | 48 |

**FA Cup**

| Date | Opponent | Venue | Result | Score |
| --- | --- | --- | --- | --- |
| Jan 13 | Bradford C (1) | A | D | 1-1 |
| Jan 17 | Bradford C (1R) | H | W | 2-0 |
| Feb 3 | Tottenham H (2) | A | L | 0-4 |

**League (Division 2)**

| Date | Opponent | Venue | Result | Score |
| --- | --- | --- | --- | --- |
| Aug 26 | Crystal Palace | H | W | 2-1 |
| Aug 28 | Sheffield W | H | L | 0-1 |
| Sep 2 | Crystal Palace | A | W | 3-2 |
| Sep 4 | Sheffield W | A | L | 0-2 |
| Sep 9 | Wolverhampton W | A | W | 1-0 |
| Sep 16 | Wolverhampton W | H | W | 1-0 |
| Sep 23 | Coventry C | A | L | 0-2 |
| Sep 30 | Coventry C | H | W | 2-1 |
| Oct 7 | Port Vale | H | L | 1-2 |
| Oct 14 | Port Vale | A | L | 0-1 |
| Oct 21 | Fulham | H | D | 1-1 |
| Oct 28 | Fulham | A | L | 0-1 |
| Nov 4 | Clapton O | H | D | 0-0 |
| Nov 11 | Clapton O | A | D | 1-1 |
| Nov 18 | Bury | A | D | 2-2 |
| Nov 25 | Bury | H | L | 0-1 |
| Dec 2 | Rotherham U | A | W | 3-0 |
| Dec 9 | Rotherham U | H | W | 3-0 |
| Dec 16 | Stockport Co | H | W | 3-0 |
| Dec 23 | Stockport Co | A | L | 0-1 |
| Dec 25 | Barnsley | H | W | 3-2 |
| Dec 26 | West Ham U | A | L | 0-1 |
| Dec 30 | Hull C | A | L | 1-2 |
| Jan 6 | Hull C | H | W | 3-2 |

### 1923-1924

All hopes of a swift return to the top flight were dispelled. It seemed the team was Division 2 material as United languished against sides which, to be honest, they would have put to the sword five years earlier. Any team fighting to win the championship cannot afford to lose 15 games and draw 13 as a shaky United did this season. Nothing about the team's performance was predictable — they thrashed Crystal Palace 5-1 at home on April 12 and then sauntered to Clapton a week later to receive a 1-0 beating. Life can be tough. Football, United were finding out, can be even tougher. They were demolished 3-0 in the FA Cup by Huddersfield in February.

**League (Division 2)**

| Date | Opponent | Venue | Result | Score |
| --- | --- | --- | --- | --- |
| Aug 25 | Bristol C | A | W | 2-1 |
| Aug 27 | Southampton | H | W | 1-0 |
| Sep 1 | Bristol C | H | W | 2-1 |
| Sep 3 | Southampton | A | D | 0-0 |
| Sep 8 | Bury | A | L | 0-2 |
| Sep 15 | Bury | H | L | 0-1 |
| Sep 22 | South Shields | A | L | 0-1 |
| Sep 29 | South Shields | H | D | 1-1 |
| Oct 6 | Oldham | A | D | 2-3 |
| Oct 13 | Oldham | H | W | 2-0 |
| Oct 20 | Stockport Co | A | W | 3-0 |
| Oct 27 | Stockport Co | H | W | 2-3 |
| Nov 3 | Leicester C | A | L | 2-3 |
| Nov 10 | Leicester C | H | W | 3-0 |
| Nov 17 | Coventry C | A | D | 2-2 |
| Nov 24 | Coventry C | H | W | 3-0 |
| Dec 1 | Leeds U | A | L | 0-1 |
| Dec 8 | Leeds U | H | D | 0-0 |
| Dec 15 | Port Vale | A | W | 3-1 |
| Dec 22 | Port Vale | H | L | 1-2 |
| Dec 25 | Barnsley | H | W | 1-0 |
| Jan 20 | Leeds U | H | D | 0-0 |
| Jan 27 | Leeds U | A | W | 1-0 |
| Feb 10 | Notts Co | A | W | 6-1 |
| Feb 17 | Notts Co | H | D | 0-0 |
| Feb 21 | Derby Co | H | D | 1-1 |
| Mar 3 | Southampton | H | L | 1-2 |

United captain Charlie Roberts raised eyebrows with his fancy short-shorts!

| | | | |
|---|---|---|---|
| Dec 26 Barnsley | A | L | 0-1 |
| Dec 29 Bradford C | A | D | 0-0 |
| Jan 2 Coventry C | H | L | 1-2 |
| Jan 5 Bradford C | H | W | 3-0 |
| Jan 19 Fulham | A | L | 1-3 |
| Jan 26 Fulham | H | D | 0-0 |
| Feb 6 Blackpool | A | L | 0-1 |
| Feb 9 Blackpool | H | D | 0-0 |
| Feb 16 Derby Co | A | L | 0-3 |
| Feb 23 Derby Co | H | D | 0-0 |
| Mar 1 Nelson | A | W | 2-0 |
| Mar 8 Nelson | H | L | 0-1 |
| Mar 15 Hull C | H | D | 1-1 |
| Mar 22 Hull C | A | D | 1-1 |
| Mar 29 Stoke C | H | D | 2-2 |
| Apr 5 Stoke C | A | L | 0-3 |
| Apr 12 Crystal Palace | H | W | 5-1 |
| Apr 18 Clapton O | A | L | 0-1 |
| Apr 19 Crystal Palace | A | D | 1-1 |
| Apr 21 Clapton O | H | D | 2-2 |
| Apr 26 Sheffield W | H | W | 2-0 |
| May 3 Sheffield W | A | L | 0-2 |

**FA Cup**

| | | | |
|---|---|---|---|
| Jan 12 Plymouth A (1) | H | W | 1-0 |
| Feb 2 Huddersfield T (2) | H | L | 0-3 |

Final League position: **14th**

| P | W | D | L | F/A | Pts |
|---|---|---|---|---|---|
| 42 | 13 | 14 | 15 | 52/44 | 40 |

# 1924-25

The season kicked off well with Ernest Mangnall's big testimonial game. In a rare display of solidarity, Manchester United teamed up with Manchester City to field a combined side against a mixture of Everton and Liverpool players. The man who had done so much for soccer was about to retire from management and try his hand at journalism. Fans packed Maine Road to say thanks. It proved to be the start of a good season for United, who won 23 of the 42 games they played, including a 5-1 defeat of Coventry City at home. The team finished 2nd to Leicester City and won promotion back into the first division after three seasons languishing in the second.

**League (Division 2)**

| | | | |
|---|---|---|---|
| Aug 30 Leicester C | H | W | 1-0 |
| Sep 1 Stockport Co | A | L | 1-2 |
| Sep 6 Stoke C | A | D | 0-0 |
| Sep 8 Barnsley | H | W | 1-0 |
| Sep 13 Coventry C | H | W | 5-1 |
| Sep 20 Oldham | A | W | 3-0 |
| Sep 27 Sheffield Wed | H | W | 2-0 |
| Oct 4 Clapton O | A | W | 1-0 |
| Oct 11 Crystal Palace | H | W | 1-0 |
| Oct 18 Southampton | A | W | 2-0 |
| Oct 25 Wolverhampton W | A | D | 0-0 |
| Nov 1 Fulham | H | W | 2-0 |
| Nov 8 Portsmouth | A | D | 1-1 |
| Nov 15 Hull C | H | W | 2-0 |
| Nov 22 Blackpool | A | D | 1-1 |
| Nov 29 Derby Co | H | D | 1-1 |
| Dec 6 South Shields | A | W | 2-1 |
| Dec 13 Bradford C | H | W | 3-0 |
| Dec 20 Port Vale | A | L | 1-2 |
| Dec 25 Middlesbrough | A | D | 1-1 |
| Dec 26 Middlesbrough | H | W | 2-0 |
| Dec 27 Leicester C | A | L | 0-3 |
| Jan 17 Chelsea | H | W | 1-0 |
| Jan 3 Stoke C | H | W | 2-0 |
| Jan 1 Coventry C | A | L | 0-1 |
| Jan 24 Oldham | H | L | 1-0 |
| Feb 7 Clapton O | H | W | 4-2 |
| Feb 14 Crystal Palace | A | L | 1-2 |
| Feb 23 Sheffield Wed | A | D | 1-1 |
| Feb 28 Wolverhampton W | H | W | 3-0 |
| Mar 7 Fulham | A | L | 0-1 |
| Mar 14 Portsmouth | H | W | 2-0 |
| Mar 21 Hull C | A | W | 1-0 |
| Mar 28 Blackpool | H | D | 0-0 |
| Apr 4 Derby Co | A | L | 0-1 |
| Apr 10 Stockport Co | H | W | 2-0 |
| Apr 11 South Shields | H | W | 1-0 |
| Apr 13 Chelsea | A | D | 0-0 |
| Apr 18 Bradford C | A | W | 1-0 |
| Apr 22 Southampton | H | D | 1-1 |
| Apr 25 Port Vale | H | W | 4-0 |
| May 2 Barnsley | A | D | 0-0 |

**FA Cup**

| | | | |
|---|---|---|---|
| Jan 10 Sheffield Wed (1) | A | L | 0-2 |

Final League position: **2nd**

| P | W | D | L | F/A | Pts |
|---|---|---|---|---|---|
| 42 | 23 | 11 | 8 | 57/23 | 57 |

# 1925-26

United celebrated their return to the first division, after three seasons away, with some thrilling matches. Having lost 5-0 to Liverpool in September, they came straight back the following week and beat Burnley 6-1. While United finished a respectable ninth, old rivals Manchester City were relegated. It was hard luck for the Maine Roaders who beat United 6-1 in the league in January and 3-0 in the semi-final of the FA Cup. However, even the silveware eluded City. When it came to the final they were beaten 1-0 by Bolton Wanderers.

**League (Division 1)**

| | | | |
|---|---|---|---|
| Aug 29 West Ham U | A | L | 0-1 |
| Sep 2 Aston Villa | H | W | 3-0 |
| Sep 5 Arsenal | H | L | 0-1 |
| Sep 9 Aston Villa | A | D | 2-2 |
| Sep 12 Manchester C | A | D | 1-1 |
| Sep 16 Leicester C | H | W | 3-2 |
| Sep 19 Liverpool | A | L | 0-5 |
| Sep 26 Burnley | H | W | 6-1 |
| Oct 3 Leeds U | A | L | 0-2 |
| Oct 10 Newcastle U | H | W | 2-1 |
| Oct 17 Tottenham H | H | D | 0-0 |
| Oct 24 Cardiff C | A | W | 2-0 |
| Oct 31 Huddersfield T | H | D | 1-1 |
| Nov 7 Everton | A | W | 3-1 |
| Nov 14 Birmingham | H | W | 3-1 |
| Nov 21 Bury | A | W | 3-1 |
| Nov 28 Blackburn R | H | W | 2-0 |
| Dec 5 Sunderland | A | L | 1-2 |
| Dec 12 Sheffield U | H | L | 1-2 |
| Dec 19 WBA | A | L | 1-5 |
| Dec 25 Bolton W | H | W | 2-1 |
| Dec 28 Leicester C | A | W | 3-1 |
| Jan 2 West Ham U | H | W | 2-1 |
| Jan 16 Arsenal | A | L | 2-3 |
| Jan 23 Manchester C | H | L | 1-6 |
| Feb 6 Burnley | A | W | 1-0 |
| Feb 13 Leeds U | H | W | 2-1 |
| Feb 27 Tottenham H | A | W | 1-0 |
| Mar 10 Liverpool | H | D | 3-3 |
| Mar 13 Huddersfield T | A | L | 0-5 |
| Mar 17 Bolton W | A | L | 1-3 |
| Mar 20 Everton | H | D | 0-0 |
| Apr 2 Notts Co | A | W | 3-0 |
| Apr 3 Bury | H | L | 0-1 |
| Apr 5 Notts Co | H | L | 0-1 |
| Apr 10 Blackburn R | A | L | 0-7 |
| Apr 14 Newcastle U | A | L | 1-4 |
| Apr 19 Birmingham | A | L | 1-2 |
| Apr 21 Sunderland | H | W | 5-1 |
| Apr 24 Sheffield U | A | L | 0-2 |
| Apr 28 Cardiff C | H | W | 1-0 |
| May 1 WBA | H | W | 3-2 |

Final League position: **9th**

| P | W | D | L | F/A | Pts |
|---|---|---|---|---|---|
| 42 | 19 | 6 | 17 | 66/73 | 44 |

**FA Cup**

| | | | |
|---|---|---|---|
| Jan 9 Port Vale (3) | A | W | 3-2 |
| Jan 30 Tottenham H (4) | A | D | 2-2 |
| Feb 3 Tottenham H (4R) | H | W | 2-0 |
| Feb 20 Sunderland (5) | A | D | 3-3 |
| Feb 24 Sunderland (5R) | H | W | 2-1 |
| Mar 6 Fulham (6) | A | W | 2-1 |
| Mar 21 Manchester C (SF) (at Brammall Lane) | N | L | 0-3 |

# 1926-27

The shock suspension by the FA of manager John Chapman for unspecified "improper conduct" in 1926 sent United into a downward spiral. Half-back Clarrie Hilditch became player- boss while the club desperately looked around for a proper replacement. Referee turned manager, Herbert Bamlett was given the job in 1927 and presided over one of the worst periods in the team's history. There was another shock for United in October of the same year, when brewer John Henry Davies, the man who rescued the club from extinction in 1902, died. The team lost 15 out of the 42 games they played and finished a disappointing 15th. In February they failed to win in a run of seven matches.

**League (Division 1)**

| | | | |
|---|---|---|---|
| Aug 28 Liverpool | A | L | 2-4 |
| Aug 30 Sheffield U | A | D | 2-2 |
| Sep 4 Leeds U | H | D | 2-2 |
| Sep 11 Newcastle U | A | L | 2-4 |
| Sep 15 Arsenal | H | D | 2-2 |
| Sep 18 Burnley | H | W | 2-1 |
| Sep 25 Cardiff C | A | W | 2-0 |
| Oct 2 Aston Villa | H | W | 2-1 |
| Oct 9 Bolton W | A | L | 0-4 |
| Oct 16 Bury | A | W | 3-0 |
| Oct 23 Birmingham | H | L | 0-1 |
| Oct 30 West Ham U | A | L | 0-4 |
| Nov 6 Sheffield Wed | H | D | 0-0 |
| Nov 13 Leicester C | A | W | 3-2 |
| Nov 20 Everton | H | W | 2-1 |
| Nov 27 Blackburn R | A | L | 1-2 |
| Dec 4 Huddersfield T | H | D | 0-0 |
| Dec 11 Sunderland | A | L | 0-6 |
| Dec 18 WBA | H | W | 2-0 |
| Dec 25 Tottenham H | A | D | 1-1 |
| Dec 27 Tottenham H | H | W | 2-1 |
| Dec 28 Arsenal | A | L | 0-1 |
| Jan 1 Sheffield U | H | W | 5-0 |
| Jan 15 Liverpool | H | L | 0-1 |
| Jan 22 Leeds U | A | W | 3-2 |
| Feb 5 Burnley | A | L | 0-1 |
| Feb 9 Newcastle U | H | W | 3-1 |
| Feb 12 Cardiff C | H | D | 1-1 |
| Feb 19 Aston Villa | A | L | 0-2 |
| Feb 26 Bolton W | H | D | 0-0 |
| Mar 5 Bury | H | L | 1-2 |
| Mar 12 Birmingham | A | L | 0-4 |
| Mar 19 West Ham U | H | L | 0-3 |
| Mar 26 Sheffield Wed | A | L | 0-2 |
| Apr 2 Leicester C | H | W | 1-0 |
| Apr 9 Everton | A | D | 0-0 |
| Apr 15 Derby Co | H | D | 2-2 |
| Apr 16 Blackburn R | H | W | 2-0 |
| Apr 18 Derby Co | A | D | 2-2 |
| Apr 23 Huddersfield T | A | D | 0-0 |
| Apr 30 Sunderland | H | D | 0-0 |
| May 7 WBA | A | D | 2-2 |

Final League position: **15th**

| P | W | D | L | F/A | Pts |
|---|---|---|---|---|---|
| 42 | 13 | 14 | 15 | 52/64 | 40 |

**FA Cup**

| | | | |
|---|---|---|---|
| Jan 8 Reading (3) | A | D | 1-1 |
| Jan 12 Reading (3R) | H | D | 2-2 |
| Jan 17 Reading (3R2) (at Villa Park) | N | L | 1-2 |

# 1927-28

More gloom for United under manager Herbert Bamlett, who had come to the club via spells in charge at Oldham Athletic, Wigan Borough and Middlesbrough. They fell to 18th in the First Division. The team's worst game was against Newcastle United in September, when they lost 7-1. There were occasional bright moments, including a 5-0 win over Derby County in October, a 5-1 defeat of Aston Villa in November and a 6-1 drubbing of Liverpool in May. However, the slide towards relegation had begun and fans began to get more and more disenchanted with the way the club was being run. The rumblings of discontent would get louder over the next few seasons.

**League (Division 1)**

| | | | |
|---|---|---|---|
| Aug 27 Middlesbrough | H | W | 3-0 |
| Aug 29 Sheffield Wed | A | W | 2-0 |
| Sep 3 Birmingham | A | D | 0-0 |
| Sep 7 Sheffield Wed | H | D | 1-1 |
| Sep 10 Newcastle U | H | L | 1-7 |
| Sep 17 Huddersfield T | A | L | 2-4 |
| Sep 19 Blackburn R | A | I | 0-3 |
| Sep 24 Tottenham H | H | W | 3-0 |
| Oct 1 Leicester C | A | L | 0-1 |
| Oct 8 Everton | A | L | 2-5 |
| Oct 15 Cardiff C | H | D | 2-2 |
| Oct 22 Derby Co | H | W | 5-0 |
| Oct 29 West Ham U | A | W | 2-1 |
| Nov 5 Portsmouth | H | W | 2-0 |
| Nov 12 Sunderland | A | L | 1-4 |
| Nov 19 Aston Villa | H | W | 5-1 |
| Nov 26 Burnley | A | L | 0-4 |
| Dec 3 Bury | H | L | 0-1 |
| Dec 10 Sheffield U | A | L | 1-2 |
| Dec 17 Arsenal | H | W | 4-1 |
| Dec 24 Liverpool | A | L | 0-2 |
| Dec 26 Blackburn R | H | D | 1-1 |
| Dec 31 Middlesbrough | A | W | 2-1 |
| Jan 7 Birmingham | H | D | 1-1 |
| Jan 21 Newcastle U | A | L | 1-4 |
| Feb 4 Tottenham H | A | L | 1-4 |
| Feb 11 Leicester C | H | W | 5-2 |
| Feb 25 Cardiff C | A | L | 0-2 |
| Mar 7 Huddersfield T | H | D | 0-0 |
| Mar 10 West Ham U | H | D | 1-1 |
| Mar 14 Everton | H | W | 1-0 |
| Mar 17 Portsmouth | A | L | 0-1 |
| Mar 28 Derby Co | A | L | 0-5 |
| Mar 31 Aston Villa | A | L | 1-3 |
| Apr 6 Bolton W | A | L | 2-3 |
| Apr 7 Burnley | H | W | 4-3 |
| Apr 9 Bolton W | H | W | 2-1 |
| Apr 14 Bury | A | L | 3-4 |
| Apr 21 Sheffield U | H | L | 2-3 |
| Apr 25 Sunderland | H | W | 2-1 |
| Apr 28 Arsenal | A | W | 1-0 |
| May 5 Liverpool | H | W | 6-1 |

Final League position: **18th**

| P | W | D | L | F/A | Pts |
|---|---|---|---|---|---|
| 42 | 16 | 7 | 19 | 72/80 | 39 |

**FA Cup**

| | | | |
|---|---|---|---|
| Jan 14 Brentford (3) | H | W | 7-1 |
| Jan 28 Bury (4) | A | D | 1-1 |
| Feb 1 Bury (4R) | H | W | 1-0 |
| Feb 18 Birmingham C (5) | H | W | 1-0 |
| Mar 3 Blackburn (6) | A | L | 0-2 |

# 1928-29

Another season in the doldrums for United. Herbert Bamlett's management style failed to inspire the team, which included legendary outside-right Joe Spence, who played for the club for 14 years and turned out for a record 510 league and cup games. They lost 15 out of 42 matches and drew 13. Between November 3 and February 13 they failed to win once during a dismal run of 16 fixtures. United's best win was 5-0 against Newcastle on September 29. The side's worst defeats were against Sheffield United in December and Derby County in March. On both occasions the Reds lost 6-1. They also went down 5-0 when they went to Newcastle in February.

**League (Division 1)**

| | | | |
|---|---|---|---|
| Aug 25 Leicester C | H | D | 1-1 |
| Aug 27 Aston Villa | A | D | 0-0 |
| Sep 1 Manchester C | A | D | 2-2 |
| Sep 8 Leeds U | A | L | 2-3 |
| Sep 15 Liverpool | H | D | 2-2 |
| Sep 22 West Ham U | A | L | 1-3 |
| Sep 29 Newcastle U | H | W | 5-0 |
| Oct 6 Burnley | A | W | 4-3 |
| Oct 13 Cardiff C | H | D | 1-1 |
| Oct 20 Birmingham | H | W | 1-0 |
| Oct 27 Huddersfield T | A | W | 2-1 |
| Nov 3 Bolton W | H | D | 1-1 |
| Nov 10 Sheffield Wed | A | L | 1-2 |
| Nov 17 Derby Co | H | L | 0-1 |
| Nov 24 Sunderland | A | L | 1-5 |
| Dec 1 Blackburn R | H | L | 1-4 |
| Dec 8 Arsenal | A | L | 1-3 |
| Dec 15 Everton | H | D | 1-1 |
| Dec 22 Portsmouth | A | L | 0-3 |
| Dec 25 Sheffield U | H | D | 1-1 |
| Dec 26 Sheffield U | A | L | 1-6 |
| Dec 29 Leicester C | A | L | 1-2 |
| Jan 1 Aston Villa | H | D | 2-2 |
| Jan 5 Manchester C | H | L | 1-2 |
| Jan 19 Leeds U | H | L | 1-2 |
| Feb 2 West Ham U | H | L | 2-3 |
| Feb 9 Newcastle U | A | L | 0-5 |
| Feb 13 Liverpool | A | W | 3-2 |
| Feb 16 Burnley | H | W | 1-0 |
| Feb 23 Cardiff C | A | D | 2-2 |
| Mar 2 Birmingham | A | D | 1-1 |
| Mar 9 Huddersfield T | H | W | 1-0 |
| Mar 16 Bolton W | A | D | 1-1 |
| Mar 23 Sheffield Wed | H | W | 2-1 |
| Mar 29 Bury | A | W | 3-1 |
| Mar 30 Derby Co | A | L | 1-6 |
| Apr 1 Bury | H | W | 1-0 |
| Apr 6 Sunderland | H | W | 3-0 |
| Apr 13 Blackburn R | A | W | 3-0 |
| Apr 20 Arsenal | H | W | 4-1 |
| Apr 27 Everton | A | W | 4-2 |
| May 4 Portsmouth | H | D | 0-0 |

Final League position: **12th**

| P | W | D | L | F/A | Pts |
|---|---|---|---|---|---|
| 42 | 14 | 13 | 15 | 66/76 | 41 |

**FA Cup**

| | | | |
|---|---|---|---|
| Jan 12 Port Vale (3) | A | W | 3-0 |
| Jan 26 Bury (4) | H | L | 0-1 |

# 1929-30

The downward slide continued. United ended the season in 17th place as the side struggled to find form. In one particularly bad patch, between September 21and October 19, the team lost six games in a row. Fans were openly criticising manager Herbert Bamlett and his future at Old Trafford looked increasingly in doubt. Their worst defeat was a 7-2 hammering by Sheffield Wednesday in November.

United's only bright spot in the results gloom was a 5-0 win against Newcastle United just after Christmas. However, it wasn't enough to lift spirits and the clamouring for changes at the top grew louder.

### League (Division 1)

| Date | Opponent | | Result | Score |
|---|---|---|---|---|
| Aug 31 | Newcastle U | A | L | 1-4 |
| Sep 2 | Leicester C | A | L | 1-4 |
| Sep 7 | Blackburn R | H | W | 1-0 |
| Sep 11 | Leicester C | H | W | 2-1 |
| Sep 14 | Middlesbrough | A | W | 3-2 |
| Sep 21 | Liverpool | H | L | 1-2 |
| Sep 28 | West Ham U | A | W | 2-1 |
| Oct 5 | Manchester C | H | L | 1-3 |
| Oct 7 | Sheffield U | A | L | 1-3 |
| Oct 12 | Grimsby T | A | L | 1-2 |
| Oct 19 | Portsmouth | A | L | 0-3 |
| Oct 26 | Arsenal | H | L | 1-2 |
| Nov 2 | Aston Villa | A | L | 0-1 |
| Nov 9 | Derby Co | H | W | 3-2 |
| Nov 16 | Sheffield Wed | A | L | 2-7 |
| Nov 23 | Sunderland | H | W | 4-2 |
| Nov 30 | Sunderland | A | L | 2-7 |
| Dec 7 | Bolton W | H | D | 1-1 |
| Dec 14 | Everton | A | D | 0-0 |
| Dec 21 | Leeds U | A | D | 0-0 |
| Dec 25 | Birmingham | H | W | 1-0 |
| Dec 26 | Birmingham | A | W | 1-0 |
| Dec 28 | Newcastle U | H | W | 5-0 |
| Jan 1 | Blackburn R | A | L | 4-5 |
| Jan 18 | Middlesbrough | H | L | 0-3 |
| Jan 25 | Liverpool | A | L | 0-1 |
| Feb 1 | West Ham U | H | W | 4-2 |
| Feb 8 | Manchester C | A | W | 1-0 |
| Feb 15 | Grimsby T | H | L | 0-6 |
| Feb 22 | Portsmouth | A | L | 0-3 |
| Mar 1 | Bolton W | A | L | 1-5 |
| Mar 8 | Aston Villa | H | L | 2-3 |
| Mar 12 | Arsenal | A | L | 1-4 |
| Mar 15 | Derby Co | A | L | 0-1 |
| Mar 29 | Burnley | H | W | 4-1 |
| Apr 5 | Sunderland | H | D | 3-3 |
| Apr 14 | Sheffield Wed | H | W | 2-1 |
| Apr 18 | Huddersfield T | A | L | 2-2 |
| Apr 19 | Everton | H | W | 3-0 |
| Apr 22 | Huddersfield T | H | D | 2-2 |
| Apr 26 | Leeds U | H | L | 1-3 |
| May 3 | Sheffield U | H | L | 1-5 |

**Final League position: 17th**

| P | W | D | L | F/A | Pts |
|---|---|---|---|---|---|
| 42 | 15 | 8 | 19 | 67/88 | 38 |

### FA Cup
Jan 11 Swindon (3) H L 0-2

## 1930-31

The team went from bad to dreadful. They lost the first 12 matches and only won seven during the whole dismal season. It was a nightmare for fans, some of whom threatened to boycott the game against Arsenal on October 18. A survival plan put forward by the supporters club included the axing of manager Herbert Bamlett. He was duly sacked on April 31, 1931, just before the last game of the season against Middlesbrough, which was watched by only a handful of die-hards. United were relegated to Division 2.

### League (Division 1)

| Date | Opponent | | Result | Score |
|---|---|---|---|---|
| Aug 30 | Aston Villa | H | L | 3-4 |
| Sep 3 | Middlesbrough | A | L | 1-3 |
| Sep 6 | Chelsea | A | L | 2-6 |
| Sep 10 | Huddersfield T | H | L | 0-6 |
| Sep 13 | Newcastle U | A | L | 4-7 |
| Sep 15 | Huddersfield T | A | L | 0-3 |
| Sep 20 | Sheffield Wed | H | L | 0-3 |
| Sep 27 | Grimsby T | A | L | 1-4 |
| Oct 4 | Arsenal | H | L | 1-2 |
| Oct 11 | Manchester C | A | L | 1-4 |
| Oct 18 | Arsenal | A | L | 1-5 |
| Oct 25 | Sunderland | H | W | 2-1 |
| Nov 1 | Birmingham | A | W | 2-0 |
| Nov 8 | Leicester C | H | L | 4-5 |
| Nov 15 | Blackpool | A | L | 1-4 |
| Nov 22 | Sheffield U | H | L | 1-3 |
| Nov 29 | Sunderland | A | L | 1-3 |
| Dec 6 | Blackburn R | H | D | 1-1 |
| Dec 13 | Derby Co | A | L | 0-5 |
| Dec 20 | Leeds U | H | W | 2-1 |
| Dec 25 | Bolton W | A | L | 1-3 |
| Dec 27 | Bolton W | H | D | 1-1 |
| Jan 1 | Portsmouth | A | L | 0-7 |
| Jan 3 | Chelsea | H | D | 0-0 |
| Jan 17 | Newcastle U | H | W | 4-1 |
| Jan 28 | Sheffield Wed | A | L | 3-4 |
| Jan 31 | Grimsby T | H | W | 1-0 |
| Feb 7 | Manchester C | H | L | 1-3 |
| Feb 21 | West Ham U | H | L | 1-3 |
| Mar 7 | Birmingham | H | L | 0-1 |
| Mar 16 | Portsmouth | H | L | 1-4 |
| Mar 21 | Blackpool | H | L | 1-5 |
| Mar 28 | Sheffield U | A | L | 1-2 |
| Apr 3 | Liverpool | A | D | 1-1 |
| Apr 4 | Sunderland | H | L | 1-2 |
| Apr 6 | Liverpool | H | W | 2-1 |
| Apr 11 | Derby Co | H | D | 0-0 |
| Apr 18 | Blackburn R | A | L | 1-5 |
| Apr 25 | Leicester C | A | L | 1-2 |
| May 2 | Middlesbrough | A | L | 3-4 |

**Final League position: 22nd**

| P | W | D | L | F/A | Pts |
|---|---|---|---|---|---|
| 42 | 7 | 8 | 27 | 53/115 | 22 |

### FA Cup
Jan 10 Stoke C (3) A D 3-3
Jan 14 Stoke C (3R) H D 0-0
Jan 19 Stoke C (3R2) N W 4-2 (at Anfield)
Jan 24 Grimsby (4) A L 0-1

## 1931-1932

Herbert Bamlett was succeeded by Walter Crickmer, aided by the crucial scout Louis Rocca, and the duo set about rescuing the club from the brink of bankruptcy after the banks lost patience and threatened to end their credit tolerance. Manchester businessman James Gibson came to the rescue with loans enabling the club to pay its way, literally week by week, until he finally achieved full control and started the search for a new manager. Ironically, Gibson was not a football man, more a lover of sports in general, but he saved the club from certain death. What would United's history have been had this quiet philanthropist not dipped into his own pocket? The team's fortunes improved, finishing in a respectable 12th place, given the financial horror story of the year, but they were still struggling in the lower league.

### League (Division 2)

| Date | Opponent | | Result | Score |
|---|---|---|---|---|
| Aug 29 | Bradford | H | L | 1-3 |
| Sep 2 | Swansea | H | L | 2-3 |
| Sep 5 | Swansea | A | L | 0-3 |
| Sep 7 | Stoke C | H | W | 3-2 |
| Sep 9 | Stoke C | A | L | 1-2 |
| Sep 12 | Tottenham H | H | D | 1-1 |
| Sep 19 | Nottingham F | A | L | 1-2 |
| Sep 26 | Chesterfield | H | W | 3-1 |
| Oct 3 | Bury | A | L | 1-2 |
| Oct 10 | Preston NE | H | W | 3-2 |
| Oct 17 | Barnsley | A | D | 0-0 |
| Oct 24 | Notts C | H | D | 0-0 |
| Oct 31 | Plymouth A | A | L | 1-3 |
| Nov 7 | Leeds U | H | L | 1-5 |
| Nov 21 | Bury | H | W | 2-1 |
| Nov 28 | Port Vale | A | W | 2-1 |
| Dec 5 | Millwall | H | W | 2-0 |
| Dec 12 | Bristol C | A | L | 3-4 |
| Dec 25 | Wolverhampton W | H | W | 3-2 |
| Dec 26 | Wolverhampton W | A | L | 0-7 |
| Jan 2 | Bradford C | A | L | 0-1 |
| Jan 16 | Swansea | H | W | 1-3 |
| Jan 23 | Tottenham H | A | L | 1-4 |
| Jan 30 | Nottingham F | H | W | 3-2 |
| Feb 6 | Chesterfield | A | L | 1-3 |
| Feb 17 | Burnley | H | W | 5-1 |
| Feb 20 | Preston NE | A | L | 0-7 |
| Feb 27 | Barnsley | H | W | 3-0 |
| Mar 5 | Notts C | A | L | 1-3 |
| Mar 12 | Plymouth A | H | W | 4-1 |
| Mar 25 | Charlton A | H | W | 4-1 |
| Mar 26 | Oldham | A | L | 0-2 |
| Mar 28 | Charlton A | A | L | 1-2 |
| Apr 2 | Bury | A | D | 0-0 |
| Apr 16 | Millwall | A | W | 1-0 |
| Apr 23 | Bradford C | H | A | 0-1 |
| Apr 30 | Bristol C | A | L | 1-2 |
| May 7 | Southampton | A | L | 1-2 |

**Final League position: 12th**

| P | W | D | L | F/A | Pts |
|---|---|---|---|---|---|
| 42 | 17 | 8 | 17 | 71/72 | 42 |

### FA Cup
Jan 9 Plymouth A (3) A L 1-4

United's Second Division Championship-winning side in 1935-36

## 1932-1933

United were finding it tough to get going in Division Two with all the internal financial problems the club faced. They improved slightly on the pitch, finishing sixth and there were some bizarre results. In September they lost to Tottenham 6-1 then thrashed Millwall 7-1 at home. Life just seemed to be one long rollercoaster ride at Old Trafford and the hope of a return to the top flight was a distant one.

### League (Division 2)

| Date | Opponent | | Result | Score |
|---|---|---|---|---|
| Aug 27 | Stoke C | H | L | 0-2 |
| Aug 29 | Charlton A | A | W | 1-0 |
| Sep 3 | Southampton | A | L | 2-4 |
| Sep 7 | Charlton A | H | L | 1-6 |
| Sep 10 | Tottenham H | A | L | 1-6 |
| Sep 17 | Grimsby T | H | D | 1-1 |
| Sep 24 | Oldham A | A | L | 1-2 |
| Oct 1 | Preston N E | H | D | 0-0 |
| Oct 8 | Burnley | A | W | 3-2 |
| Oct 15 | Bradford Park Ave | H | W | 3-2 |
| Oct 22 | Millwall | A | W | 7-1 |
| Oct 29 | Port Vale | A | D | 3-3 |
| Nov 5 | Notts C | H | W | 2-0 |
| Nov 12 | Bury | A | L | 1-3 |
| Nov 19 | Fulham | H | W | 4-3 |
| Nov 26 | Chesterfield | A | D | 1-1 |
| Dec 3 | Bradford C | H | W | 2-1 |
| Dec 10 | West Ham U | A | L | 1-3 |
| Dec 17 | Lincoln C | H | W | 4-1 |
| Dec 24 | Swansea T | A | L | 1-2 |
| Dec 26 | Plymouth Argyle | A | W | 3-2 |
| Dec 31 | Plymouth Argyle | H | D | 0-0 |
| Jan 2 | Stoke C | A | D | 0-1 |
| Jan 7 | Southampton | H | L | 1-2 |
| Jan 21 | Grimsby T | A | L | 2-3 |
| Jan 28 | Oldham A | H | W | 4-0 |
| Feb 4 | Preston N E | A | L | 1-2 |
| Feb 22 | Burnley | H | W | 2-1 |
| Mar 4 | Millwall | H | D | 3-3 |
| Mar 11 | Port Vale | H | W | 2-1 |
| Mar 18 | Notts C | A | L | 0-2 |
| Mar 25 | Bradford Park Ave | A | L | 1-2 |
| Apr 1 | Fulham | A | L | 1-3 |
| Apr 5 | Chesterfield | H | W | 2-1 |
| Apr 8 | Bradford C | A | L | 0-2 |
| Apr 14 | Nottingham F | H | W | 2-1 |
| Apr 15 | West Ham U | H | W | 2-1 |
| Apr 17 | Nottingham F | A | L | 0-2 |
| Apr 22 | Lincoln C | A | L | 2-3 |
| Apr 29 | Swansea T | H | L | 0-1 |
| May 6 | Swansea T | H | D | 1-1 |

**Final League position: 6th**

| P | W | D | L | F/A | Pts |
|---|---|---|---|---|---|
| 42 | 15 | 13 | 14 | 71/68 | 43 |

### FA Cup
Jan 14 Middlesbrough (3) H L 1-4

## 1933-1934

The previous season's battles with Millwall were to take on a very special significance for United this year. With their fortunes sinking fast, United finished the season at their lowest in the 20th position, a disaster for a club of its supposed status. They were hovering on the brink of the unthinkable. Millwall were one place above them and the two teams met in May. The United players had to fight for their lives against the London team, eventually winning a thrilling encounter 2-0. They were saved from the ignominy of relegation – at a time when rivals Manchester City won the FA Cup with none other than Matt Busby!

**League (Division 2)**

| | | | | |
|---|---|---|---|---|
| Aug 26 | Plymouth Argyle | A | L | 0-4 |
| Aug 30 | Nottingham F | h | L | 0-1 |
| Sep 2 | Lincoln C | H | D | 1-1 |
| Sep 7 | Nottingham f | H | L | 0-1 |
| Sep 12 | Bolton W | H | L | 1-5 |
| Sep 16 | Brentford | A | W | 4-3 |
| Sep 23 | Burnley | H | W | 5-2 |
| Sep 30 | Oldham A | A | L | 0-2 |
| Oct 7 | Preston N E | H | W | 1-0 |
| Oct 14 | Bradford Park Ave | A | L | 1-6 |
| Oct 21 | Bury | A | L | 1-2 |
| Oct 28 | Hull C | H | W | 4-1 |
| Nov 4 | Fulham | A | W | 2-0 |
| Nov 11 | Southampton | H | W | 1-0 |
| Nov 18 | Blackpool | A | L | 1-3 |
| Nov 25 | Bradford C | H | W | 2-1 |
| Dec 2 | Port Vale | A | W | 3-2 |
| Dec 9 | Notts C | H | L | 1-2 |
| Dec 16 | Swansea T | A | L | 1-2 |
| Dec 23 | Millwall | H | D | 1-1 |
| Dec 25 | Grimsby T | H | L | 1-1 |
| Dec 26 | Grimsby T | A | L | 3-7 |
| Dec 30 | Plymouth Argyle | H | L | 0-3 |
| Jan 6 | Lincoln C | A | L | 1-5 |
| Jan 20 | Bolton W | A | L | 1-3 |
| Jan 27 | Brentford | H | L | 1-3 |
| Feb 3 | Burnley | A | W | 4-1 |
| Feb 10 | Oldham A | H | L | 2-3 |
| Feb 21 | Preston N E | A | L | 2-3 |
| Feb 24 | Bradford Park Ave | H | L | 0-4 |
| Mar 3 | Bury | H | W | 2-1 |
| Mar 10 | Hull C | A | L | 1-4 |
| Mar 17 | Fulham | H | W | 1-0 |
| Mar 24 | Southampton | A | L | 0-1 |
| Mar 30 | West Ham U | H | L | 0-1 |
| Mar 31 | Blackpool | H | W | 2-0 |
| Apr 2 | West Ham U | A | L | 1-2 |
| Apr 7 | Bradford C | A | D | 1-1 |
| Apr 14 | Port Vale | H | W | 2-0 |
| Apr 21 | Notts C | A | D | 0-0 |
| Apr 28 | Swansea T | H | D | 1-1 |
| May 5 | Millwall | A | W | 2-0 |

Final League position: **20th**

| P | W | D | L | F/A | Pts |
|---|---|---|---|---|---|
| 42 | 14 | 6 | 22 | 59/85 | 34 |

**FA Cup**

| | | | | |
|---|---|---|---|---|
| Jan 13 | Portsmouth (3) | H | D | 1-1 |
| Jan 17 | Portsmouth (3R) | A | L | 1-4 |

## 1934-1935

After the trauma of the last season, things could only start to look up for United. Manager Scott Duncan still had a fight on his hands but the team had at least turned the corner. October and November saw them hit their best patch for years with six straight victories and then another four in December. They also improved in the FA Cup, eventually going out in January after taking Nottingham Forrest to a replay. United finished a creditable fifth in the League. It seemed things were back on track at last and the fans started to flock back to Old Trafford.

**League (Division 2)**

| | | | | |
|---|---|---|---|---|
| Aug 25 | Bradford C | H | W | 2-0 |
| Sep 1 | Sheffield U | A | L | 2-3 |
| Sep 3 | Bolton W | A | L | 1-3 |
| Sep 8 | Barnsley | H | W | 4-1 |
| Sep 12 | Bolton w | H | L | 0-3 |
| Sep 15 | Port Vale | A | L | 2-3 |
| Sep 22 | Norwich C | H | W | 5-0 |
| Sep 29 | Swansea T | H | W | 3-1 |
| Oct 6 | Burnley | A | W | 2-1 |
| Oct 13 | Oldham A | H | W | 4-0 |
| Oct 20 | Newcastle U | A | W | 1-0 |
| Oct 27 | West Ham U | H | W | 3-1 |
| Nov 3 | Blackpool | A | w | 2-1 |
| Nov 10 | Bury | H | W | 1-0 |
| Nov 17 | Hull C | A | L | 2-3 |
| Nov 24 | Nottingham F | H | W | 3-2 |
| Dec 1 | Brentford | A | L | 1-3 |
| Dec 8 | Fulham | H | W | 1-0 |
| Dec 15 | Bradford Park Ave | A | W | 2-1 |
| Dec 22 | Plmouth Argyle | H | W | 3-1 |
| Dec 25 | Notts C | H | W | 2-1 |
| Dec 26 | Notts C | A | L | 0-1 |
| Dec 29 | Bradford C | A | L | 0-2 |
| Jan 1 | Southampton | H | W | 3-0 |
| Jan 5 | Sheffield U | H | D | 3-3 |
| Jan 19 | Barnsley | A | W | 2-0 |
| Feb 2 | Norwich C | A | L | 2-3 |
| Feb 6 | Port Vale | H | W | 2-1 |
| Feb 9 | Swansea T | A | L | o-1 |
| Feb 23 | Oldham A | A | L | 1-3 |
| Mar 2 | Newcastle U | H | L | 0-1 |
| Mar 9 | West Ham U | A | D | 0-0 |
| Mar 16 | Blackpool | H | W | 3-2 |
| Mar 23 | Bury | A | W | 1-0 |
| Mar 27 | Burnley | H | L | 3-4 |
| Mar 30 | Hull C | H | W | 3-0 |
| Apr 6 | Nottingham F | A | D | 2-2 |
| Apr 13 | Brentford | H | D | 0-0 |
| Apr 20 | Fulham | A | L | 1-3 |
| Apr 22 | Southampton | A | L | 0-1 |
| Apr 27 | Bradford Park Ave | H | W | 2-0 |
| May 4 | Plymouth Argyle | A | W | 2-0 |

Final League position: **5th**

| P | W | D | L | F/A | Pts |
|---|---|---|---|---|---|
| 42 | 23 | 4 | 15 | 76/55 | 50 |

**FA Cup**

| | | | | |
|---|---|---|---|---|
| Jan 12 | Bristol R (3) | A | W | 3-1 |
| Jan 26 | Nottingham F (4) | A | D | 0-0 |
| Jan 30 | Nottingham F (4R) | H | L | 0-3 |

## 1935-1936

What joy and relief was experienced by the fans this season. From the pit of despair two years earlier, United had hauled themselves back to glory by taking the Championship. It was the end of the season which saw United hit a purple patch. They ran up 19 victories on the trot – nobody could live with them. When the title was won with a 3-2 win at Bury, over 31,000 fans invaded the pitch to celebrate a return to the big time. It had been a long time coming and they were going to enjoy every minute of the winning of a major piece of silverware at last.

**League (Division 2)**

| | | | | |
|---|---|---|---|---|
| Aug 31 | Plymouth Argyle | A | L | 1-3 |
| Sep 4 | Charlton A | H | W | 3-0 |
| Sep 7 | Bradford C | H | W | 3-1 |
| Sep 9 | Charlton A | A | D | 0-0 |
| Sep 14 | Newcastle U | A | W | 2-0 |
| Sep 18 | Hull C | H | W | 2-0 |
| Sep 21 | Tottenham H | H | D | 0-0 |
| Sep 28 | Southampton | A | L | 1-2 |
| Oct 5 | Port Vale | A | W | 3-0 |
| Oct 12 | Fulham | H | W | 1-0 |
| Oct 19 | Sheffield U | H | W | 3-1 |
| Oct 26 | Bradford Park Ave | A | L | 0-1 |
| Nov 2 | Leicester C | H | L | 0-1 |
| Nov 9 | Swansea T | A | L | 1-2 |
| Nov 16 | West Ham U | H | L | 2-3 |
| Nov 23 | Norwich C | A | W | 5-3 |
| Nov 30 | Doncaster R | H | D | 0-0 |
| Dec 7 | Blackpool | A | L | 1-4 |
| Dec 14 | Nottingham F | H | W | 5-0 |
| Dec 26 | Barnsley | H | D | 1-1 |
| Dec 28 | Plymouth Argyle | H | W | 3-2 |
| Jan 1 | Barnsley | A | W | 3-0 |
| Jan 4 | Bradford C | A | L | 0-1 |
| Jan 18 | Newcastle U | H | W | 3-1 |
| Feb 1 | Southampton | H | W | 4-0 |
| Feb 5 | Tottenham H | A | D | 0-0 |
| Feb 8 | Port Vale | H | W | 7-2 |
| Feb 22 | Sheffield U | A | D | 1-1 |
| Feb 29 | Blackpool | H | W | 3-2 |
| Mar 7 | West Ham U | A | W | 2-1 |
| Mar 14 | Swansea T | H | W | 3-0 |
| Mar 21 | Leicester C | A | D | 1-1 |
| Mar 28 | Norwich C | H | W | 2-1 |
| Apr 1 | Fulham | A | D | 2-2 |
| Apr 4 | Doncaster R | A | D | 0-0 |
| Apr 10 | Burnley | A | D | 2-2 |
| Apr 11 | Bradford Park Ave | H | W | 4-0 |
| Apr 13 | Burnley | H | W | 4-0 |
| Apr 18 | Nottingham F | A | D | 1-1 |
| Apr 25 | Bury | H | W | 2-1 |
| Apr 29 | Bury | A | W | 3-2 |
| May 2 | Hull C | A | D | 1-1 |

Final League position: **1st**

| P | W | D | L | F/A | Pts |
|---|---|---|---|---|---|
| 42 | 22 | 12 | 8 | 85/43 | 56 |

**FA Cup**

| | | | | |
|---|---|---|---|---|
| Jan 11 | Reading (3) | A | W | 3-1 |
| Jan 25 | Stoke C (4) | A | D | 0-0 |
| Jan 29 | Stoke C (4R) | H | L | 0-2 |

## 1936-1937

The euphoria of the previous season quickly wore off as United found themselves fighting to stay up. A famous name of the future appeared in his first League game for the club, Walter Winterbottom. Although he never shone particularly brightly on the pitch, he was manager of England from 1946 to 1963. As the season drew to a close, United had managed to win only ten games. They were relegated and Scott Duncan resigned. He went on to manage Ipswich Town. Striker George Mutch also left to play for Preston.

**League (Division 1)**

| | | | | |
|---|---|---|---|---|
| Aug 29 | Wolverhampton W | H | D | 1-1 |
| Sep 2 | Huddersfield T | A | L | 1-3 |
| Sep 5 | Derby C | A | L | 4-5 |
| Sep 9 | Huddersfield | H | W | 3-1 |
| Sep 12 | Manchester C | H | W | 3-2 |
| Sep 19 | Sheffield w | H | D | 1-1 |
| Sep 26 | Preston N E | A | L | 1-3 |
| Oct 3 | Arsenal | H | W | 2-0 |
| Oct 10 | Brentford | A | L | 0-4 |
| Oct 17 | Portsmouth | A | L | 1-2 |
| Oct 24 | Chelsea | H | D | 0-0 |
| Oct 31 | Stoke C | A | L | 0-3 |
| Nov 7 | Charlton A | H | D | 0-0 |
| Nov 14 | Grimsby T | A | L | 2-6 |
| Nov 21 | Liverpool | H | L | 2-5 |
| Nov 28 | Leeds U | A | L | 1-2 |
| Dec 5 | Birmingham | H | L | 1-2 |
| Dec 12 | Midlesborough | A | L | 2-3 |
| Dec 19 | WBA | H | D | 2-2 |
| Dec 25 | Bolton W | A | W | 4-0 |
| Dec 26 | Wolverhampton W | A | L | 1-3 |
| Jan 1 | Sunderland | H | W | 2-1 |
| Jan 2 | Derby C | H | D | 2-2 |
| Jan 9 | Manchester C | A | L | 0-1 |
| Jan 23 | Sheffield W | A | L | 0-1 |
| Feb 3 | Preston N E | H | D | 1-1 |
| Feb6 | Arsenal | A | D | 1-1 |
| Feb 13 | Brentford | H | L | 1-3 |
| Feb 20 | Portsmouth | H | L | 0-1 |
| Feb 27 | Chelsea | A | L | 2-4 |
| Mar 6 | Stoke C | H | W | 2-1 |
| Mar 13 | Charlton A | A | L | 0-3 |
| Mar 20 | Grimsby T | H | D | 1-1 |
| Mar 26 | Everton | H | W | 2-1 |
| Mar 27 | Liverpool | A | L | 0-2 |
| Mar 29 | Everton | A | W | 3-2 |
| Apr 3 | Leeds U | H | D | 0-0 |
| Apr 10 | Birmingham | A | D | 2-2 |
| Apr 17 | Middlesbrough | H | W | 2-1 |
| Apr 21 | Sunderland | A | D | 1-1 |
| Apr 24 | WBA | A | L | 0-1 |

Final League position: **21st**

| P | W | D | L | F/A | Pts |
|---|---|---|---|---|---|
| 42 | 10 | 12 | 20 | 55/78 | 32 |

**FA Cup**

| | | | | |
|---|---|---|---|---|
| Jan 16 | Reading (3) | H | W | 1-0 |
| Jan 30 | Arsenal (4) | A | L | 0-5 |

## 1937-1938

Walter Crickmer took over as temporary manager following the departure cf Scott Duncan. Young Irish striker Johnny Carey made his debut in the game against Southampton in September. Just after Christmas he scored when United beat Nottingham Forest, the side he would later manage, 3-2. Although he started out as a forward, Carey eventually found his true niche, becoming one of the finest full-backs in history. United's line-up also benefited from the presence of ace marksman Jack Rowley, who was purchased from Bournemouth and Stan Pearson. United finally found their winning form in November when they thrashed Chesterfield 7-1. At the end of the season they were promoted back into Division One

**League (Division 2)**

| | | | | |
|---|---|---|---|---|
| Aug 28 | Newcastle U | H | W | 3-0 |
| Aug 30 | Coventry C | A | L | 0-1 |
| Sep 4 | Luton T | A | L | 0-1 |
| Sep 8 | Coventry C | H | D | 2-2 |
| Sep 11 | Barnsley | H | w | 4-1 |
| Sep 13 | Bury | A | W | 2-1 |
| Sep 18 | Stockport C | A | L | 0-1 |
| Sep 25 | Southampton | H | L | 1-2 |
| Oct 2 | Sheffield U | H | L | 0-1 |
| Oct 9 | Tottenham H | A | W | 1-0 |
| Oct 16 | Blackburn R | A | D | 1-1 |
| Oct 23 | Sheffield W | H | W | 1-0 |
| Oct 30 | Fulham | A | L | 0-1 |
| Nov 6 | Plymouth Argyle | H | D | 0-0 |
| Nov 13 | Chesterfield | A | W | 7-1 |
| Nov 20 | Aston Villa | H | W | 3-1 |
| Nov 27 | Norwich c | A | W | 3-2 |
| Dec 4 | Swansea T | H | W | 5-1 |
| Dec 11 | Bradford Park Ave | A | L | 0-4 |
| Dec 27 | Nottingham F | H | W | 4-3 |
| Dec 28 | Nottingham F | A | w | 3-2 |
| Jan 1 | Newcastle U | A | D | 2-2 |
| Jan 15 | Luton T | H | w | 4-2 |
| Jan 29 | Stockport C | h | W | 3-1 |
| Feb 2 | Barnsley | A | D | 2-2 |
| Feb 5 | Southampton | A | D | 3-3 |
| Feb 17 | Sheffield U | A | W | 2-1 |
| Feb 19 | Tottenham H | H | L | 0-1 |
| Feb 23 | West Ham U | H | W | 4-0 |
| Feb 26 | Blackburn R | H | W | 2-1 |
| Mar 4 | Sheffield W | A | W | 3-1 |
| Mar 12 | Fulham | H | w | 1-0 |
| Mar 19 | Plymouth Argyle | A | D | 1-1 |
| Mar 26 | Chesterfield | H | W | 4-1 |
| Apr 2 | Aston Villa | A | L | 0-3 |
| Apr 9 | Norwich C | H | D | 0-0 |
| Apr 15 | Burnley | A | L | 0-1 |
| Apr 16 | Swansea T | A | D | 2-2 |
| Apr 18 | Burnley | H | W | 4-0 |
| Apr 23 | Bradford Park Ave | H | W | 3-1 |
| Apr 30 | West Ham U | A | L | 0-1 |
| May 7 | Bury | H | W | 2-0 |

Final League position: **2nd**

| P | W | D | L | F/A | Pts |
|---|---|---|---|---|---|
| 42 | 22 | 9 | 11 | 82/50 | 53 |

**FA Cup**

| | | | | |
|---|---|---|---|---|
| Jan 8 | Yeovil T (3) | H | W | 3-0 |
| Jan 22 | Barnsley (4) | A | D | 2-2 |
| Jan 26 | Barnsley (4R) | H | W | 1-0 |
| Feb 12 | Brentford (5) | A | L | 0-2 |

## 1938-1939

War clouds were looming over Europe as United approached what was to be the final season before League football was suspended. When it returned after the war, the club was to embark on the new era, depeleted in terms of playing staff and Old Trafford in ruins, but with the guidance of a great man – Matt Busby. At least United were back in the First Division now, with a different line-up but hopes of a stable period of football. The team finished the season in 14th place and, ironically, it was Manchester City's turn to suffer as they crashed into Division Two. United, however, were to remain in the top flight for the next 36 years.

**League (Division 1)**

| | | | | |
|---|---|---|---|---|
| Aug 27 | Middlesbrough | A | L | 1-3 |
| Aug 31 | Bolton W | H | D | 2-2 |
| Sep 3 | Birmingham | H | W | 4-1 |
| Sep 7 | Liverpool | A | L | 0-1 |
| Sep 10 | Grimsby T | A | L | 0-1 |
| Sep 17 | Stoke C | A | D | 1-1 |
| Sep 24 | Chelsea | H | W | 5-1 |
| Oct 1 | Preston N E | A | D | 1-1 |
| Oct 8 | Charlton A | H | L | 0-2 |
| Oct 15 | Blackpool | H | D | 0-0 |
| Oct 22 | Derby C | A | L | 1-5 |
| Oct 29 | Sunderland | H | L | 0-1 |
| Nov 5 | Aston Villa | A | W | 2-0 |
| Nov 12 | Wolverhampton W | H | L | 1-3 |
| Nov 19 | Everton | A | L | 0-3 |
| Nov 26 | Huddersfield T | H | D | 1-1 |
| Dec 3 | Portsmouth | A | D | 0-0 |
| Dec 10 | Arsenal | H | W | 1-0 |
| Dec 17 | Brentford | A | W | 5-2 |
| Dec 24 | Middlesbrough | H | D | 1-1 |
| Dec 26 | Leicester C | H | W | 3-0 |
| Dec 27 | Leicester C | A | D | 11 |
| Dec 31 | Birmingham | A | d | 3-3 |
| Jan 14 | Grimsby T | H | W | 3-1 |
| Jan 21 | Stoke C | H | L | 0-1 |
| Jan 28 | Chelsea | A | W | 1-0 |
| Feb 4 | Preston N E | H | D | 1-1 |
| Feb 11 | Charlton A | A | L | 1-7 |
| Feb 18 | Blackpool | A | W | 5-3 |
| Feb 25 | Derby C | H | D | 1-1 |
| Mar 4 | Sunderland | A | L | 2-5 |
| Mar 11 | Aston Villa | H | D | 1-1 |
| Mar 18 | Wolverhampton W | A | L | 0-3 |
| Mar 29 | Everton | H | L | 0-2 |
| Apr 1 | Huddersfield T | A | D | 1-1 |
| Apr 7 | Leeds U | H | D | 0-0 |
| Apr 8 | Portsmouth | H | D | 1-1 |
| Apr 10 | Leeds U | A | L | 1-3 |
| Apr 15 | Arsenal | A | L | 1-2 |
| Apr 22 | Brentford | H | W | 3-0 |
| Apr 29 | Bolton W | A | D | 0-0 |
| May 6 | Liverpool | H | W | 2-0 |

Final League position: **14th**

| P | W | D | L | F/A | Pts |
|---|---|---|---|---|---|
| 42 | 11 | 16 | 15 | 57/65 | 38 |

**FA Cup**

| | | | | |
|---|---|---|---|---|
| Jan 7 | WBA (3) | A | D | 0-0 |
| Jan 11 | WBA (3R) | H | L | 1-5 |

## 1946-47

United resumed football in Division One after the war with a new man, Matt Busby, at the helm. His task was to rebuild a shattered club which was playing its games at Manchester City's Maine Road ground because Old Trafford had been bombed. He brought in Jimmy Murphy as his assistant to help develop the team and bring on any youngsters who showed promise. The partnership produced immediate results with United chalking up five straight victories, most notably a 5-0 thrashing of Liverpool – Busby's former club. With the likes of Rowley, Mitten and Aston leading the challenge, The Reds finished second in the championship race, a remarkable achievement for a new manager who arrived at a club that was almost bankrupt.

### League (Division 1)

| Aug 31 | Grimsby Town | H | W | 2-1 |
|---|---|---|---|---|
| Sep 4 | Chelsea | A | W | 3-0 |
| Sep 7 | Charlton A | A | W | 3-1 |
| Sep 11 | Liverpool | H | W | 5-0 |
| Sep 14 | Middlesbrough | H | W | 1-0 |
| Sep 18 | Chelsea | H | D | 1-1 |
| Sep 21 | Stoke C | A | L | 2-3 |
| Sep 28 | Arsenal | H | W | 5-2 |
| Oct 5 | Preston NE | H | D | 1-1 |
| Oct 12 | Sheffield U | A | D | 2-2 |
| Oct 19 | Blackpool | A | L | 1-3 |
| Oct 26 | Sunderland | A | L | 0-3 |
| Nov 2 | Aston Villa | H | D | 0-0 |
| Nov 9 | Derby Co | H | W | 4-1 |
| Nov 16 | Everton | A | D | 2-2 |
| Nov 23 | Huddersfield T | H | W | 5-2 |
| Nov 30 | Wolverhampton WA | L | 2-3 | |
| Dec 7 | Brentford | H | W | 4-1 |
| Dec 14 | Blackburn R | A | L | 1-2 |
| Dec 25 | Bolton W | A | D | 2-2 |
| Dec 26 | Bolton W | H | W | 1-0 |
| Dec 28 | Grimsby T | A | D | 0-0 |
| Jan 4 | Charlton A | H | W | 4-1 |
| Jan 18 | Middlesbrough | A | W | 4-2 |
| Feb 1 | Arsenal | A | L | 2-6 |
| Feb 5 | Stoke C | H | D | 1-1 |
| Feb 22 | Blackpool | H | W | 3-0 |
| Mar 1 | Sunderland | A | D | 1-1 |
| Mar 8 | Aston Villa | H | W | 2-1 |
| Mar 15 | Derby Co | A | L | 3-4 |
| Mar 22 | Everton | A | L | 3-0 |
| Mar 29 | Huddersfield T | A | D | 2-2 |
| Apr 5 | Wolverhampton WH | D | 3-1 | |
| Apr 7 | Leeds U | H | W | 3-1 |
| Apr 8 | Leeds U | A | W | 2-0 |
| Apr 12 | Brentford | A | D | 0-0 |
| Apr 19 | Blackburn R | H | W | 4-0 |
| Apr 26 | Portsmouth | A | W | 1-0 |
| May 3 | Liverpool | A | L | 0-1 |

# Back From The Brink

During the war years, Old Trafford was reduced to a shell, the glories and disappointments of what had gone before still ringing through its skeletal, burned-out structure. 'The ground, and the club, was in need of a saviour, someone with vision and tenacity to revive the club's dignity against seemingly impossible odds. On February 15, 1945, a certain Scotsman arrived at Old Trafford. Looking around the ruins, he felt the frisson of expectation and hope which has so pervaded the club throughout its history. Little did he know then what glory he would bring to this ground and what joy – and tragedy – its fans would experience with him every inch of the way.

Matt Busby, The Godfather as he became known, had arrived. The former Liverpool, Scotland and Manchester City player had a massive task ahead of him. Because of the state of the ground, matches had to be played at City's Maine Road base, the club was in debt to the banks and many of the pre-war team members were still serving in the forces. He had, however, the nucleus of a strong team in the likes of Jack Rowley, Charlie Mitten, John Aston and goalkeeper Jack Crompton and it was upon this foundation he set about creating a squad capable of returning United to its previous strength. But he needed a good right-hand man to help him mould the team, and in signing Jimmy Murphy as assistant manager Busby pulled off a masterstroke of football management. Murphy, it seemed, was perfect for the role of supporter to the boss – a quiet but determined man, he loved working on the field with the players, watching their progress, assessing their potential. The Busby-Murphy connection was to become one the most durable and effective partnerships in football history.

But Busby himself was not averse to the hands-on style – donning a track suit and mixing it with his players on the pitch, something which amazed the squad members brought up on the stiff-collared, suited approach to management in the past. It also forged a bond between manager and players which was to reap huge dividends for the Scot over the following decades. To this day, stars such as Best, Law, Charlton and Stiles – the players who were to bring him such success – will hear nothing ill said of the man and in Alex Ferguson's relationship with United of today there is a distinct echo of the Busby approach.

The effect of all this was immediate, United were growing in confidence with every season. Football is full of ironies, and when the League returned in the 1946-47 season, The Reds finished second in the Championship race to Liverpool, the club which had been so reluctant to let Busby go after his return from active duty. Indeed, trophy success was not far away and in 1948, just three years after arriving, United lifted the FA Cup with a 4-2 victory over Blackpool in a classic contest. For any manager though, past or present, the one confirmation of success is the League Championship and Busby and Murphy set their sights on that goal. Over the next four years the big prize was to elude them, United finishing runners-up three times, but as the new decade dawned they cracked it, becoming Champions in 1952 with London's best, Spurs and Arsenal, four points behind. It had been 41 years since United had won the title and now they were about to start the march towards a destiny which was to leave a profound mark on British football history.

By now, United had the basis of what was to be dubbed in the press "the Busby Babes", a term disliked by the manager for its child-like connotations. His players were anything but and he preferred The Red Devils. The likes of Jackie Blanchflower and Roger Byrne were emerging under Busby's guidance but he also raided the market with a keen eye for young talent, bringing in the tricky winger Johnny Berry and Tommy Taylor from Barnsley in 1953. That was also the year which saw the emergence of Duncan Edwards, a player many still say was the best ever to wear United's strip and certainly one of Busby's greatest discoveries. With the addition of Dennis Viollet and David Pegg the

| | | | |
|---|---|---|---|
| May 10 Preston NE | A | D | 1-1 |
| May 17 Portsmouth | H | W | 3-0 |
| May 26 Sheffield U | H | W | 6-2 |

**Final League position: 2nd**

| P | W | D | L | F/A | Pts |
|---|---|---|---|---|---|
| 42 | 22 | 12 | 8 | 96/54 | 56 |

## 1947-1948

As the fans started to flock back to football, United didn't disappoint on the pitch. The team maintained a level of consistency this season which saw them again finish second, aided by a flourish mid-season with five straight wins between December and the New Year. But the real bonus came at the end when Busby watched with satisfaction as the team lifted the FA Cup, beating Blackpool – which boasted one of "the greats" Stan Mortensen – 4-2 in a game regarded as a football classic. It was Busby's first trophy since taking over at Old Trafford. The feeling among the fans was that something special was happening at last.

### League (Division 1)

| | | | |
|---|---|---|---|
| Aug 23 Middlesbrough | A | D | 2-2 |
| Aug 27 Liverpool | H | W | 2-0 |
| Aug 30 Charlton A | H | W | 6-2 |
| Sep 3 Liverpool | A | D | 2-2 |
| Sep 6 Arsenal | A | L | 1-2 |
| Sep 8 Burnley | A | D | 0-0 |
| Sep 13 Sheffield U | H | L | 0-1 |
| Sep 20 Manchester C | A | D | 0-0 |
| Sep 27 Preston NE | A | L | 1-2 |
| Oct 4 Stoke C | H | D | 1-1 |
| Oct 11 Grimsby T | H | L | 3-4 |
| Oct 18 Sunderland | A | L | 0-1 |
| Oct 25 Aston Villa | H | W | 6-2 |
| Nov 1 Wolverhampton W | A | W | 6-2 |
| Nov 8 Huddersfield T | H | D | 4-4 |
| Nov 15 Derby Co | A | D | 1-1 |
| Nov 22 Everton | H | D | 2-2 |
| Nov 29 Chelsea | A | W | 4-0 |
| Dec 6 Blackpool | H | D | 1-1 |
| Dec 13 Blackburn R | A | D | 1-1 |
| Dec 20 Middlesbrough | H | W | 2-1 |
| Dec 25 Portsmouth | H | W | 3-2 |
| Dec 27 Portsmouth | A | W | 3-1 |
| Jan 1 Burnley | H | W | 5-0 |
| Jan 3 Charlton A | A | W | 2-1 |
| Jan 17 Arsenal | H | D | 1-1 |
| Jan 31 Sheffield U | A | L | 1-2 |
| Feb 14 Preston NE | H | D | 1-1 |
| Feb 21 Stoke C | A | W | 2-0 |
| Mar 6 Sunderland | H | W | 3-1 |
| Mar 17 Grimsby T | A | D | 1-1 |
| Mar 20 Wolverhampton W | H | W | 3-2 |
| Mar 22 Aston Villa | A | W | 1-0 |
| Mar 26 Bolton W | H | L | 0-2 |
| Mar 27 Huddersfield T | A | W | 2-0 |
| Mar 29 Bolton W | A | W | 1-0 |
| Apr 3 Derby Co | H | W | 1-0 |
| Apr 7 Manchester C | H | D | 1-1 |
| Apr 10 Everton | A | L | 0-2 |

It's 4-you! The United team returns with the Cup after a thrilling 4-2 victory over Blackpool in 1948.

United side which had lifted the Championship in 1952 had virtually disappeared. In many ways, football is a reflection of social change and fifties Britain, for all the rationing and austerity, was heading for tremendous change with youth leading the way. The "Babes" were born and Busby was hungry to capitalise on the success he had already enjoyed with the old school.

Immediate success on the pitch, however, was not forthcoming. The team need time to gel and though always pushing for honours, United were still hovering around fifth place in the league by the end of the 1955 season. The following year saw the Babes come into their own, sweeping to the 1955-56 Championship with a commanding 11 point lead at the end. Busby had created a formidable footballing force and an academy of excellence which was still producing talents like Eddie Colman and Geoff Bent, and the loyalty of the players to their mentor was unswerving. Few teams in the First Division could live with this United side, especially when Busby unveiled his latest young weapon Bobby Charlton, the mild-mannered striker with a lethal right foot shot. The team won the title for the second successive season and continued the assault on other trophies at home and abroad.

By now, Busby had a taste for European success, despite the football authorities' resistance to English teams becoming involved abroad, and wanted no more than to pit his youngsters against the best in Continental football. By the start of the 1957 season he felt the team was ready and it was with an air of supreme confidence that he embarked on a European campaign. His dream seemed tantalisingly close when United played the European Cup quarter final first leg against Red Star of Belgrade and won 2-1.

Now they had to travel behind the Iron Curtain to finish the job. The game in Belgrade was a stern test of United's youthful resilience. They won through, drawing the match 3-3 but reaching the semi-final 5-4 on aggregate. Busby, and United fans back home, were ecstatic but the manager was aware that the team had to return as soon as possible to England to resume League commitments.

The United squad, its officials and a bevy of reporters who had followed the team abroad landed at Munich airport for refuelling still full of the events of Belgrade. As they waited in the airport lounge in anticipation of the final flight back to England, Matt Busby could reflect on a job well done after 13 years as the driving force of Manchester United and ponder with excitement what the future would hold for the young team surrounding him.

What was to happen next, as the aircraft made its way down a snow-choked runway was to stun not only a nation but the entire world of football and tragically deprive the game of a host of its brightest stars.

# 1948-1949

Though the team was flying on the pitch, United and Busby were hit by a pay wrangle between the club and the players which threatened to break the squad and severely tested the manager's determination to stick to the rules. To this day, United have a strict wage structure but back then, clubs were paying illegal bonuses to players to supplement their wages. United's players wanted the same, but Busby refused. He knew that many members of the team were reaching the end of their careers in the top flight and that a string of youngsters were coming through. He even stamped his authority on one player, Johnny Morris, by selling him to Derby after rows on the training field. Despite the rumblings, United went on to finish second again and even reached the FA Cup semi-final, losing 1-0 to Wolves at Goodison.

## Final League position: 2nd

| P | W | D | L | F/A | Pts |
|---|---|---|---|---|---|
| 42 | 19 | 14 | 9 | 81/48 | 52 |

## FA Cup

| | | | | |
|---|---|---|---|---|
| Jan 10 | Aston Villa (3) | A | W | 6-4 |
| Jan 24 | Liverpool (4) | H | W | 3-0 |
| | (at Goodison Park) | | | |
| Feb 7 | Charlton A (5) | H | W | 2-0 |
| Feb 28 | Preston NE (6) | H | W | 4-1 |
| | (at Maine Road) | | | |
| Mar 13 | Derby Co (SF) | N | W | 3-1 |
| | (at Hillsborough) | | | |
| Apr 24 | Blackpool (F) | N | W | 4-2 |
| | (at Wembley) | | | |

## League (Division 1)

| | | | | |
|---|---|---|---|---|
| Aug 21 | Derby Co | H | L | 1-2 |
| Aug 23 | Blackpool | A | W | 3-0 |
| Aug 28 | Arsenal | A | W | 1-0 |
| Sep 1 | Blackpool | H | L | 3-4 |
| Sep 4 | Huddersfield T | H | W | 4-1 |
| Sep 8 | Wolverhampton WA | L | | 2-3 |
| Sep 11 | Manchester C | A | D | 0-0 |
| Sep 15 | Wolverhampton WH | A | D | 2-0 |
| Sep 18 | Sheffield U | A | D | 2-2 |
| Sep 25 | Aston Villa | H | W | 3-1 |
| Oct 2 | Sunderland | A | L | 1-2 |
| Oct 9 | Charlton A | H | D | 1-1 |
| Oct 16 | Stoke C | A | L | 1-2 |
| Oct 23 | Burnley | H | D | 1-1 |
| Oct 30 | Preston NE | H | D | 1-1 |
| Nov 6 | Everton | H | W | 2-0 |
| Nov 13 | Chelsea | A | D | 1-1 |
| Nov 20 | Birmingham C | H | W | 3-0 |
| Apr 17 | Chelsea | H | W | 5-0 |
| Apr 28 | Blackpool | A | L | 0-1 |
| May 1 | Blackburn | H | W | 4-0 |

Matt Busby turns to reporters at United's training ground after being told he was to be made a Freeman Of The City in 1961. "Don't let the boys know yet", he said. "They'll stop training."

| | | | | | |
|---|---|---|---|---|---|
| Nov 27 | Middlesbrough | A | W | 4-1 |
| Dec 4 | Newcastle U | H | D | 1-1 |
| Dec 11 | Portsmouth | A | D | 2-2 |
| Dec 18 | Derby Co | A | W | 3-1 |
| Dec 25 | Liverpool | H | D | 0-0 |
| Dec 26 | Liverpool | A | W | 2-0 |
| Jan 1 | Arsenal | H | W | 2-0 |
| Jan 22 | Manchester C | H | D | 0-0 |
| Feb 19 | Aston Villa | A | L | 1-2 |
| Mar 5 | Charlton A | A | W | 3-2 |
| Mar 12 | Stoke C | H | W | 3-0 |
| Mar 19 | Birmingham C | A | L | 0-1 |
| Apr 6 | Huddersfield T | A | L | 1-2 |
| Apr 9 | Chelsea | H | D | 1-1 |
| Apr 15 | Bolton W | A | W | 2-0 |
| Apr 16 | Burnley | A | W | 2-0 |
| Apr 18 | Bolton W | H | W | 3-0 |
| Apr 21 | Sunderland | H | L | 1-2 |
| Apr 23 | Preston NE | H | D | 2-2 |
| Apr 27 | Everton | A | L | 0-2 |
| Apr 30 | Newcastle U | A | W | 1-0 |
| May 2 | Middlesbrough | H | W | 1-0 |
| May 4 | Sheffield U | H | W | 3-2 |
| May 7 | Portsmouth | H | W | 3-2 |

## FA Cup

| | | | | |
|---|---|---|---|---|
| Jan 8 | Bournemouth (3) | H | W | 6-0 |
| Jan 29 | Bradford (4) | H | D | 1-1 |
| Feb 5 | Bradford (4R) | A | D | 1-1 |
| Feb 7 | Bradford (42R) | H | W | 5-0 |
| Feb 12 | Yeovil (5) | H | W | 8-0 |
| Feb 26 | Hull C (6) | A | W | 1-0 |
| Mar 26 | Wolves (SF) | N | D | 1-1 |
| | (at Hillsborough) | | | |
| Apr 2 | Wolves (SFR) | | L | 0-1 |
| | (at Goodison Park) | | | |

**Final League position: 2nd**

| P | W | D | L | F/A | Pts |
|---|---|---|---|---|---|
| 42 | 21 | 11 | 10 | 77/44 | 53 |

# 1949-1950

The youngsters Busby was nurturing now started to blossom with the likes of Roger Byrne, Jackie Blanchflower and Mark Jones making an impact in the reserve team and pressing for first team places. It was a season of minor transition with United finishing fourth in the League and going out of the Cup to Chelsea in the sixth round. Too many draws held United back in terms of the Championship but there were some notable victories, in particular a 7-0 beating of Aston Villa at Old Trafford in March. That completed a double over Villa after October's 4-0 win.

## League (Division 1)

| | | | | |
|---|---|---|---|---|
| Aug 20 | Derby Co | A | W | 1-0 |
| Aug 24 | Bolton W | H | W | 3-0 |
| Aug 27 | WBA | H | D | 1-2 |
| Aug 31 | Bolton W | A | W | 2-1 |
| Sep 3 | Manchester C | H | W | 2-1 |
| Sep 7 | Liverpool | A | D | 1-1 |
| Sep 10 | Chelsea | A | D | 1-1 |
| Sep 17 | Stoke C | H | D | 2-2 |
| Sep 24 | Burnley | A | L | 0-1 |

| Oct 1 | Sunderland | H | L | 1-3 |
| Oct 8 | Charlton A | H | W | 3-2 |
| Oct 15 | Aston Villa | A | W | 4-0 |
| Oct 22 | Wolverhampton W | H | W | 3-0 |
| Oct 29 | Portsmouth | A | D | 0-0 |
| Nov 5 | Huddersfield T | H | W | 6-0 |
| Nov 12 | Everton | A | D | 0-0 |
| Nov 19 | Middlesbrough | H | W | 2-0 |
| Nov 26 | Blackpool | A | D | 3-3 |
| Dec 3 | Newcastle U | H | D | 1-1 |
| Dec 10 | Fulham | A | L | 0-1 |
| Dec 17 | Derby C | H | L | 0-1 |
| Dec 24 | WBA | A | W | 2-1 |
| Dec 26 | Arsenal | H | W | 2-0 |
| Dec 27 | Arsenal | A | D | 0-0 |
| Dec 31 | Manchester C | A | W | 2-1 |
| Jan 14 | Chelsea | H | W | 1-0 |
| Jan 21 | Stoke C | A | L | 1-3 |
| Feb 4 | Burnley | H | W | 3-2 |
| Feb 18 | Sunderland | A | D | 2-2 |
| Feb 25 | Charlton A | A | W | 2-1 |
| Mar 8 | Aston Villa | H | W | 7-0 |
| Mar 11 | Middlesbrough | A | W | 3-2 |
| Mar 15 | Liverpool | H | D | 0-0 |
| Mar 18 | Blackpool | H | L | 1-2 |
| Mar 25 | Huddersfield T | A | L | 1-3 |
| Apr 1 | Everton | H | D | 1-1 |
| Apr 7 | Birmingham C | H | L | 0-2 |
| Apr 8 | Wolverhampton W | A | D | 0-0 |
| Apr 10 | Birmingham C | A | D | 0-0 |
| Apr 15 | Portsmouth | H | L | 0-2 |
| Apr 22 | Newcastle U | A | L | 1-2 |
| Apr 29 | Fulham | H | W | 3-0 |

## 1950-1951

In the summer of 1950, United lost one of its key players in Charlie Mitten in circumstances which today sound familiar but in those days was bizarre. The club travelled to South America for an end-of-season tour and Mitten was approached by the Colombian club Sante Fe with the promise of money way beyond United's means. He was warned by Busby that the domestic rules meant he would be automatically suspended at home. Mitten, however, accepted Santa Fe's offer but returned home a year later disillusioned. He was duly banned in England and after serving his suspension left United to join Fulham. The Reds finished the season second yet again and were knocked out of the FA Cup in the sixth round by Birmingham.

**Final League position: 4th**

| P | W | D | L | F/A | Pts |
|---|---|---|---|---|---|
| 42 | 18 | 14 | 10 | 69/44 | 50 |

### FA Cup

| Jan 7 | Weymouth (3) | H | W | 4-0 |
| Jan 28 | Watford (4) | A | W | 1-0 |
| Feb 11 | Portsmouth (5) | H | D | 3-3 |
| Feb 15 | Portsmouth (5R) | A | W | 3-1 |
| Mar 4 | Chelsea (6) | A | L | 0-2 |

United goalkeeper Jack Crompton in 1946. He was a crucial factor in Busby's rebuilding of the side after the war.

Winger Billy McGlenn is put through his paces.

United half-back Henry Cockburn in 1946.

Charlie Mitten was a rebel in 1950 when he signed for Colombia's Santa Fe.

## League (Division 1)

| Date | Opponent | H/A | Result | Score |
|---|---|---|---|---|
| Aug 19 | Fulham | H | W | 1-0 |
| Aug 23 | Liverpool | A | L | 1-2 |
| Aug 26 | Bolton W | A | L | 1-0 |
| Aug 30 | Liverpool | H | W | 1-0 |
| Sep 2 | Blackpool | H | W | 1-0 |
| Sep 4 | Aston Villa | A | W | 3-1 |
| Sep 9 | Tottenham H | A | L | 0-1 |
| Sep 13 | Aston Villa | H | D | 0-0 |
| Sep 16 | Charlton A | H | W | 3-0 |
| Sep 23 | Middlesbrough | A | W | 2-1 |
| Sep 30 | Wolverhampton W | A | D | 0-0 |
| Oct 7 | Sheffield W | H | W | 3-1 |
| Oct 14 | Arsenal | A | L | 0-3 |
| Oct 21 | Portsmouth | H | D | 0-0 |
| Oct 28 | Everton | A | W | 4-1 |
| Nov 4 | Burnley | H | D | 1-1 |
| Nov 11 | Chelsea | A | L | 0-1 |
| Nov 18 | Stoke C | H | D | 0-0 |
| Nov 25 | WBA | A | W | 1-0 |
| Dec 2 | Newcastle U | H | L | 1-2 |
| Dec 9 | Huddersfield T | A | W | 3-2 |
| Dec 16 | Fulham | A | D | 2-2 |
| Dec 23 | Bolton W | H | L | 2-3 |
| Dec 25 | Sunderland | A | L | 1-2 |
| Dec 26 | Sunderland | H | L | 3-5 |
| Jan 13 | Tottenham H | H | W | 2-1 |
| Jan 20 | Charlton A | A | W | 2-1 |
| Feb 3 | Middlesbrough | H | W | 1-0 |
| Feb 17 | Wolverhampton W | H | W | 2-1 |
| Feb 26 | Sheffield W | A | W | 4-0 |
| Mar 3 | Arsenal | H | W | 3-1 |
| Mar 10 | Portsmouth | A | D | 0-0 |
| Mar 17 | Everton | H | W | 3-0 |
| Mar 23 | Derby Co | H | W | 2-0 |
| Mar 24 | Burnley | A | W | 2-1 |
| Mar 26 | Derby Co | A | W | 4-2 |
| Mar 31 | Chelsea | H | W | 4-1 |
| Apr 7 | Stoke C | A | W | 2-1 |
| Apr 14 | WBA | A | L | 0-2 |
| Apr 21 | Newcastle U | H | W | 3-0 |
| Apr 28 | Huddersfield T | A | W | 2-0 |
| May 5 | Blackpool | H | W | 6-0 |
|  | Blackpool | A | D | 1-1 |

## FA Cup

| Date | Round | Opponent | H/A | Result | Score |
|---|---|---|---|---|---|
| Jan 6 | Oldham (3) |  | H | W | 4-1 |
| Jan 27 | Leeds U (4) |  | H | W | 4-0 |
| Feb 10 | Arsenal (5) |  | H | W | 1-0 |
| Feb 24 | Birmingham C (6) | A | L | 0-1 |

## Final League position: **2nd**

| P | W | D | L | F/A | Pts |
|---|---|---|---|---|---|
| 42 | 24 | 8 | 10 | 74/40 | 56 |

# 1951-1952

After several seasons as runners-up in the Championship, United fans were left wondering if the coveted title would ever return to Old Trafford. Their dreams were about to be realised as the team flourished at last, losing just eight games all season with Jack Rowley notching a club record of 30 goals. Roger Byrne made his full League debut in November, going on to score seven goals in the last six games, and 18-year-old Jackie Blanchflower came into the side. This was the season when the press dubbed the

One of the greats. Johnny Carey was the Roy Keane of the 40s. He brought passion and style to the side for 20 years from 1936.

Johnny Hanlon in the 1946 team.

Jack Rowley was United's 50's hit-man.

Top scorer Stan Pearson in 1946.

## 1952-1953

This year was to hold a very special significance in the history of Manchester United – the arrival on the scene of one of the club's greatest names, Duncan Edwards. In him, and players like Bobby Charlton a few years later, Matt Busby reaped the rewards of his investment in youth and set the club on the road to unparalleled success both at home and abroad. Edwards made his first-team debut in April after arriving at the ground expecting nothing more

team The Busby Babes. United went on to win the Championship in style, four points clear of Spurs.

### League (Division 1)

| | | | | |
|---|---|---|---|---|
| Aug 18 | WBA | A | D | 3-3 |
| Aug 22 | Middlesbrough | H | W | 4-2 |
| Aug 25 | Newcastle U | H | W | 2-1 |
| Aug 29 | Middlesbrough | A | W | 4-1 |
| Sep 1 | Bolton W | A | L | 0-1 |
| Sep 5 | Charlton A | H | W | 3-2 |
| Sep 8 | Stoke C | H | W | 4-0 |
| Sep 12 | Charlton A | A | D | 2-2 |
| Sep 15 | Manchester C | A | W | 2-1 |
| Sep 22 | Tottenham H | A | L | 0-2 |
| Sep 29 | Preston NE | H | L | 1-2 |
| Oct 6 | Derby Co | H | W | 2-1 |
| Oct 13 | Aston Villa | A | W | 5-2 |
| Oct 20 | Sunderland | H | L | 0-1 |
| Oct 27 | Wolverhampton WA | W | 2-0 |
| Nov 3 | Huddersfield T | H | D | 1-1 |
| Nov 10 | Chelsea | A | L | 2-4 |
| Nov 17 | Portsmouth | H | L | 1-3 |
| Nov 24 | Liverpool | A | D | 0-0 |
| Dec 1 | Blackpool | H | W | 3-1 |
| Dec 8 | Arsenal | A | W | 3-1 |
| Dec 15 | WBA | H | W | 5-1 |
| Dec 22 | Newcastle U | A | D | 2-2 |
| Dec 25 | Fulham | H | W | 3-2 |
| Dec 26 | Fulham | A | D | 3-3 |
| Dec 29 | Bolton W | H | W | 1-0 |
| Jan 5 | Stoke C | A | D | 0-0 |
| Jan 19 | Manchester C | H | D | 1-1 |
| Jan 25 | Tottenham H | H | W | 2-0 |
| Feb 9 | Preston NE | A | W | 2-1 |
| Feb 16 | Derby Co | A | W | 3-0 |
| Mar 1 | Aston Villa | H | D | 1-1 |
| Mar 8 | Sunderland | A | W | 2-1 |
| Mar 15 | Wolverhampton WH | W | 2-0 |
| Mar 22 | Huddersfield T | A | L | 2-3 |
| Apr 5 | Portsmouth | A | L | 0-1 |
| Apr 11 | Burnley | A | D | 1-1 |
| Apr 12 | Liverpool | H | W | 4-0 |
| Apr 14 | Burnley | H | W | 6-1 |
| Apr 19 | Blackpool | A | D | 2-2 |
| Apr 21 | Chelsea | H | W | 3-0 |
| Apr 26 | Arsenal | H | W | 6-1 |

### FA Cup

| | | | | |
|---|---|---|---|---|
| Jan 12 | Hull C (3) | H | L | 0-2 |

Final League position: **1st**

| P | W | D | L | F/A | Pts |
|---|---|---|---|---|---|
| 42 | 23 | 11 | 8 | 95/52 | 57 |

than to continue his duties as a junior with the ground staff. Busby however, had other ideas and threw him straight into the team to play Cardiff City. It was also the season that another great player, Tommy Taylor arrived from Barnsley. A formidable team was nearing completion.

Man City threaten United keeper Crompton's goal in the derby game of 1951. United won 2-1 with goals from Johnny Berry and Harry McShane – father of today's "Lovejoy" TV star Ian McShane.

## League (Division 1)

|  |  | |  | |
|---|---|---|---|---|
| Aug 23 | Chelsea | H | W | 2-0 |
| Aug 27 | Arsenal | A | L | 1-2 |
| Aug 30 | Manchester C | A | L | 1-2 |
| Sep 3 | Arsenal | H | D | 0-0 |
| Sep 6 | Portsmouth | A | L | 0-2 |
| Sep 10 | Derby Co | A | W | 3-2 |
| Sep 13 | Bolton W | H | W | 1-0 |
| Sep 20 | Aston Villa | A | D | 3-3 |
| Sep 27 | Sunderland | H | L | 0-1 |
| Oct 4 | Wolverhampton W | A | L | 2-6 |
| Oct 11 | Stoke C | H | L | 0-2 |
| Oct 18 | Preston NE | H | W | 5-0 |
| Oct 25 | Burnley | H | L | 1-3 |
| Nov 1 | Tottenham H | A | W | 2-1 |
| Nov 8 | Sheffield W | H | D | 1-1 |
| Nov 15 | Cardiff C | A | W | 2-1 |
| Nov 22 | Newcastle U | H | D | 2-2 |
| Nov 29 | WBA | A | L | 1-3 |
| Dec 6 | Middlesbrough | H | W | 3-2 |
| Dec 13 | Liverpool | A | W | 2-1 |
| Dec 20 | Chelsea | A | W | 3-2 |
| Dec 25 | Blackpool | A | D | 0-0 |
| Dec 26 | Blackpool | H | W | 2-1 |
| Jan 1 | Derby Co | H | W | 1-0 |
| Jan 3 | Manchester C | H | D | 1-1 |
| Jan 17 | Portsmouth | H | W | 1-0 |
| Jan 24 | Bolton W | A | L | 1-2 |
| Feb 7 | Aston Villa | H | W | 3-1 |
| Feb 18 | Sunderland | A | D | 2-2 |
| Feb 21 | Wolverhampton W | H | L | 0-3 |
| Feb 28 | Stoke C | A | L | 1-3 |
| Mar 7 | Preston NE | A | L | 1-2 |
| Mar 14 | Burnley | H | W | 3-2 |
| Mar 25 | Tottenham H | H | W | 2-1 |
| Mar 28 | Sheffield W | A | D | 0-0 |
| Apr 3 | Charlton A | A | D | 2-2 |
| Apr 4 | Cardiff C | H | L | 1-4 |
| Apr 6 | Charlton A | H | W | 3-2 |
| Apr 11 | Newcastle U | A | W | 2-1 |
| Apr 18 | WBA | H | D | 2-2 |
| Apr 20 | Liverpool | H | W | 3-1 |
| Apr 25 | Middlesbrough | A | L | 0-6 |

## FA Cup

|  |  | |  | |
|---|---|---|---|---|
| Jan 10 | Millwall (3) | A | W | 1-0 |
| Jan 31 | Walthamstow A (4) | H | D | 1-1 |
| Feb 5 | Walthamstow A (4R) (at Highbury) | A | W | 5-2 |
| Feb 14 | Everton (5) | A | L | 1-2 |

Final League position: **8th**

| P | W | D | L | F/A | Pts |
|---|---|---|---|---|---|
| 42 | 18 | 10 | 14 | 69/72 | 46 |

# 1953-1954

United's captain and stalwart Johnny Carey had retired in May, 1953, at the age of 34 and the honour would be shared by Pearson and Chilton. until 1955 when Roger Byrne emerged as a natural

# BACK FROM THE BRINK BUSBY ARRIVES

leader in 1955. The club's future was now firmly in the hands of the youngsters and Busby devoted himself to their development. The Youth team was sweeping all before it, beating Wolves to win the FA Youth Cup and even taking their first steps into Europe when Busby took his Babes to Zurich to play in an international competition for young talent. The first team was steady on the pitch, finishing with Wolves taking the title, but it was an improvement on the eighth slot the previous season.

## 1954-1955

Chelsea won the League this season with United this season.

### League (Division 1)

| | | | | |
|---|---|---|---|---|
| Aug 19 | Chelsea | H | D | 1-1 |
| Aug 22 | Liverpool | A | D | 4-4 |
| Aug 26 | WBA | H | L | 1-0 |
| Aug 29 | Newcastle U | H | D | 1-1 |
| Sep 2 | WBA | A | L | 0-2 |
| Sep 5 | Manchester C | A | L | 0-2 |
| Sep 9 | Middlesbrough | H | D | 2-2 |
| Sep 12 | Bolton W | A | D | 0-0 |
| Sep 16 | Middlesbrough | A | W | 4-1 |
| Sep 19 | Preston NE | H | W | 1-0 |
| Sep 26 | Tottenham H | A | D | 1-1 |
| Oct 3 | Burnley | H | L | 1-2 |
| Oct 10 | Sunderland | H | W | 1-0 |
| Oct 17 | Wolverhampton W | A | L | 1-3 |
| Oct 24 | Aston Villa | H | W | 1-0 |
| Oct 31 | Huddersfield T | A | D | 0-0 |
| Nov 7 | Arsenal | H | D | 2-2 |
| Nov 14 | Cardiff C | A | W | 6-1 |
| Nov 21 | Blackpool | H | W | 4-1 |
| Nov 28 | Portsmouth | A | D | 1-1 |
| Dec 5 | Sheffield U | H | D | 2-2 |
| Dec 12 | Chelsea | A | L | 1-3 |
| Dec 19 | Liverpool | H | W | 5-1 |
| Dec 25 | Sheffield W | H | W | 5-2 |
| Dec 26 | Sheffield W | A | W | 1-0 |
| Jan 2 | Newcastle | A | W | 2-1 |
| Jan 16 | Manchester C | H | L | 0-1 |
| Jan 23 | Bolton W | H | L | 1-0 |
| Feb 6 | Preston NE | A | W | 3-1 |
| Feb 13 | Tottenham H | H | W | 2-0 |
| Feb 20 | Burnley | A | L | 0-2 |
| Feb 27 | Sunderland | A | W | 2-0 |
| Mar 6 | Wolverhampton W | H | W | 1-0 |
| Mar 13 | Aston Villa | A | D | 2-2 |
| Mar 20 | Huddersfield T | H | W | 3-1 |
| Mar 27 | Arsenal | A | L | 1-3 |
| Apr 3 | Cardiff C | H | L | 2-3 |
| Apr 10 | Blackpool | A | L | 0-2 |
| Apr 16 | Charlton A | H | W | 2-0 |
| Apr 17 | Portsmouth | H | W | 2-0 |
| Apr 19 | Charlton A | A | W | 0-1 |
| Apr 24 | Sheffield U | A | W | 3-1 |

### FA Cup

| | | | | |
|---|---|---|---|---|
| Jan 9 | Burnley (3) | A | L | 3-5 |

### Final League position: 4th

| P | W | D | L | F/A | Pts |
|---|---|---|---|---|---|
| 42 | 18 | 12 | 12 | 72/58 | 48 |

Johnny Berry fires at goal in the 1955 clash with Bolton. United won 1-0 in front of 45,000 fans.

A product of Busby's youth policy, Johnny Byrne became a real United star, a player of great flair who became captain of the side in the '50s and an England regular.

finishing fifth, but not before The Reds won a momentous game in London 6-5 with Viollet scoring a hat-trick and Tommy Taylor grabbing two, and then taking the return match at Old Trafford in May 2-1. The duo were proving to be United's hot-shots, both notching 20 goals apiece over the season and they were soon to come into their own in the next year. But in 1954, United said goodbye to another of the old school, Stan Pearson, after 17 years at Old Trafford. He was transferred to Bury and ended up managing Chester.

## League (Division 1)

| Date | Opponent | Venue | Result | Score |
|---|---|---|---|---|
| Aug 21 | Portsmouth | H | L | 1-3 |
| Aug 23 | Sheffield W | A | W | 4-2 |
| Aug 28 | Blackpool | A | W | 4-2 |
| Sep 1 | Sheffield W | H | W | 2-0 |
| Sep 4 | Charlton A | H | W | 3-1 |
| Sep 8 | Tottenham H | A | W | 2-0 |
| Sep 11 | Bolton W | A | D | 1-1 |
| Sep 15 | Tottenham H | H | W | 2-1 |
| Sep 18 | Huddersfield T | H | D | 1-1 |
| Sep 25 | Manchester C | A | L | 2-3 |
| Oct 2 | Wolverhampton W | A | L | 2-4 |
| Oct 9 | Cardiff C | H | W | 5-2 |
| Oct 16 | Chelsea | A | W | 6-5 |
| Oct 23 | Newcastle U | H | D | 2-2 |
| Oct 30 | Everton | A | L | 2-4 |
| Nov 6 | Preston NE | H | W | 2-1 |
| Nov 13 | Sheffield U | A | L | 0-3 |
| Nov 20 | Arsenal | H | W | 2-1 |
| Nov 27 | WBA | A | L | 0-2 |
| Dec 4 | Leicester C | H | W | 3-1 |
| Dec 11 | Burnley | A | W | 4-2 |
| Dec 18 | Portsmouth | A | D | 0-0 |
| Dec 27 | Aston Villa | A | L | 0-1 |
| Dec 28 | Aston Villa | H | L | 0-1 |
| Jan 1 | Blackpool | H | W | 4-1 |
| Jan 22 | Bolton W | H | D | 1-1 |
| Feb 5 | Huddersfield T | A | W | 3-1 |
| Feb 12 | Manchester C | H | L | 0-5 |
| Feb 23 | Wolverhampton W | H | L | 2-4 |
| Feb 26 | Cardiff C | A | L | 0-3 |
| Mar 5 | Burnley | H | W | 1-0 |
| Mar 19 | Everton | H | L | 1-2 |
| Mar 26 | Preston NE | A | W | 2-0 |
| Apr 2 | Sheffield U | H | W | 5-0 |
| Apr 8 | Sunderland | A | L | 3-4 |
| Apr 9 | Leicester C | A | L | 0-1 |
| Apr 11 | Sunderland | H | D | 2-2 |
| Apr 16 | WBA | H | W | 3-0 |
| Apr 18 | Newcastle U | A | L | 0-2 |
| Apr 23 | Arsenal | A | W | 3-2 |
| Apr 26 | Charlton A | A | D | 1-1 |
| Apr 30 | Chelsea | H | W | 2-1 |

## FA Cup

| Date | Opponent | Venue | Result | Score |
|---|---|---|---|---|
| Jan 6 | Reading (3) | A | D | 1-1 |
| Jan 12 | Reading (3R) | H | W | 4-1 |
| Feb 29 | Manchester C (4) | A | L | 0-2 |

Final League position: **5th**

| P | W | D | L | F/A | Pts |
|---|---|---|---|---|---|
| 42 | 20 | 7 | 15 | 84/74 | 47 |

Suits you sir! Busby, Edwards and Byrne try on the new style tracksuits in 1955.

# BACK FROM THE BRINK BUSBY ARRIVES

## 1955-1956

United raced to the top of the League and lost only two games in the latter half of the year. Nothing would stop them and they strolled to another Championship title with two games to spare. It was down to Taylor, now at the peak of his scoring power with 25 goals and 20 more from Dennis Viollet. They were the most prolific goalscoring duo in the League and the envy of club managers throughout the country. Busby had bought well in Taylor and now sat back to watch his team destroy the opposition with considerable flair. The Reds were on a roll.

### League (Division 1)

| | | | | |
|---|---|---|---|---|
| Aug 31 | Tottenham H | A | W | 2-1 |
| Sep 3 | Manchester C | A | L | 0-1 |
| Sep 7 | Everton | H | W | 2-1 |
| Sep 10 | Sheffield U | A | L | 0-1 |
| Sep 14 | Everton | A | L | 2-4 |
| Sep 17 | Preston NE | A | L | 3-2 |
| Sep 24 | Burnley | A | D | 0-0 |
| Oct 1 | Luton T | H | W | 3-1 |
| Oct 8 | Wolverhampton W | H | W | 4-3 |
| Oct 15 | Aston Villa | A | D | 4-4 |
| Oct 22 | Huddersfield T | H | W | 3-0 |
| Oct 29 | Cardiff C | A | W | 1-0 |
| Nov 5 | Arsenal | H | D | 1-1 |
| Nov 12 | Bolton W | A | L | 1-3 |
| Nov 19 | Chelsea | H | W | 3-0 |
| Nov 26 | Blackpool | A | D | 0-0 |
| Dec 3 | Sunderland | H | W | 2-1 |
| Dec 10 | Portsmouth | A | L | 2-3 |
| Dec 17 | Birmingham C | H | W | 2-1 |
| Dec 24 | WBA | A | W | 4-1 |
| Dec 26 | Charlton A | H | W | 5-1 |
| Dec 27 | Charlton A | A | L | 0-3 |
| Dec 31 | Manchester C | H | W | 2-1 |
| Jan 14 | Sheffield U | H | W | 3-1 |
| Jan 21 | Preston NE | H | L | 1-3 |
| Feb 4 | Burnley | H | W | 2-0 |
| Feb 11 | Luton T | A | W | 2-0 |

### FA Cup

| | | | | |
|---|---|---|---|---|
| Jan 7 | Bristol R (3) | A | L | 0-4 |

Final League position: **1st**

| P | W | D | L | F/A | Pts |
|---|---|---|---|---|---|
| 42 | 25 | 10 | 7 | 85/51 | 60 |

## 1956-57

Matt Busby's dream of taking on the cream of Continental football came to fruition as United entered the European Cup, progressing to the semi-final before losing to Real Madrid. It was a great season for the fans. Taylor was on form again with 22, Whelan scored 26 and the young Bobby Charlton grabbed 10. At home, United stormed to a second

Men at the top. United directors: (Back) Walter Crickmer, Matt Busby (Front) George Whitaker and Alan Gibson in 1958.

Club secretary Walter Crickmer was a staunch ally of Busby as he rebuilt the team after the war.

A rare shot of Bobby Charlton trying to get the better of brother Jack in United's clash with Leeds at Elland Road in 1958.

successive Championship and were robbed of the League and FA Cup double by Aston Villa at Wembley, losing 2–1 after goalkeeper Ray Wood suffered a broken cheek bone in a clash with Villa striker Peter McParland.

## League (Division 1)

| | | | | | |
|---|---|---|---|---|---|
| Aug 18 | Birmingham C | H | D | 2-2 | |
| Aug 20 | Preston NE | A | W | 3-1 | |
| Aug 25 | WBA | A | W | 3-2 | |
| Aug 29 | Preston NE | H | W | 3-0 | |
| Sep 1 | Portsmouth | H | W | 3-0 | |
| Sep 5 | Chelsea | A | W | 2-1 | |
| Sep 8 | Newcastle U | A | D | 1-1 | |
| Sep 15 | Sheffield W | H | W | 4-1 | |
| Sep 22 | Manchester C | H | W | 2-0 | |
| Sep 29 | Arsenal | A | W | 2-1 | |
| Oct 6 | Charlton A | H | W | 4-2 | |
| Oct 13 | Sunderland | A | W | 3-1 | |
| Oct 20 | Everton | H | L | 2-5 | |
| Oct 27 | Blackpool | A | D | 2-2 | |
| Nov 3 | Wolverhampton W | H | W | 3-0 | |
| Nov 10 | Bolton W | A | L | 0-2 | |
| Nov 17 | Leeds U | H | W | 3-2 | |
| Nov 24 | Tottenham H | A | D | 2-2 | |
| Dec 1 | Luton T | H | W | 3-1 | |
| Dec 8 | Aston Villa | A | W | 3-1 | |
| Dec 15 | Birmingham C | A | L | 1-3 | |
| Dec 26 | Cardiff C | H | W | 3-1 | |
| Dec 29 | Portsmouth | A | W | 3-1 | |
| Jan 1 | Chelsea | H | W | 3-0 | |
| Jan 12 | Newcastle U | H | W | 6-1 | |
| Jan 19 | Sheffield W | A | L | 1-2 | |
| Feb 2 | Manchester C | A | W | 4-2 | |
| Feb 9 | Arsenal | H | W | 6-2 | |
| Feb 18 | Charlton A | A | W | 5-1 | |
| Feb 23 | Blackpool | H | L | 0-2 | |
| Mar 6 | Everton | A | W | 2-1 | |
| Mar 9 | Aston Villa | H | D | 1-1 | |
| Mar 16 | Wolverhampton W | A | D | 1-1 | |
| Mar 25 | Bolton W | H | L | 0-2 | |
| Mar 30 | Leeds U | A | W | 2-1 | |
| Apr 6 | Tottenham H | H | D | 0-0 | |
| Apr 13 | Luton T | A | W | 2-0 | |
| Apr 19 | Burnley | A | W | 3-1 | |
| Apr 20 | Sunderland | H | W | 4-0 | |
| Apr 22 | Burnley | H | W | 2-0 | |
| Apr 27 | Cardiff C | A | W | 3-2 | |
| Apr 29 | WBA | H | D | 1-1 | |

## FA Cup

| | | | | | |
|---|---|---|---|---|---|
| Jan 5 | Hartlepool U (3) | A | W | 4-3 | |
| Jan 26 | Wrexham (4) | A | W | 5-0 | |
| Feb 16 | Everton (5) | H | W | 1-0 | |
| Mar 2 | Bournemouth (6) | A | W | 2-1 | |
| Mar 23 | Birmingham C (SF) | N | W | 2-0 | (at Hillsborough) |
| May 4 | Aston Villa (F) | N | L | 1-2 | (at Wembley) |

## European Cup

| | | | | | |
|---|---|---|---|---|---|
| Sep 12 | RSC Anderlecht | A | W | 2-1 | |
| Sep 26 | RSC Anderlecht | H | W | 10-0 | |
| Oct 17 | Borussia D | H | W | 3-2 | |
| Nov 21 | Borussia D | A | D | 0-0 | |
| Jan 16 | Athletico Bilbao | A | L | 3-5 | |
| Feb 6 | Athletico Bilbao | H | W | 3-0 | |
| Apr 11 | Real Madrid | A | L | 1-3 | |
| Apr 25 | Real Madrid | H | D | 2-2 | |

**Final League position: 1st**

| P | W | D | L | F/A | Pts |
|---|---|---|---|---|---|
| 42 | 28 | 8 | 6 | 103/54 | 64 |

Charlton turns on the style in the 1958 derby against City.

Bill Foulkes. Few will forget his Munich heroics – or his game.

Dennis Viollet (left) and Tommy Taylor were a deadly double act for United.

# Young, Gifted And Red

## "

**"L**egs like tree trunks and an unforgettable zest for the game". That was how Jimmy Murphy described the boy who was only 15 when he made his debut

**L**among the men of Old Trafford on Easter Monday, 1953. He was a club junior and though Busby and Murphy knew full well he had the potential to become a major force for the team, Edwards had all the mundane duties to perform – cleaning the players boots and helping the ground staff. When he arrived that morning expecting to do just that, Busby told him to get his boots on, he was facing Cardiff City.

That was the moment when United created a real legend talked about by fans today. He became one of the most formidable left-half players in the country but he could run for 90 minutes non-stop, covering just about every area of the pitch if necessary. Word soon spread around other clubs that United had found a youngster who was destined for the England shirt, but rivals were amazed when the international call-up came at the age of 17, by which time

Edwards was a fully seasoned club player. It is almost unthinkable, even in these days, that one so young could handle the responsibility of senior appearances and yet be so unfazed by the experience. In many ways, the likes of Paul Scholes of today's team is the successor – quiet, skillful, assured of his own abilities and with a determination and physical strength that gives him an immediate advantage over the opposition. Legend has it that Edwards once broke the scoreboard with a shot at Old Trafford that whizzed past the goal.

Edwards' first game for England was against Scotland at Wembley and the home side thrashed the Scots

**E**7-2. The youngster was a brick wall at the back, mopping up Scottish attacks and then giving England the chance to sweep forward with his sublime distribution. Over the following years, he was to play in just about every position for United because he loved to attack. He had a hunger for goals

Busby takes his new discovery through the finer details of his contract with United. It was to prove a monumental signing.

and his very presence on the pitch, his team-mates said at the time, would inspire a confidence in the whole team before a game. During his time, Edwards won two Championship medals, making 175 appearances in the League and Cup and reaped 21 goals. He was one of those players the United fans expected to score every week.

With Edwards, Eddie Colman and Mark Jones at the back, United rarely leaked unnecessary goals and that defensive partnership was to prove vital when United went into Europe in the 1957-1958 season. The prospect held no fear for Edwards, to him they were just another challenge to be met. United strolled through the initial rounds and then faced Red Star of Belgrade in the quarter final. The events of that fateful trip to Yugoslavia are recorded elsewhere, but the fight Edwards put up to survive was typical of the man.

The player had been expecting to return to England to marry his fiancee and, still only 21, had a momentous football career

ahead of him. After 15 days in intensive care in a German hospital and with doctors fighting for him, Edwards succumbed to kidney failure and died. When his coffin returned to Manchester, thousand of traumatised fans lined the streets. Nobody could believe that players of the stature of Edwards had been taken in such a way. Duncan Edwards was to become a part of the fabric of Manchester United's history.

It took Matt Busby and Jimmy Murphy years to come to terms with the loss and talk about players like Edwards but when they did, they put his contribution to football in general and United in particular, in perspective.

"He was a players' player", recalled Jimmy Murphy. "The greatest. There was only one and that was Duncan Edwards."

A rock in defence, Edwards clears a dangerous ball against Scotland at Wembley in 1957.

Towering inferno. He was superb in aerial combat.

Edwards' courage became legendary at Old Trafford. He feared nobody.

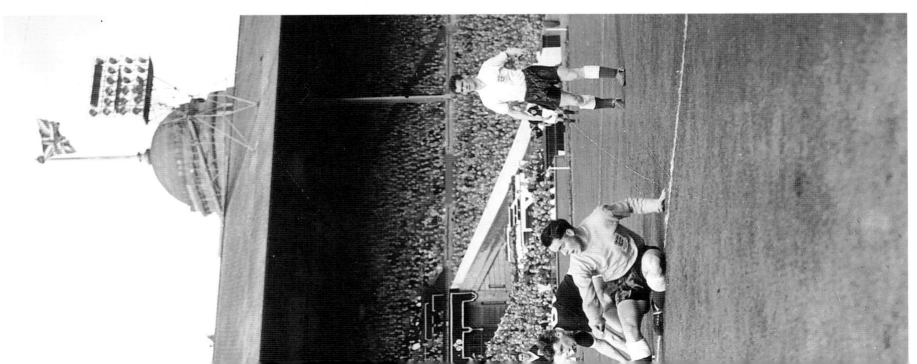

"Legs like tree-trunks", said Jimmy Murphy. Edwards was a giant of a player.

Besides his physical prowess, he displayed some silky skills. Here he is in goalmouth action at Villa in 1957.

## 1957-58

By now, the "Busby Babes" — the manager actually preferred the title Red Devils — were beginning their domination of English football despite having lost the FA Cup Final the previous season and being robbed of the Double by Aston Villa at Wembley. It was recognised that the team was by far the best in Britain, yet it was still a young side and fans sensed that greater honours were on the way.

United were League Champions and heading into Europe this season with no fear of the Continental sides. They got off to a great start, thrashing Manchester City 4-1, Leeds 5-0 and Blackpool 4-1. February 1 saw The Reds face Arsenal at Highbury in one the greatest games ever seen with 60,000 watching a monumental tussle. Edwards, Charlton, Taylor and Viollet all hit the net as United took the game 5-4. A week later, the cream of British football was to be tragically destroyed at Munich airport.

### League (Division 1)

| | | | | |
|---|---|---|---|---|
| Aug 28 | Everton | H | W | 3-0 |
| Aug 31 | Manchester C | H | W | 4-1 |
| Sep 4 | Everton | A | D | 3-3 |
| Sep 7 | Leeds Utd | H | W | 5-0 |
| Sep 9 | Blackpool | A | W | 4-1 |
| Sep 14 | Bolton W | A | L | 0-4 |
| Sep 18 | Blackpool | H | L | 1-2 |
| Sep 21 | Arsenal | H | W | 4-2 |
| Sep 28 | Wolverhampton W | A | L | 1-3 |
| Oct 5 | Aston Villa | H | W | 4-1 |
| Oct 12 | Nottingham F | A | W | 2-1 |
| Oct 19 | Portsmouth | H | L | 0-3 |
| Oct 28 | WBA | A | L | 3-4 |
| Nov 2 | Burnley | H | W | 1-0 |
| Nov 9 | Preston NE | A | D | 1-1 |
| Nov 16 | Sheffield W | H | W | 2-1 |
| Nov 23 | Newcastle U | A | W | 2-1 |
| Nov 30 | Tottenham H | H | L | 3-4 |
| Dec 7 | Birmingham C | A | D | 3-3 |
| Dec 14 | Chelsea | H | L | 0-1 |
| Dec 21 | Leicester C | H | W | 4-0 |
| Dec 25 | Luton Town | H | W | 3-0 |
| Dec 26 | Luton Town | A | D | 2-2 |
| Dec 28 | Manchester C | A | D | 2-2 |
| Jan 11 | Leeds U | A | D | 1-1 |
| Jan 18 | Bolton W | H | W | 7-2 |
| Feb 1 | Arsenal | A | W | 5-4 |
| Feb 22 | Nottingham F | H | D | 1-1 |
| Mar 8 | WBA | H | L | 0-4 |
| Mar 15 | Burnley | A | L | 0-3 |
| Mar 29 | Sheffield W | A | L | 0-1 |

# Munich's Dark Shadow

White snowflakes tumble down on to the blackened wreckage of a plane. It's a chilling scene and one that froze the soul of United for years.

The disaster at Munich airport on February 6, 1958, claimed 21 lives, including those of seven Busby babes. It was an appalling tragedy and one that still haunts the hearts and minds of everyone connected with the club. Decades later fans still dream of what could have been if the doomed squad had returned safely to Manchester after their European Cup quarter-final against Red Star Belgrade. It's a story of horror and great heroism. The chartered aircraft had only stopped off at Munich to take on more fuel and should have been safely on its way within minutes. However, after two aborted take-offs it was clear there was something wrong with one of the engines.

While the passengers kicked their heels in the airport café, the pilots had talks with the ground staff about what to do. The make of plane, an Elizabethan, had the power to lift-off on a single engine, so the fateful decision was taken to push on for home. As the aircraft roared down the runway for the last time, fear was etched on the faces of the players. Johnny Berry even declared: "We're going to die!" Instead of soaring into the sky, the plane ploughed through a fence, shot across a road and smashed into a house. A wing and

part of the tail were ripped clean away, leaving the cockpit to career on into a tree. The fuselage then demolished a hut packed with tyres and fuel, sparking a fireball inferno.

Goalkeeper Harry Gregg emerged as the hero of the hour. After kicking his way out of the wreckage, he risked his life by going back to rescue a badly injured mother and her baby. Then, despite the threat of more explosions, he grabbed hold of Bobby Charlton and Dennis Viollet by the waistbands of their trousers and hauled them to safety. It was a scene of dreadful carnage that sent shock waves round the world. Among the dead were the cream of English football. Forward Tommy Taylor perished at the age of 26 along with strikers Liam Whelan, aged 22 and David Pegg, also 22. Loved ones and fans back home listened in stunned disbelief as the names were read out on the TV news. It couldn't be true that full backs Roger Byrne, aged 28 and Geoff Bent, aged 25 would never put on a pair of boots again, or that half-backs Eddie Colman, aged 21, and Mark Jones, aged 24, would never see another Old Trafford crowd. It was too awful to take in. United also lost three stalwarts, coach Bert Whalley, trainer Tom Curry, and club secretary Walter Crickmer. The crash ripped the heart out of the club. Half-back Duncan Edwards, aged 22, eventually lost a gallant 15 day hospital battle for life against dreadful wounds.

The Elizabethan airliner still burns 12 hours after smashing into a house at the end of the runway

At one time it was also touch and go whether manager Matt Busby would make it. He suffered severe chest injuries in the crash and doctors were so worried about his condition, he was given the last rites twice. The day after the disaster, assistant manager Jimmy Murphy flew out to comfort the injured.

He had been working with the Welsh squad and missed out on the fateful trip to Belgrade. Despite his immense grief, Jimmy shouldered the burden of keeping the club alive. With Matt Busby recovering in hospital, he set about making sure the memory of those who died would be honoured in the best way possible – by fielding a team.

U nited were allowed to postpone their next match, an FA Cup tie against Sheffield Wednesday, until February 19. Right up until the last minute fans didn't know who would be playing. Jimmy signed up Blackpool's Ernie Taylor and, only hours before kick-off, managed to get Aston Villa's Stan Crowther on board too. The rest of the team was made up of players taken from the youth and reserve ranks. Munich survivors Harry Gregg and Bill Foulkes were given a rapturous reception when they came out on to the pitch ahead of the scratch side. The historic game was so charged with emotion, United couldn't fail to

win. They beat Wednesday 3-0 and demonstrated to the world that the show would go on. With Manchester still in deep shock, Jimmy based the team in Blackpool. The FA Cup gave them something to aim at and, despite all the pressures, United made it to the final. A win would have been the perfect tonic for the club, but Bolton Wanderers proved too strong and took the trophy by beating the new Reds 2-0. It was a controversial game. When crash hero Harry Gregg leapt to snatch a cross, Bolton's Nat Lofthouse barged him over the line. Gregg was knocked cold during the clash and Wanderers were awarded their second goal. It still rankles with some fans. Matt Busby spent over 10 weeks in the Rechts der Isar hospital in Munich recovering from his injuries. On his return to Manchester he predicted it would take five years to put a new winning team together. Slowly but surely Matt set the club on the road to glory. One of his first moves was to sign left-back Noel Cantwell in November 1960. Then, two years later, began the reign of "The King," Denis Law, who joined United for a record fee of £115,000 and scored during his first game for the club. Next came Pat Crerand in 1963. The team was growing in strength all the time and toasted it's first real success since the disaster when they beat Leicester 3-1 to take the FA Cup in May 1963. United were back in the spotlight and the days of Best were yet to come.

| Mar 31 | Aston Villa | A | L | 2-3 |
| Apr 4 | Sunderland | H | D | 2-2 |
| Apr 5 | Preston NE | H | D | 0-0 |
| Apr 7 | Sunderland | A | W | 2-1 |
| Apr 12 | Tottenham H | A | L | 0-1 |
| Apr 16 | Portsmouth | A | D | 3-3 |
| Apr 19 | Birmingham C | H | L | 0-2 |
| Apr 21 | Wolverhampton WH | | L | 0-4 |
| Apr 23 | Newcastle U | H | D | 1-1 |
| Apr 26 | Chelsea | A | L | 1-2 |

Final League position: **9th**

| P | W | D | L | F/A | Pts |
|---|---|---|---|-----|-----|
| 42 | 16 | 11 | 15 | 85/75 | 43 |

### FA Cup

| Jan 4 | Workington T (3) | A | W | 3-1 |
| Jan 25 | Ipswich T (4) | H | W | 2-0 |
| Feb 19 | Sheffield W (5) | H | W | 3-0 |
| Mar 1 | WBA (6) | A | D | 2-2 |
| Mar 5 | WBA (6R) | H | W | 1-0 |
| Mar 22 | Fulham (SF) | N | D | 2-2 |
| | (at Villa Park) | | | |
| Mar 26 | Fulham (SFR) | N | W | 5-3 |
| | (at Highbury) | | | |
| May 3 | Bolton W (F) | N | L | 0-2 |
| | (at Wembley) | | | |

ffff7

### European Cup

| Sep 25 | Shamrock R (P) | A | W | 6-0 |
| Oct 2 | Shamrock R (P) | H | W | 3-2 |
| Nov 21 | Dukla Pague (1) | H | W | 3-0 |
| Dec 4 | Dukla Pague (1) | A | L | 0-1 |
| Jan 14 | RS Belgrade (2) | H | W | 2-1 |
| Feb 5 | RS Belgrade (2) | A | D | 3-3 |
| May 8 | AC Milan (SF) | H | W | 2-1 |
| May 14 | AC Milan (SF) | A | L | 0-4 |

The faces still haunt United fans. Taken in 1957 these were the pride of the Championship side who took on Red Star Belgrade.
*Back row:* Eddie Colman, Bill Foulkes, Ray Wood, Johnny Byrne, Mark Jones, Duncan Edwards.
*Front row:* Dennis Viollet, Johnny Berry, Tommy Taylor, Liam Whelan, David Pegg.

Jimmy Murphy puts Bobby Charlton and his team-mates through their paces at the Blackpool training ground.

Harry Gregg dives in despair as Bolton score in the home game just two weeks before Munich

The cockpit of the Elizabethan lies a twisted wreck in the snow after failing to take off at Muncih Airpport. Several United players had left the front of the plane

ke-off and moved to the back because they thought it was safer.

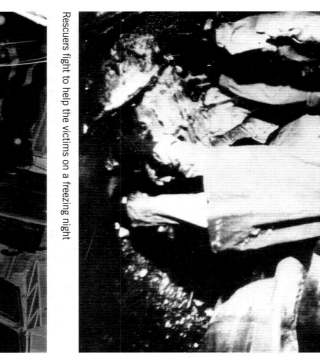

The mangled interior of the plane behind the cockpit door

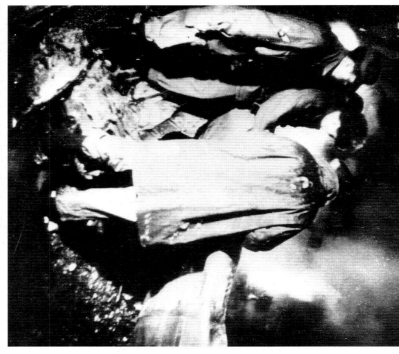

Rescuers fight to help the victims on a freezing night

The wreckage still smoulders hours after the crash

The shattered plane lies silently in the snow-covered field the morning after careering off the runway. By now, the world knew the full extent of the crash.

Rescuers and investigators carry out the tragic task of identifying victims lying in the snow.

The detailed quest for reasons why the plane crashed begins immediately

The terrible sight that met rescuers when they got near the plane

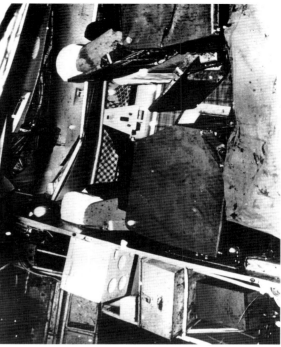

The stewards' section inside the Elizabethan

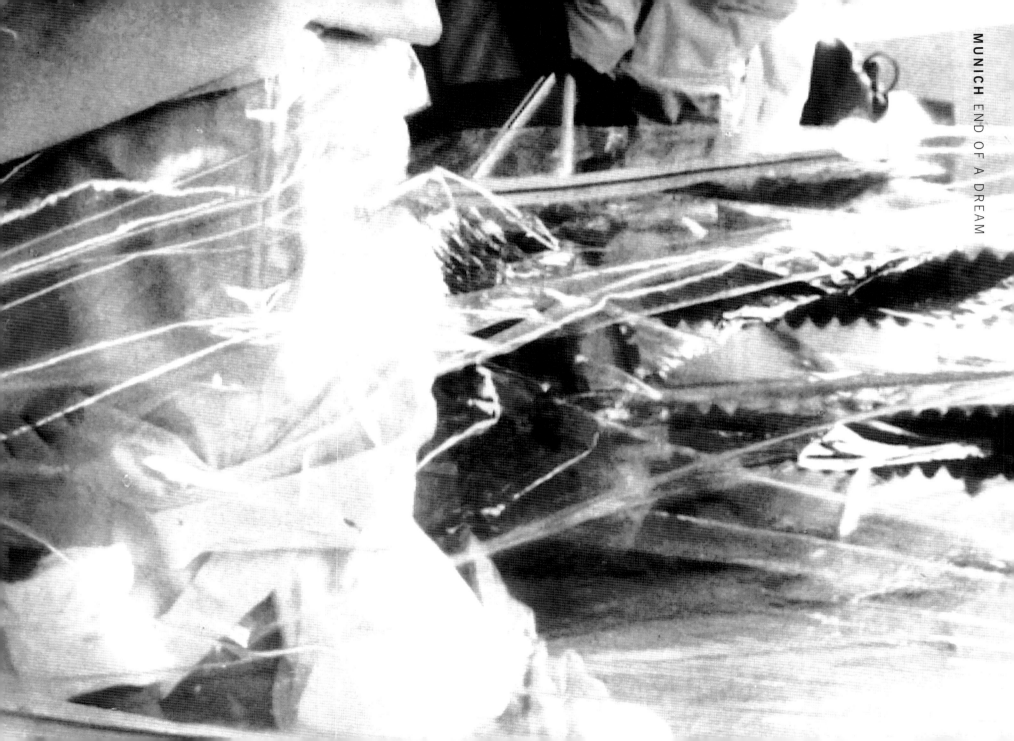

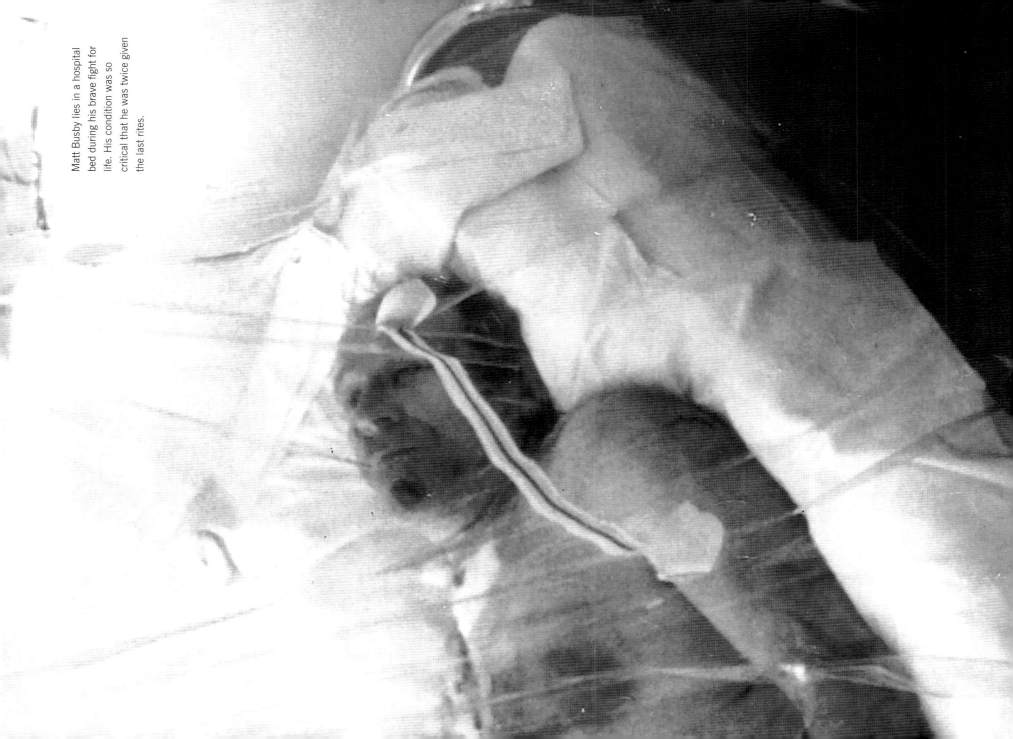

Matt Busby lies in a hospital bed during his brave fight for life. His condition was so critical that he was twice given the last rites.

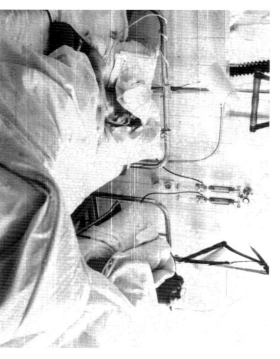

Duncan Edwards (right) lost his two-week fight for life

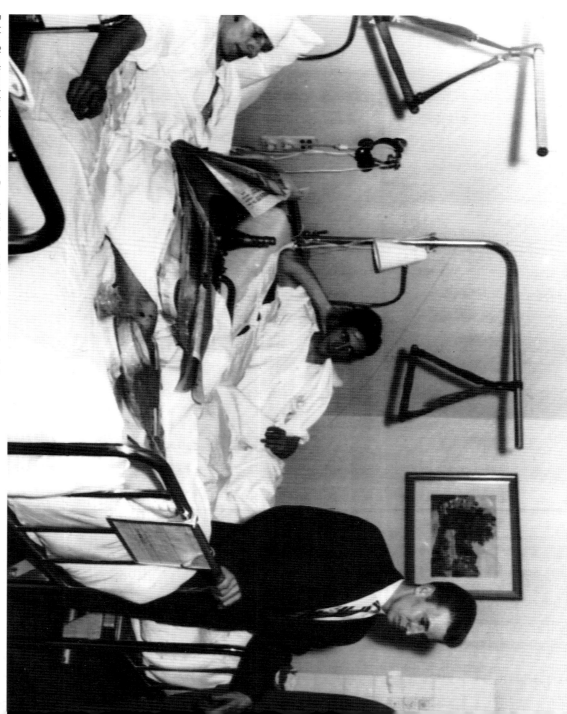

Bobby Charlton visits his team-mates Dennis Viollet and Albert Scanlon in hospital

Duncan Edwards' parents receive the terrible news at home in Manchester

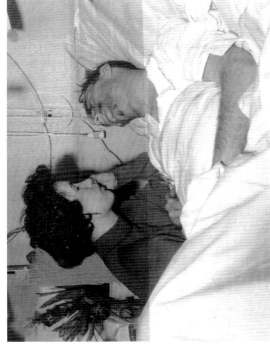

Goalkeeper Ray Wood receives a visit from his wife

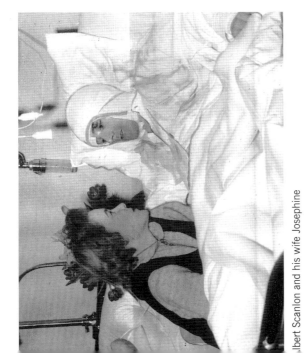

Albert Scanlon and his wife Josephine

The wives of Harry Gregg and Bill Foulkes call for news

Grief-stricken fans flocked to Old Trafford desperate for the latest news of their heroes. Many stayed for days unable to believe the scale of the tragedy

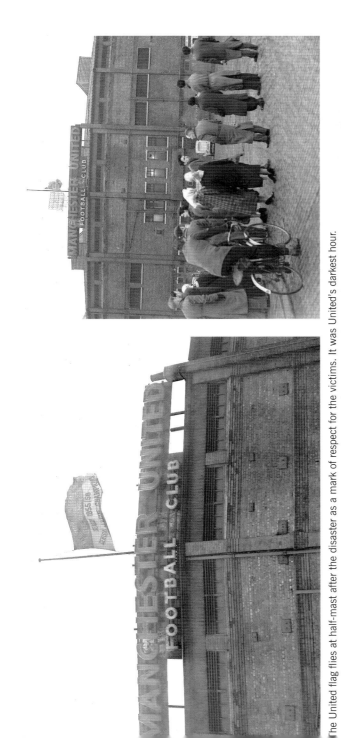

The United flag flies at half-mast after the disaster as a mark of respect for the victims. It was United's darkest hour.

Jimmy Murphy, who didn't travel to Europe with the team, phones Munich from Old Trafford on the night of the crash

Relatives of survivors
prepare to fly to Munich in
the aftermath of the crash

Harry Gregg, one of the heroes of the crash, is greeted by a young German nurse who tended the victims

Thousands pay their respects as Duncan Edwards is brought home

Those who survived begin to return to Manchester

Matt Busby returns to his Manchester home to a hero's welcome after winning his battle in Munich

Professor Maurer, the man whose skill as a surgeon saved lives at Munich, and his wife Erica on a visit to Old Trafford in March 1958

United players Ron Cope and Freddie Goodwin head for Milan for the semi-final of the European Cup in 1958. They kept the dream alive.

Busby unveils the memorial plaque to the victims of Munich at Old Trafford. It is still a moving sight today

Keeping the dream alive. Wesley Bent, 5, and Roger Jones, 3, nephews of Munich victims Mark Jones and Geoff Bent.

Pilot Capt James Thain (far left) and his crew who survived the crash

Surgeon Professor Maurer sifts the hundreds of thank you letters he received from around the world

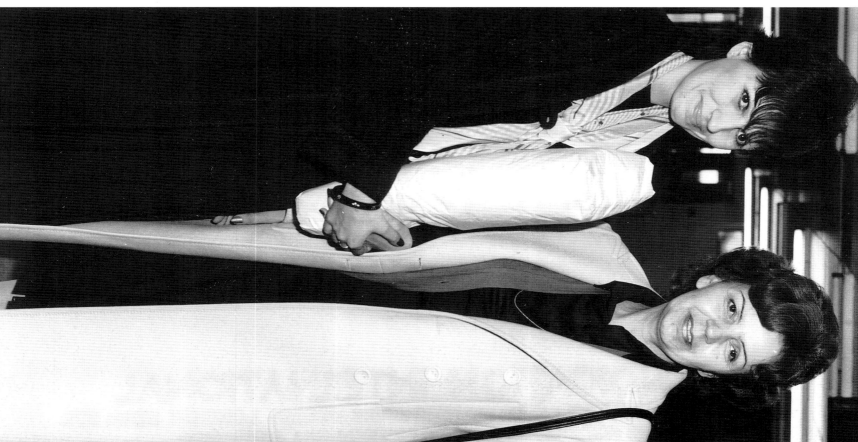

Vesna Lukic (left) was two-years-old when she was pulled from the wreckage of United's plane by Harry Gregg. The two became good friends after the disaster

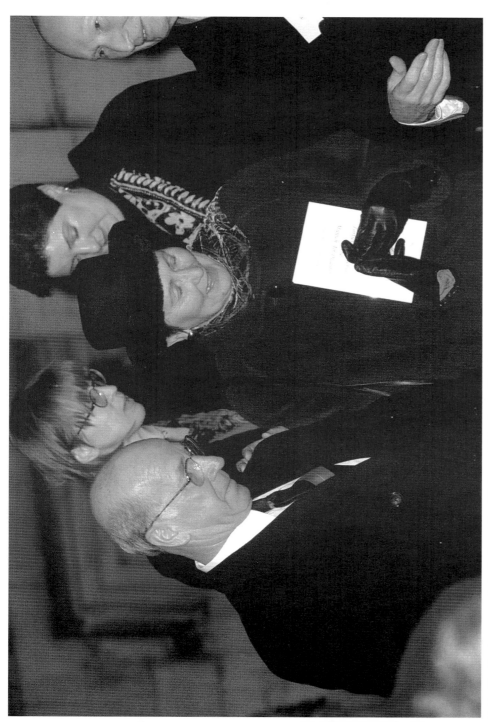

Bobby Charlton in a moment of reflection at the 40th Memorial Service for Munich

Paddy Crerand waves to fans as he arrives

The Future. David Beckham pays his respects

In Busby's footsteps. Alex Ferguson at the service.

## 1958-1959

With the entire country still stunned by the Munich tragedy and Busby recovering, Jimmy Murphy took on the task of taking United forward. A reassembled team had lost in the controversial 1958 Cup Final when Bolton forward Nat Lofthouse bundled Munich survivor Harry Gregg into the net to clinch a 2-0 victory. Any success from now on was viewed as a tribute to those who had died and every game took on a special significance with fans flocking to Old Trafford every week to show their support. Given the circumstances, it was an astonishing achievement for the team to finish the League in second place behind Wolves with 103 goals scored. United were on the way back.

**League (Division 1)**

| | | | | |
|---|---|---|---|---|
| Aug 23 | Chelsea | H | W | 5-2 |
| Aug 27 | Nottingham F | A | W | 3-0 |
| Aug 30 | Blackpool | A | L | 1-2 |
| Sep 3 | Nottingham F | H | D | 1-1 |
| Sep 6 | Blackburn R | H | W | 6-1 |
| Sep 8 | West Ham U | A | L | 2-3 |
| Sep 13 | Newcastle U | A | D | 1-1 |
| Sep 17 | West Ham U | H | W | 4-1 |
| Sep 20 | Tottenham H | H | D | 2-2 |
| Sep 27 | Manchester C | A | D | 1-1 |
| Oct 4 | Wolverhampton W | A | L | 0-4 |
| Oct 8 | Preston NE | H | L | 0-2 |
| Oct 11 | Arsenal | H | D | 1-1 |
| Oct 18 | Everton | H | L | 2-3 |
| Oct 25 | WBA | H | L | 1-2 |
| Nov 1 | Leeds U | A | W | 2-1 |
| Nov 8 | Burnley | H | L | 1-3 |
| Nov 15 | Bolton W | A | L | 3-6 |
| Nov 22 | Luton Town | H | W | 2-1 |
| Nov 29 | Birmingham C | A | W | 4-0 |
| Dec 6 | Leicester C | H | W | 4-1 |
| Dec 13 | Preston NE | A | W | 4-3 |
| Dec 20 | Chelsea | A | W | 3-2 |
| Dec 26 | Aston Villa | H | W | 2-1 |
| Dec 27 | Aston Villa | A | W | 2-0 |
| Jan 3 | Blackpool | H | W | 3-1 |
| Jan 31 | Newcastle U | H | D | 4-4 |
| Feb 7 | Tottenham H | A | W | 3-1 |
| Feb 16 | Manchester C | H | W | 4-1 |
| Feb 21 | Wolverhampton WH | A | L | 2-1 |
| Feb 28 | Arsenal | A | L | 2-3 |
| Mar 2 | Blackburn R | A | W | 3-1 |
| Mar 7 | Everton | H | W | 2-1 |
| Mar 14 | WBA | A | W | 3-1 |
| Mar 21 | Leeds U | H | W | 4-0 |
| Mar 27 | Portsmouth | H | W | 6-1 |
| Mar 28 | Burnley | A | L | 2-4 |
| Mar 30 | Portsmouth | A | W | 3-1 |
| Apr 4 | Bolton W | H | W | 3-0 |
| Apr 11 | Luton Town | A | D | 0-0 |
| Apr 18 | Birmingham C | H | W | 1-0 |
| Apr 25 | Leicester C | A | L | 1-2 |

# In Pursuit Of Glory

They say that football is just a game, but all supporters of every club know this is simply not true. They love it and whatever misfortune may blight their lives, the team they follow is always there.

A distraction it may be, but it's a crucial one.

And so it was with United after the terrible events of 1958. Old Trafford became a shrine for the club's faithful – not least the city itself – and the players who arrived as the new decade dawned were soon to discover a weight of hope and expectation which would live with them for the rest of their lives. Some would excel in the pressure-cooker atmosphere, indeed become national heroes, others would wilt under the enormity of it all.

Though so much young talent had been lost in the wrecked Elizabethan on the Munich airport runway, a typical British resolve surfaced at the club. As Matt Busby recovered, his loyal assistant Jimmy Murphy took control. Not only was there a business to run, a great tradition had to be maintained. He was to admit years later: "I felt as if I was going out of my mind".

Thankfully, he stayed sane and put out a patched-up side with Munich heroes Harry Gregg and Bill Foulkes, Shay Brennan and Ronnie Cope to play Sheffield Wednesday in the FA Cup fifth round on Feb 19, 1958. They won 3-0, Brennan scoring two. It was against all expectations, but fans everywhere applauded the victory. The weakened side could never sustain a level of performance necessary to win the championship – they finished ninth – but they went to the Cup Final, losing to Bolton Wanderers. In the following season, United finished second to Wolves, a remarkable result given the trauma of the previous years. As the country moved into a period of huge social change with the dawn of the sixties, so the club embarked on a new era which would echo down the decades until May 26, 1999, at Barcelona's Nou Camp stadium. We record the events of that famous night later.

By 1960, Matt Busby was back in the driving seat at Old Trafford. One of his first moves was to sign left-back Noel Cantwell from West Ham. Two years later, a legend arrived in the form of Denis Law, signed from Italian club Torino in 1962 for a record £115,000. Next

**FA Cup**

Jan 10 Norwich C (3)    A   L   0-3

## 1959-1960

Matt Busby was slowly taking the reigns of the club and began a steady rebuilding with the emphasis once more on youth. He had little choice, but with the likes of Charlton starting to grow in stature the future seemed brighter. The shadow of Munich still hung over the club, but he once again started the search for talent, bringing in the dynamic Albert Quixall from Sheffield Wednesday and Noel Cantwell from West Ham. Dennis Viollet was on top form but United as a unit was not ready to challenge for the title yet. Their worst defeat was a 7-2 drubbing by Newcastle and United finished seventh, no-man's-land for a club of United's stature.

### League (Division 1)

| | | | |
|---|---|---|---|
| Aug 22 | WBA | A | L 2-3 |
| Aug 26 | Chelsea | H | L 0-1 |
| Aug 29 | Newcastle U | H | W 3-2 |
| Sep 2 | Chelsea | A | W 6-3 |
| Sep 5 | Birmingham C | A | D 1-1 |
| Sep 9 | Leeds U | H | W 6-0 |
| Sep 12 | Tottenham H | H | L 5-1 |
| Sep 16 | Leeds U | A | D 2-2 |
| Sep 19 | Manchester C | A | L 0-3 |
| Sep 26 | Preston NE | A | L 0-4 |
| Oct 3 | Leicester C | H | W 4-1 |
| Oct 10 | Arsenal | H | W 4-2 |
| Oct 17 | Wolverhampton WA | L | 2-3 |
| Oct 24 | Sheffield W | H | W 3-1 |
| Oct 31 | Blackburn R | A | D 1-1 |
| Nov 7 | Fulham | H | D 3-3 |
| Nov 14 | Bolton W | A | D 1-1 |
| Nov 21 | Luton Town | H | W 4-1 |
| Nov 28 | Everton | A | L 1-2 |
| Dec 5 | Blackpool | H | W 3-1 |
| Dec 12 | Nottingham F | A | W 5-1 |
| Dec 19 | WBA | H | L 2-3 |
| Dec 26 | Burnley | H | L 1-2 |
| Dec 28 | Burnley | A | W 4-1 |
| Jan 2 | Newcastle U | A | L 3-7 |
| Jan 16 | Birmingham C | H | W 2-1 |
| Jan 23 | Tottenham H | A | L 1-2 |
| Feb 6 | Manchester C | H | D 0-0 |
| Feb 13 | Preston NE | H | D 1-1 |
| Feb 24 | Leicester C | A | L 1-3 |
| Feb 27 | Blackpool | A | W 6-0 |
| Mar 5 | Wolverhampton W | H | L 0-2 |
| Mar 19 | Nottingham F | H | W 3-1 |
| Mar 26 | Fulham | A | W 5-0 |
| Mar 30 | Sheffield W | A | L 2-4 |
| Apr 7 | Bolton W | H | W 2-0 |
| Apr 9 | Luton Town | A | W 3-2 |
| Apr 15 | West Ham U | A | L 1-2 |

A superb portrait of Busby in 1968. Fans rightly dubbed him The Godfather – he laid the foundations of the modern superclub.

U nited fans, however, craved the return of the Championship and it was on Busby's mind as well. He brought in a young Irishman, George Best, and a much-needed winger John Connelly from Burnley. He now had a line-up that was to prove too much for the opposition and in the 1964-65 season they were champions again – the first time since Munich.

Now the scene was set for a remarkable period at United. There are times in any football club's history when fans can sense success and this was it for Busby and his Babes. Law was prolific with 28 goals and Herd was the staunch back-up man, adding 20 to the tally of 89 that season. But most important, they were back

came Pat Crerand, a sturdy Scot from Glasgow Celtic. Busby had a game-plan and though the League Championship was beyond the team – by 1963 they were in 19th position – they were a classic Cup side, storming to the '63 Final and winning it 3-1 against Leicester, David Herd scoring two.

in Europe in 1966, producing some magical performances such as the 5-1 demolition of Benfica in Portugal. The team was to lose out when they met Partizan Belgrade at Old Trafford a month later, but as fans left the ground that night, there was a feeling that the club was on the right track.

They were to be proved right. The 1966-1967 season saw United romp away with the League title again and enter yet another European campaign, but this time far better equipped to take on the flair teams from abroad. This is exactly what Busby had dreamed of and United strolled through the preliminary rounds against the likes of the Maltese team Hibernians until they faced the quality of Real Madrid. A 1-0 win in Spain and a sensational 3-3 draw at home in the return leg saw United through to face Benfica at Wembley.

Much has been said about the game that was to follow, but it was simply the culmination of a dream held by Matt Busby since the day he lay in a hospital bed in Germany after the crash 10 years earlier and whispered to his assistant Jimmy Murphy: "Keep the flag flying".

# 1960-61

In a bid to strengthen the side, Busby signed two important players in 1960. He spent £30,000 on the bandy-legged West Bromwich Albion midfield hardman Maurice Setters and £29,000 on West Ham's Irish international left-back Noel Cantwell.

Although they were sound long-term investments, the arrival of fresh blood failed to give the club an immediate leg-up in the league. Despite a sparkling mid-season run of five wins on the trot, United remained seventh overall. They were also knocked out of the FA Cup in the fourth round by Sheffield Wednesday.

**Final League position: 7th**

| P | W | D | L | F/A | Pts |
|---|---|---|---|---|---|
| 42 | 19 | 7 | 16 | 102/80 | 45 |

**FA Cup**

| | | | |
|---|---|---|---|
| Jan 9 | Derby C (3) | A | W 4-2 |
| Jan 30 | Liverpool (4) | H | W 3-1 |
| Feb 20 | Sheffield W (5) | A | L 0-1 |

**League (Division 1)**

| | | | |
|---|---|---|---|
| Aug 20 | Blackburn R | H | L 1-3 |
| Aug 24 | Everton | A | L 0-4 |
| Aug 31 | Everton | H | W 4-0 |
| Sep 3 | Tottenham H | A | L 1-4 |
| Sep 5 | West Ham U | A | L 1-2 |
| Sep 10 | Leicester C | H | D 1-1 |
| Sep 14 | West Ham U | H | W 6-1 |
| Sep 17 | Aston Villa | A | L 1-3 |
| Sep 24 | Wolverhampton WH | A | L 1-3 |
| Oct 1 | Bolton W | A | D 1-1 |
| Oct 15 | Burnley | A | L 3-5 |
| Oct 22 | Newcastle U | H | W 3-2 |
| Oct 29 | Arsenal | A | L 1-2 |
| Nov 5 | Sheffield W | H | D 0-0 |
| Nov 12 | Birmingham C | A | L 1-3 |
| Nov 19 | WBA | H | W 3-0 |
| Nov 26 | Cardiff C | A | L 0-3 |
| Dec 3 | Preston N E | H | W 1-0 |
| Dec 10 | Fulham | A | D 4-4 |
| Dec 17 | Blackburn R | A | W 2-1 |
| Dec 24 | Chelsea | A | W 2-1 |
| Dec 26 | Chelsea | H | W 6-0 |
| Dec 31 | Manchester C | H | W 5-1 |
| Jan 16 | Tottenham H | H | W 2-0 |
| Jan 21 | Leicester C | A | L 0-6 |
| Feb 4 | Aston Villa | H | D 1-1 |
| Feb 11 | Wolverhampton W | A | L 1-2 |
| Feb 18 | Bolton W | H | W 3-1 |
| Feb 25 | Nottingham F | A | L 2-3 |
| Mar 4 | Manchester C | A | W 3-1 |
| Mar 11 | Newcastle U | A | W 3-1 |
| Mar 18 | Arsenal | H | D 1-1 |
| Mar 25 | Sheffield W | A | L 1-5 |
| Mar 31 | Blackpool | A | L 0-2 |
| Apr 16 | Blackburn R | H | W 1-0 |
| Apr 18 | West Ham U | H | W 5-3 |
| Apr 23 | Arsenal | A | L 2-5 |
| Apr 30 | Everton | H | W 5-0 |

1963: Busby brought in the Best – along with the deadly duo Albert Quixall and Denis Law.

David Herd came in to add beef to the front line. He shows why against Blackburn in 1965

Pitches were atrocious in 1962 when this was taken showing referee J. Cattlin giving the all clear to Jimmy Murphy (centre).

# 1961-1962

The arrival of striker David Herd, just before the season kicked off, was the only ray of sunshine. The son of Matt Busby's old Arsenal team-mate Alex scored 14 goals. However, they weren't enough to stop United's slide down the division to 15th. High hopes for FA Cup glory were dashed too when United lost a semi-final clash against Tottenham Hotspur at Hillsborough 3-1. It was time for Busby to think again about the line-up and persuade the board to come up with some more cash for top class talent.

| | | | |
|---|---|---|---|
| Apr 1 | Fulham | H | W 3-1 |
| Apr 3 | Blackpool | H | W 2-0 |
| Apr 8 | WBA | A | D 1-1 |
| Apr 12 | Burnley | H | W 6-0 |
| Apr 15 | Birmingham C | H | W 4-1 |
| Apr 22 | Preston N E | A | W 4-2 |
| Apr 29 | Cardiff C | H | D 3-3 |

**FA Cup**

| | | | |
|---|---|---|---|
| Jan 7 | Middlesbrough (3)H | W | W 3-0 |
| Jan 28 | Sheffield W (4) | A | D 1-1 |
| Feb 1 | Sheffield W (4R) | H | L 2-7 |

**League Cup**

| | | | |
|---|---|---|---|
| Oct 19 | Exeter C (1) | A | D 1-1 |
| Oct 26 | Exeter C (1R) | H | W 4-1 |
| Nov 2 | Bradford C (2) | A | L 1-2 |

Final League position: **7th**

| P | W | D | L | F/A | Pts |
|---|---|---|---|---|---|
| 42 | 18 | 9 | 15 | 88/76 | 45 |

**League (Division 1)**

| | | | |
|---|---|---|---|
| Aug 19 | West Ham U | A | D 1-1 |
| Aug 23 | Chelsea | H | W 3-2 |
| Aug 26 | Blackburn R | H | W 6-1 |
| Aug 30 | Chelsea | A | L 0-2 |
| Sep 2 | Blackpool | A | W 3-2 |
| Sep 9 | Tottenham H | H | W 1-0 |
| Sep 16 | Cardiff C | A | W 2-1 |
| Sep 18 | Aston Villa | A | D 1-1 |
| Sep 23 | Manchester C | H | W 3-2 |
| Sep 30 | Wolverhampton W | H | L 0-2 |
| Oct 7 | WBA | A | D 1-1 |
| Oct 14 | Birmingham C | H | L 0-2 |
| Oct 21 | Arsenal | A | L 1-5 |
| Oct 28 | Bolton W | H | L 0-3 |
| Nov 4 | Sheffield W | A | L 1-3 |
| Nov 11 | Leicester C | H | D 2-2 |
| Nov 18 | Ipswich T | A | L 1-4 |
| Nov 25 | Burnley | H | L 1-4 |
| Dec 2 | Everton | A | L 1-5 |
| Dec 9 | Fulham | H | W 3-0 |
| Dec 16 | West Ham U | H | L 1-2 |
| Dec 26 | Nottingham F | H | W 6-3 |
| Jan 13 | Blackpool | H | L 0-1 |
| Jan 15 | Aston Villa | H | W 2-0 |
| Jan 20 | Tottenham H | A | D 2-2 |
| Feb 3 | Cardiff C | H | W 3-0 |
| Feb 10 | Manchester C | A | W 2-0 |
| Feb 24 | WBA | H | W 4-1 |
| Feb 28 | Wolverhampton W | A | D 2-2 |
| Mar 3 | Birmingham C | A | D 1-1 |
| Mar 17 | Bolton W | A | L 0-1 |

## 1962-1963

A season of FA Cup highs and League lows. Determined to improve United's fortunes, Busby brought The King back from foreign exile in the summer of 1962. Striker Denis Law agreed to leave Italy's Torino and return to Britain for a bumper £115,000 fee. Although it was a record amount at the time, fans quickly came to realise they had been presented with a bargain. All Busby needed was somebody to help improve the supply of good balls to a formidable front line. He found the perfect candidate in Celtic right-half Pat Crerand, who joined in February 1963 for £43,000. Although The Reds finished the season in 19th place, their worst showing since the Busby era began, they won the FA Cup decisively, beating a tough Leicester City side 3-1.

Final League position: **5th**

| P | W | D | L | F/A | Pts |
|---|---|---|---|-----|-----|
| 42 | 15 | 9 | 18 | 72/75 | 39 |

### FA Cup

| Jan 6 | Bolton W (3) | H | W | 2-1 |
|---|---|---|---|---|
| Jan 31 | Arsenal (4) | H | W | 1-0 |
| Feb 17 | Sheffield W (5) | H | D | 0-0 |
| Feb 21 | Sheffield W (5R) | A | W | 2-0 |
| Mar 10 | Preston N E (6) | A | D | 0-0 |
| Mar 14 | Preston N E (6R) | H | W | 2-1 |
| Mar 31 | Tottenham H (SF) N | L | 1-3 | (Hillsborough) |

### League (Division 1)

| Aug 18 | WBA | H | D | 2-2 |
|---|---|---|---|---|
| Aug 22 | Everton | A | L | 1-3 |
| Aug 25 | Arsenal | A | W | 3-1 |
| Aug 29 | Everton | H | L | 0-1 |
| Sep 1 | Birmingham C | H | W | 2-0 |
| Sep 5 | Bolton W | A | L | 0-3 |
| Sep 8 | Leyton Orient | A | L | 0-1 |
| Sep 12 | Bolton W | H | W | 3-0 |
| Sep 15 | Manchester C | H | L | 2-3 |
| Sep 22 | Burnley | H | L | 2-5 |
| Sep 29 | Sheffield W | H | L | 0-1 |
| Oct 6 | Blackpool | A | D | 2-2 |
| Oct 13 | Blackburn R | H | L | 0-3 |
| Oct 24 | Tottenham H | A | L | 2-6 |
| Oct 27 | West Ham U | H | W | 3-1 |
| Nov 3 | Ipswich T | A | W | 5-3 |
| Nov 10 | Liverpool | H | D | 3-3 |
| Nov 17 | Wolverhampton W | A | W | 3-2 |
| Mar 20 | Nottingham F | A | L | 0-1 |
| Mar 24 | Sheffield W | H | D | 1-1 |
| Apr 4 | Leicester C | A | L | 3-4 |
| Apr 7 | Ipswich T | H | W | 5-0 |
| Apr 10 | Blackburn R | A | L | 0-3 |
| Apr 14 | Burnley | A | W | 3-1 |
| Apr 16 | Arsenal | H | L | 2-3 |
| Apr 21 | Everton | H | D | 1-1 |
| Apr 23 | Sheffield U | H | L | 0-1 |
| Apr 24 | Sheffield U | A | W | 3-2 |
| Apr 28 | Fulham | A | L | 0-2 |

Hard man – soft centre. Paddy Crerand gave United tremendous steel at the back. With fiancee Noreen Ferrie in 1963

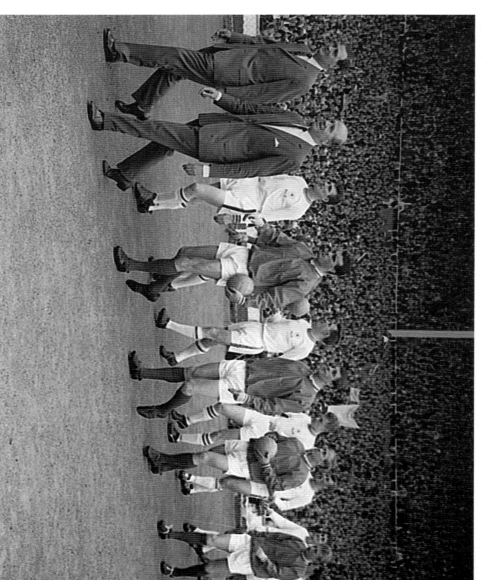

Five years after Munich and a proud Matt Busby leads his team out in the '63 Cup Final against Leicester.

| | | | | |
|---|---|---|---|---|
| Nov 24 | Aston Villa | H | D | 2-2 |
| Dec 1 | Sheffield U | A | D | 1-1 |
| Dec 8 | Nottingham F | H | W | 5-1 |
| Dec 15 | WBA | A | L | 0-3 |
| Dec 26 | Fulham | H | D | 1-1 |
| Feb 23 | Blackpool | H | D | 1-1 |
| Mar 2 | Blackburn R | A | D | 2-2 |
| Mar 9 | Tottenham H | H | L | 0-2 |
| Mar 18 | West Ham U | A | L | 1-3 |
| Mar 23 | Ipswich T | H | L | 0-1 |
| Apr 1 | Fulham | H | L | 0-2 |
| Apr 9 | Aston Villa | A | W | 2-1 |
| Apr 13 | Liverpool | A | L | 0-1 |
| Apr 15 | Leicester C | H | D | 2-2 |
| Apr 16 | Leicester C | A | L | 3-4 |
| Apr 20 | Sheffield U | H | D | 1-1 |
| Apr 22 | Wolverhampton WH | | W | 2-1 |
| May 1 | Sheffield W | H | L | 1-3 |
| May 4 | Burnley | A | W | 1-0 |
| May 6 | Arsenal | H | L | 2-3 |
| May 10 | Birmingham C | A | L | 1-2 |
| May 15 | Manchester C | A | D | 1-1 |
| May 18 | Leyton Orient | H | W | 3-1 |
| May 20 | Nottingham F | A | L | 2-3 |

Final League position: **19th**

| P | W | D | L | F/A | Pts |
|---|---|---|---|---|---|
| 42 | 12 | 12 | 20 | 67/81 | 34 |

**FA Cup**

| | | | | |
|---|---|---|---|---|
| Mar 4 | Huddersfield T (3) | H | W | 5-0 |
| Mar 11 | Aston Villa (40) | H | W | 1-0 |
| Mar 16 | Chelsea (5) | H | W | 2-1 |
| Mar 30 | Coventry C (6) | A | W | 3-1 |
| Apr 27 | Southampton | N | W | 1-0 |
| | (at Villa Park) | | | |
| May 25 | Leicester C (F) | N | W | 3-1 |
| | (at Wembley) | | | |

## 1963-1964

The desolation of Munich was now replaced by high hopes. Busby's plans for a new team seemed to be coming to fruition. Law amazed fans by netting 46 goals, and Best made his debut against West Brom. The dark-haired Irishman, who played as though he had glue on the toes of his boots, scored his first goal for United during a 5-1 demolition of Burnley on December 28. Apart from a European Cup Winner's Cup upset, when they beat Sporting Lisbon 4-1 then lost 0-5 to the same team, United did well. They came second in the League and reached the semi-finals of the FA Cup.

**League (Division 1)**

| | | | | |
|---|---|---|---|---|
| Aug 24 | Sheffield W | A | D | 3-3 |
| Aug 28 | Ipswich T | H | W | 2-0 |
| Aug 31 | Everton | H | W | 5-1 |
| Sep 3 | Ipswich T | A | W | 7-2 |
| Sep 7 | Birmingham C | A | D | 1-1 |
| Sep 11 | Blackpool | H | W | 3-0 |
| Sep 14 | WBA | H | W | 1-0 |
| Sep 16 | Blackpool | A | L | 0-1 |
| Sep 21 | Arsenal | A | L | 1-2 |
| Sep 28 | Leicester C | H | W | 3-1 |
| Oct 2 | Chelsea | A | D | 1-1 |

The "work ethic" was Busby's philosophy. Players were expected to fight for every ball.

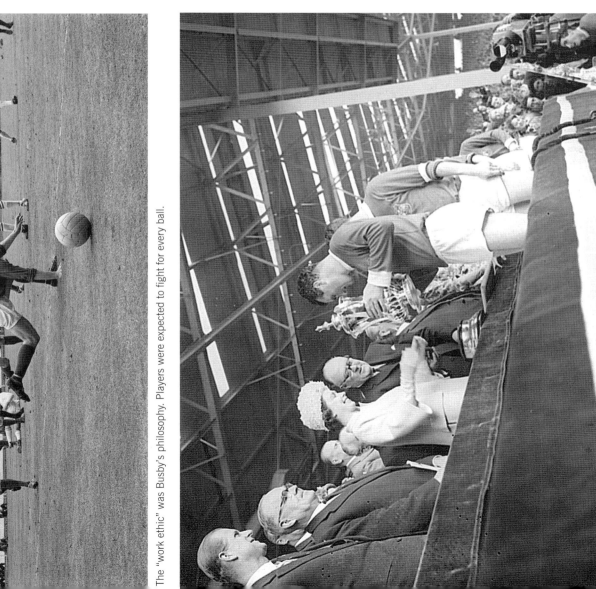

...y Royal Command. Noel Cantwell accepts the FA Cup from The Queen in 1963 and United are back on track.

# 1964-1965

Although United were doing well, Busby wasn't content. He continued to improve the team by signing Burnley's ace winger John Connelly in the summer of 1964. He cost the club £60,000 and proved to be worth his weight in gold. When United were crowned League champions for the first time since Munich, he was third highest goal scorer with 15, ahead of Charlton and Best, who each netted 10. During one blistering mid-season spell, from September 8 to December 5, the team didn't lose once in 15 games. The highlight of the

| | | | |
|---|---|---|---|
| Oct 5 | Bolton W | A | W 1-0 |
| Oct 19 | Nottingham F | A | W 2-1 |
| Oct 26 | West Ham U | H | L 0-1 |
| Oct 28 | Blackburn R | H | D 2-2 |
| Nov 2 | Wolverhampton W | A | L 0-2 |
| Nov 9 | Tottenham H | H | W 4-1 |
| Nov 16 | Aston Villa | A | L 0-4 |
| Nov 23 | Liverpool | H | L 0-1 |
| Nov 30 | Sheffield U | H | W 2-1 |
| Dec 7 | Stoke C | H | W 5-2 |
| Dec 14 | Sheffield W | H | W 3-1 |
| Dec 21 | Everton | A | L 0-4 |
| Dec 26 | Burnley | A | L 1-6 |
| Dec 28 | Burnley | H | W 5-1 |
| Jan 11 | Birmingham C | H | L 1-2 |
| Jan 18 | WBA | A | W 4-1 |
| Feb 1 | Arsenal | H | W 3-1 |
| Feb 8 | Leicester C | A | L 2-3 |
| Feb 19 | Bolton W | H | W 5-0 |
| Feb 22 | Blackburn R | A | W 3-1 |
| Mar 7 | West Ham U | A | W 2-0 |
| Mar 21 | Tottenham H | A | W 3-2 |
| Mar 23 | Chelsea | H | D 1-1 |
| Mar 27 | Fulham | A | D 2-2 |
| Mar 28 | Wolverhampton W | H | D 2-2 |
| Mar 30 | Fulham | H | W 3-0 |
| Apr 4 | Liverpool | A | L 0-3 |
| Apr 6 | Aston Villa | H | W 1-0 |
| Apr 13 | Sheffield U | A | W 2-1 |
| Apr 18 | Stoke C | A | L 1-3 |
| Apr 25 | Nottingham F | H | W 3-1 |

**Final League position: 2nd**

| P | W | D | L | F/A | Pts |
|---|---|---|---|---|---|
| 42 | 23 | 7 | 12 | 90/62 | 53 |

## FA Cup

| | | | |
|---|---|---|---|
| Jan 4 | Southampton (3) | A | W 3-2 |
| Jan 25 | Bristol R (4) | H | W 4-1 |
| Feb 15 | Barnsley (5) | A | W 4-0 |
| Feb 29 | Sunderland (6) | H | D 3-3 |
| Mar 4 | Sunderland (6R) | A | D 2-2 |
| Mar 9 | Sunderland (62R) | N | W 5-1 |
| | (at Leeds Road) | | |
| Mar 14 | West Ham U (SF) | N | L 1-3 |
| | (at Hillsborough) | | |

## European Cup Winners' Cup

| | | | |
|---|---|---|---|
| Sep 25 | Willem II (1) | A | D 1-1 |
| Oct 15 | Willem II (1R) | H | W 6-1 |
| Dec 3 | Tottenham H (2) | A | L 0-2 |
| Dec 10 | Tottenham H (2) | H | W 4-1 |
| Feb 26 | Sporting Lisbon (3) | H | W 4-1 |
| Mar 18 | Sporting Lisbon (3) | A | L 0-5 |

Top that! United skipper Cantwell on his way back from the '63 Final with the Cup and Bill Foulkes' four-year-old son Stephen.

amazing run of 13 wins and two draws was a 7-0 blitz of Aston Villa in front of a delirious Old Trafford crowd. United also reached the semi-finals of the FA and European Fairs Cups.

## League (Division 1)

| Aug 22 | WBA | H | D | 2-2 |
|---|---|---|---|---|
| Aug 24 | West Ham U | A | L | 1-3 |
| Aug 29 | Leicester C | A | D | 2-2 |
| Sep 2 | West Ham U | H | W | 3-1 |
| Sep 5 | Fulham | A | L | 1-2 |
| Sep 8 | Everton | A | D | 3-3 |
| Sep 12 | Nottingham F | H | W | 3-0 |
| Sep 16 | Everton | H | W | 2-1 |
| Sep 19 | Stoke C | A | W | 2-1 |
| Sep 26 | Tottenham H | H | W | 4-1 |
| Sep 30 | Chelsea | A | W | 2-0 |
| Oct 6 | Burnley | A | D | 0-0 |
| Oct 10 | Sunderland | H | W | 1-0 |
| Oct 17 | Wolverhampton W | A | W | 4-2 |
| Oct 24 | Aston Villa | H | W | 7-0 |
| Oct 31 | Liverpool | A | W | 2-0 |
| Nov 7 | Sheffield W | H | W | 1-0 |
| Nov 14 | Blackpool | A | W | 2-1 |
| Nov 21 | Blackburn R | H | W | 3-0 |
| Nov 28 | Arsenal | A | W | 3-2 |
| Dec 5 | Leeds U | H | L | 0-1 |
| Dec 12 | WBA | A | D | 1-1 |
| Dec 16 | Birmingham C | H | D | 1-1 |
| Dec 26 | Sheffield U | A | W | 1-0 |
| Dec 28 | Sheffield U | H | D | 1-1 |
| Jan 16 | Nottingham F | A | D | 2-2 |
| Jan 23 | Stoke C | H | D | 1-1 |
| Feb 6 | Tottenham H | A | L | 0-1 |
| Feb 13 | Burnley | H | W | 3-2 |
| Feb 24 | Sunderland | A | L | 0-1 |
| Feb 27 | Wolverhampton W | H | W | 3-0 |
| Mar 13 | Chelsea | H | W | 4-0 |
| Mar 15 | Fulham | H | W | 4-1 |
| Mar 20 | Sheffield W | A | L | 0-1 |
| Mar 22 | Blackpool | H | W | 2-0 |
| Apr 3 | Blackburn R | A | W | 5-0 |
| Apr 12 | Leicester C | H | W | 1-0 |
| Apr 17 | Leeds U | A | W | 1-0 |
| Apr 19 | Birmingham C | A | W | 4-2 |
| Apr 24 | Liverpool | H | W | 3-0 |
| Apr 26 | Arsenal | H | W | 3-1 |
| Apr 28 | Aston Villa | A | L | 1-2 |

**Final League position: 1st**

| P | W | D | L | F/A | Pts |
|---|---|---|---|---|---|
| 42 | 26 | 9 | 7 | 89/39 | 61 |

## FA Cup

| Jan 9 | Chester (3) | H | W | 2-1 |
|---|---|---|---|---|
| Jan 30 | Stoke C (4) | A | D | 0-0 |
| Feb 3 | Stoke C (4R) | H | W | 1-0 |
| Feb 20 | Burnley (5) | H | W | 2-1 |
| Mar 10 | Wolves (6) | A | W | 5-3 |
| Mar 27 | Leeds U (SF) | N | D | 0-0 |
| | (at Hillsborough) | | | |
| Mar 31 | Leeds U (SFR) | A | L | 0-1 |
| | (at City Ground) | | | |

## Inter-Cities Fairs Cup

| Sep 23 | Djurgaarden (1) | A | D | 1-1 |
|---|---|---|---|---|
| Oct 27 | Djurgaarden (1) | H | W | 6-1 |
| Nov 11 | B Dortmund (2) | A | W | 6-1 |
| Dec 2 | B Dortmund (2) | H | W | 4-1 |
| Jan 20 | Everton (3) | H | D | 1-1 |
| Feb 9 | Everton (3) | A | W | 2-1 |
| Mar 12 | R Strasbourg (4) | A | W | 5-0 |
| May 19 | R Strasbourg (4) | H | D | 0-0 |
| May 31 | Ferencvaros (5) | H | W | 3-2 |
| Jun 6 | Ferencvaros (5) | A | L | 0-1 |
| Jun 16 | Ferencvaros (5R) | A | L | 1-2 |

Bobby Charlton, exhausted as ever, after the Cup Final victory over Leicester in 1963.

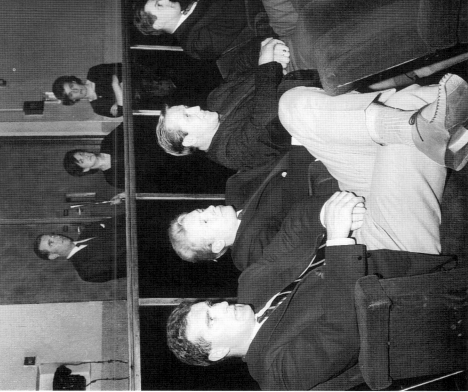

Hey, we were pretty good! Cantwell, Law and Setters watch a special film of the '63 Final.

for the youngster.

# 1965-1966

Although United finished the season in fourth place, ten points behind the winners Liverpool, they played well. The team made it through to the semi-finals of the FA Cup for the fifth season in a row. During one classic match against Wolves they came back from two-nil down, after just nine minutes, to win 4-2. They also reached the semi-finals of the European Cup. Despite the lack of silverware, fans had plenty to cheer about when two club stalwarts, Bobby Charlton and Nobby Stiles, helped England carry off the World Cup in 1966.

## League (Division 1)

| | | | |
|---|---|---|---|
| Aug 21 | Sheffield W | H | W 1-0 |
| Aug 24 | Nottingham F | A | L 2-4 |
| Aug 28 | Northampton T | A | D 1-1 |
| Sep 1 | Nottingham F | H | D 0-0 |
| Sep 4 | Stoke C | A | W 2-1 |
| Sep 8 | Newcastle U | A | W 2-1 |
| Sep 11 | Burnley | A | L 0-3 |
| Sep 15 | Newcastle U | H | D 1-1 |
| Sep 18 | Chelsea | H | W 4-1 |
| Sep 25 | Arsenal | A | L 2-4 |
| Oct 9 | Liverpool | H | W 2-0 |
| Oct 16 | Tottenham H | A | L 1-5 |
| Oct 23 | Fulham | H | W 4-1 |
| Oct 30 | Blackpool | A | W 2-1 |
| Nov 6 | Blackburn R | H | D 2-2 |
| Nov 13 | Leicester C | A | W 5-0 |
| Nov 20 | Sheffield U | H | W 3-1 |
| Dec 4 | West Ham U | H | D 0-0 |
| Dec 11 | Sunderland | A | W 3-2 |
| Dec 15 | Everton | H | W 3-0 |
| Dec 18 | Tottenham H | H | W 5-1 |
| Dec 27 | WBA | H | D 1-1 |
| Jan 1 | Liverpool | A | L 1-2 |
| Jan 8 | Sunderland | H | D 1-1 |
| Jan 12 | Leeds U | A | D 1-1 |
| Jan 15 | Fulham | A | W 1-0 |
| Jan 29 | Sheffield W | A | D 0-0 |
| Feb 5 | Northampton T | H | W 6-2 |
| Feb 18 | Stoke C | A | D 2-2 |
| Feb 26 | Burnley | H | W 4-2 |
| Mar 12 | Chelsea | A | L 0-2 |
| Mar 19 | Arsenal | H | W 2-1 |
| Apr 6 | Aston Villa | A | D 1-1 |
| Apr 9 | Leicester C | H | L 1-2 |
| Apr 16 | Sheffield U | A | L 1-3 |
| Apr 25 | Everton | A | D 0-0 |
| Apr 27 | Blackpool | H | W 2-1 |
| Apr 30 | West Ham U | A | L 2-3 |
| May 4 | WBA | A | D 3-3 |
| May 7 | Blackburn R | A | W 4-1 |
| May 9 | Aston Villa | H | W 6-1 |
| May 19 | Leeds U | H | D 1-1 |

**Final League position: 4th**

| P | W | D | L | F/A | Pts |
|---|---|---|---|---|---|
| 42 | 18 | 15 | 9 | 84/59 | 51 |

## FA Cup

| | | | |
|---|---|---|---|
| Jan 22 | Derby C (3) | A | W 5-2 |
| Feb 12 | Rotherham U (4) | H | D 0-0 |
| Feb 15 | Rotherham U (4R)A | W 1-0 |

United didn't have it all their own way. Leeds' boss Don Revie walks away with a real prize in Johnny Giles in 1963.

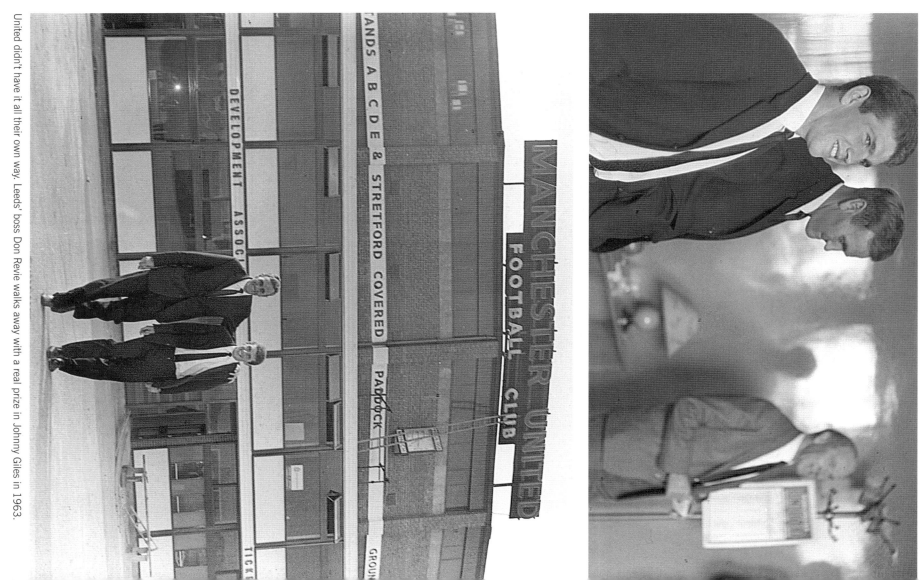

# 1966-1967

After a patchy start, Busby shook up the side again. He brought in his rising young stars Bobby Noble and Johnny Aston. Matt also invested £50,000 in Chelsea's goalkeeper Alex Stepney. Noble played left-back and Aston came into the first team as outside left. Having been knocked out of the FA and League Cups early, the side had few distractions. They weren't playing in Europe either and were able to concentrate on the title race. United went unbeaten in their last 20 games and made sure of the top spot by thrashing West Ham 6-1 away in London.

## League (Division 1)

| Date | Opponent | | | Score |
|---|---|---|---|---|
| Aug 20 | WBA | H | W | 5-3 |
| Aug 23 | Everton | A | W | 2-1 |
| Aug 27 | Leeds U | A | L | 1-3 |
| Aug 31 | Everton | H | W | 3-0 |
| Sep 3 | Newcastle U | H | W | 3-2 |
| Sep 7 | Stoke C | A | L | 0-3 |
| Sep 10 | Tottenham H | A | L | 1-2 |
| Sep 17 | Manchester C | H | W | 1-0 |
| Sep 24 | Burnley | H | W | 4-1 |
| Oct 1 | Nottingham F | A | W | 2-1 |
| Oct 8 | Blackpool | H | D | 1-1 |
| Oct 15 | Chelsea | H | D | 1-1 |
| Oct 29 | Arsenal | H | W | 1-0 |
| Nov 5 | Chelsea | A | W | 3-1 |
| Nov 12 | Sheffield W | H | W | 2-0 |
| Nov 19 | Southampton | A | W | 2-1 |
| Nov 26 | Sunderland | A | W | 5-0 |
| Nov 30 | Leicester C | A | W | 2-1 |
| Dec 3 | Aston Villa | A | L | 1-2 |
| Dec 10 | Liverpool | H | D | 2-2 |
| Dec 17 | WBA | A | W | 4-3 |
| Dec 26 | Sheffield U | A | L | 1-2 |
| Dec 27 | Sheffield U | H | W | 2-0 |
| Dec 31 | Leeds U | H | D | 0-0 |
| Jan 14 | Tottenham H | H | W | 1-0 |
| Jan 21 | Manchester C | A | D | 1-1 |
| Feb 4 | Burnley | A | D | 1-1 |
| Feb 11 | Nottingham F | H | W | 1-0 |
| Feb 25 | Blackpool | H | W | 4-0 |
| Mar 3 | Arsenal | A | D | 1-1 |
| Mar 11 | Newcastle U | A | D | 0-0 |
| Mar 18 | Leicester C | H | W | 5-2 |
| Mar 25 | Liverpool | A | D | 0-0 |
| Mar 5 | Wolves (5) | A | W | 4-2 |
| Mar 26 | Preston N E (6) | A | D | 1-1 |
| Mar 30 | Preston N E (6R) | H | W | 3-1 |
| Apr 23 | Everton (SF) | N | L | 0-1 |
|  | (at Burnden Park) | | | |

## European Cup

| Date | Opponent | | | Score |
|---|---|---|---|---|
| Sep 22 | HJK Helsinki (P) | A | W | 3-2 |
| Oct 6 | HJK Helsinki (P) | H | W | 6-0 |
| Nov 17 | ASK Vorwaerts (1) | A | W | 2-0 |
| Dec 1 | ASK Vorwaerts (1) | H | W | 3-1 |
| Feb 2 | Benfica (2) | H | W | 3-2 |
| Mar 9 | Benfica (2) | A | W | 5-1 |
| Apr 13 | Partizan Belgrade (SF) | A | L | 0-2 |
| Apr 20 | Partizan Belgrade (SF) | H | W | 1-0 |

Strength at the back was the key to United's success in the '60s. 'Keeper David Gaskell and Bill Foulkes keep Burnley out in 1963

## 1967-1968

Matt Busby finally achieved his ambition when United beat the Portuguese giants Benfica 4-1 to become the first English team to lift the European Cup. The triumph overshadowed Manchester City's celebrations. After many years in the football wilderness they had snatched the League title, beating United into second place. Young newcomer Brian Kidd, aged just 19, proved his talent by scoring a wonderful goal in a Wembley match that was supercharged throughout. Charlton netted two goals and Best, at his peak, danced round the Portuguese goalkeeper. Sadly, Denis Law missed the magical match because of a knee injury and had to watch it on TV in hospital.

### Final League position: 1st

| P | W | D | L | F/A | Pts |
|---|---|---|---|-----|-----|
| 42 | 24 | 12 | 6 | 84/45 | 60 |

### FA Cup

| | | | |
|---|---|---|---|
| Jan 28 | Stoke C (3) | H W | 2-0 |
| Feb 18 | Norwich C (3) | H L | 1-2 |

### League Cup

| | | | |
|---|---|---|---|
| Sep 14 | Blackpool (2) | A L | 1-5 |

### League (Division 1)

| | | | |
|---|---|---|---|
| Aug 19 | Everton | A L | 1-3 |
| Aug 23 | Leeds U | H W | 1-0 |
| Aug 26 | Leicester C | H D | 1-1 |
| Sep 2 | West Ham U | A W | 3-1 |
| Sep 6 | Sunderland | A D | 1-1 |
| Sep 9 | Burnley | H D | 2-2 |
| Sep 16 | Sheffield W | H D | 2-2 |
| Sep 23 | Tottenham H | H W | 3-1 |
| Sep 30 | Manchester C | A W | 2-1 |
| Oct 7 | Arsenal | H W | 1-0 |
| Oct 14 | Sheffield U | A W | 3-0 |
| Oct 25 | Coventry C | H W | 4-0 |
| Oct 28 | Nottingham F | A L | 1-3 |
| Nov 4 | Stoke C | H W | 1-0 |
| Nov 8 | Leeds U | A L | 0-1 |
| Nov 11 | Liverpool | A W | 2-1 |
| Nov 18 | Southampton | H W | 3-2 |
| Nov 25 | Chelsea | A D | 1-1 |
| Dec 2 | WBA | H W | 2-1 |
| Dec 9 | Newcastle U | A D | 2-2 |
| Mar 27 | Fulham | A D | 2-2 |
| Mar 28 | Fulham | H W | 2-1 |
| Apr 1 | West Ham U | H W | 3-0 |
| Apr 10 | Sheffield W | A D | 2-2 |
| Apr 18 | Southampton | H W | 3-0 |
| Apr 22 | Sunderland | A D | 0-0 |
| Apr 29 | Aston Villa | H W | 3-1 |
| May 6 | West Ham U | A W | 6-1 |
| May 13 | Stoke C | H D | 0-0 |

He's the leader; he's the leader! Charlton brings out the team to face Leicester at Old Trafford for the last game of the '69 season. T

| | | | | |
|---|---|---|---|---|
| Dec 16 | Everton | H | W | 3-1 |
| Dec 23 | Leicester C | A | D | 2-2 |
| Dec 26 | Wolverhampton W | H | W | 4-0 |
| Dec 30 | Wolverhampton W | A | W | 3-2 |
| Jan 6 | West Ham U | H | W | 3-1 |
| Jan 20 | Sheffield W | H | W | 4-2 |
| Feb 3 | Tottenham H | A | W | 2-1 |
| Feb 17 | Burnley | A | L | 1-2 |
| Feb 24 | Arsenal | A | W | 2-0 |
| Mar 2 | Chelsea | H | L | 1-3 |
| Mar 16 | Coventry C | A | L | 0-2 |
| Mar 23 | Nottingham F | H | W | 3-0 |
| Mar 27 | Manchester C | H | L | 1-3 |
| Mar 30 | Stoke C | A | W | 4-2 |
| Apr 6 | Liverpool | H | L | 1-2 |
| Apr 12 | Fulham | A | W | 4-0 |
| Apr 13 | Southampton | A | D | 2-2 |
| Apr 15 | Fulham | H | W | 3-0 |
| Apr 20 | Sheffield U | H | W | 1-0 |
| Apr 29 | WBA | A | L | 3-6 |
| May 4 | Newcastle U | H | W | 6-0 |
| May 11 | Sunderland | H | L | 1-2 |

**Final League position: 0th**

| P | W | D | L | F/A | Pts |
|---|---|---|---|---|---|
| 42 | 24 | 8 | 10 | 89/55 | 56 |

**FA Cup**

| | | | | |
|---|---|---|---|---|
| Jan 27 | Tottenham H (3) | H | D | 2-2 |
| Jan 31 | Tottenham H (3R) | A | L | 0-1 |

**European Cup**

| | | | | |
|---|---|---|---|---|
| Sep 20 | Hibernian Malta (1) | H | W | 4-0 |
| Sep 27 | Hibernian Malta (1) | A | D | 0-0 |
| Nov 15 | Sarajevo (2) | A | D | 0-0 |
| Nov 29 | Sarajevo (2) | H | W | 2-1 |
| Feb 28 | Gornik Zabrze (3) | H | W | 2-0 |
| Mar 13 | Gornik Zabrze (3) | A | L | 0-1 |
| Apr 24 | Real Madrid (SF) | H | W | 1-0 |
| May 15 | Real Madrid (SF) | A | D | 3-3 |
| May 29 | Benfica (F) | N | W | 4-1 |
| | (at Wembley) | | | |

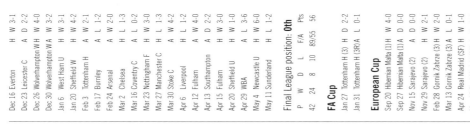

Paddy Crerand and Maurice Setters run out to face Leicester in 1969.

Reserve Dogs! A stray hound gave United more problems than Leyton Orient in 1963.

...ypical scrap with the midlanders 3-2.

Touché. Matt Busby receives a special Sword For Service to United in October, 1964. But he knew his best weapons were on the pitch.

Gregg, Stiles, Foulkes, Herd and Connelly meet royalty while Busby looks to divine support in 1964.

Busby was no ivory-tower man, he loved the odd ha

hampions! Busby and Murphy with United staff celebrate the League title after beating Arsenal 3-1 in 1965. Future manager McGuinness could smile then.

Dynamic duo. Noel Cantwell and Tony Dunne were the Jaap Stam and Dennis Irwin of United's sixties team. Here, they foil a Fulham raid in 1965.

In 1963, United were chasing Liverpool for the title, eventually finishing 2nd – but not before this Charlton blinder against Sheffield Wednesday in January.

es, even Harry Gregg was sent off. Here he watches from the touchline as United battle back against Blackburn in 1965.

A PHOTOGRAPHIC HISTORY OF MANCHESTER UNITED **79**

Herd and Charlton get tough in defence.

Hit men Herd and Law haunt the goal against Leeds in the '65 Cup semi.

Games against Leeds are always a tough battle and Law reels away with a rip

uck with Big Jack Charlton in 1965. The pitch looks like The Somme – and the games were just as confrontational.

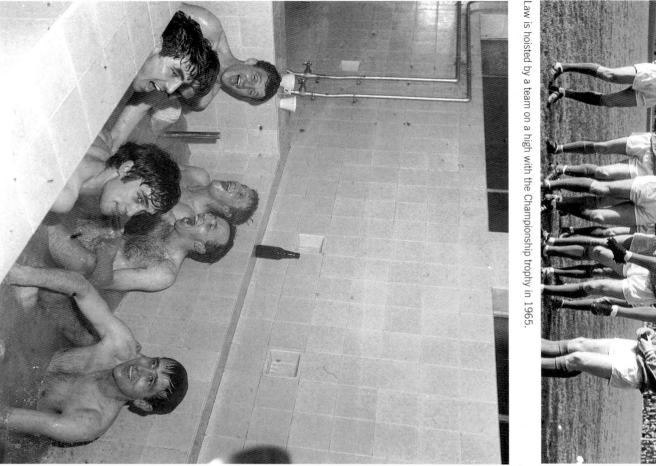

United had beaten Blackpool 2-1 at home in 1965 and the bath was the only place to celebrate.

Law is hoisted by a team on a high with the Championship trophy in 1965.

Together, Anderson, Stiles, Setters and Crerand in a moment which captures the team spirit of United.

Denis Law scored a sensational overhead goal against Chelsea in 1965.

Touting for ticket business. They existed back in 1965 outside Old Trafford.

Bill Foulkes fends off
Liverpool's Ian St John
in a typical battle with
Merseyside in 1965.

Maestro David Herd takes on the Burnley defence at Old Trafford in 1966 – and wins. United finished 4-2 victors.

Bill Foulkes clears for United in the match against Burnley in 1966.

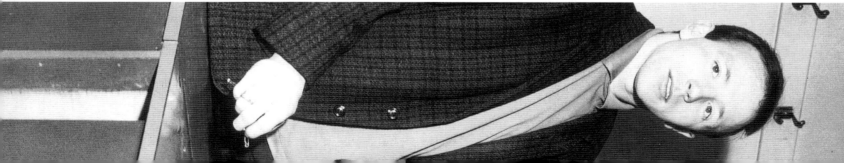

Charlton and the team listen to the FA Cup draw in March, 1966. It came out Manchester City or Everton.

One of the great United 'keepers, Alex Stepney, surveys Old Trafford on arriving in 1966.

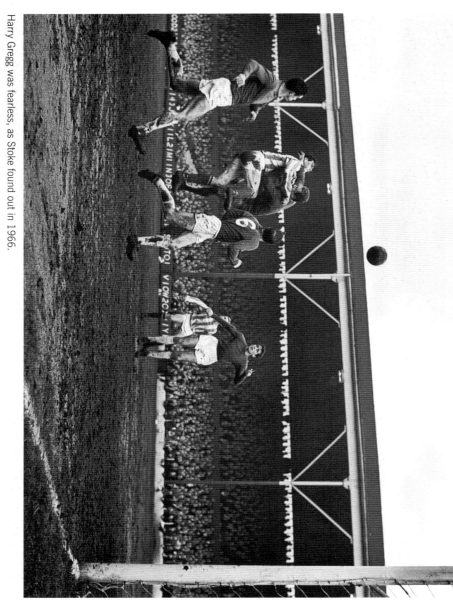

Harry Gregg was fearless, as Stoke found out in 1966.

City's Mike Summerbee was a class player, but United's defence was solid in 1966.

Pomp and ceremony. Busby collects his well-deserved award.

He never lost the passion for United or the game. Matt in 1967.

The players toast Busby after he is awarded Freeman Of The City in 1967.

We'll drink to that! The United squad celebrate a 6-1 demolition of West Ham in May 1967. They were flying high now, and European glory was not far awa

Sky high... Best, Crerand and Kidd duel with John Radford and Frank McLintock of Arsenal in 1967

What's your problem? Best and United were at their peak in 1967 and George faced a real trial every week with defenders. But he always he gave as good as he got.

Bill Foulkes marshalls the United defence to cope with Chelsea's Osgood.

Pick that one out! Law nets against West Ham in a 1-1 draw in 1968.

Police keep and eye on United's army of supporters in 1967.

A young Brian Kidd gets the better of Liverpool's Tommy Smith in 1970 – no mean feat because Smith was *the* hard man of football in those days.

Kiddo goes down in the box against West Ham in 1968. He was a powerful front man for United.

Kidd being led away after being sent off in a 1968 game against Spurs.

Pot shot! Kidd relaxes with a game of snooker in 1969.

Celebration time. Kidd turns 19 – and United are European kings in 1968!

Gold hunt. Kidd lost a medallion at Wembley in 1968 and phones the groun

Spurs player Joe Kinnear at the Brian Kidd FA disciplinary hearing in 1968.

United full back John Fitzpatrick with Busby at an FA hearing in 1969.

A PHOTOGRAPHIC HISTORY OF MANCHESTER UNITED 107

Aston followed in his father's footsteps at Old Trafford, but he never won over the crowds like John Snr had.

Aston was a goalscorer despite the fans' disapproval of him. He celebrates netting one against Newcastle in 1968.

Cantwell passes on tips to his son Robert at home in 1966.

Lover boy. United's David Sadler with fiancee Christine Halliday after the European Cup win in 1968. A quiet but deadly front man.

The Aston family talk through Johnny's two goals at Chelsea in 1966.

...own the ages. John Aston
...nr with his son after the
...oungster helped United
...estroy Benfica at Wembley.

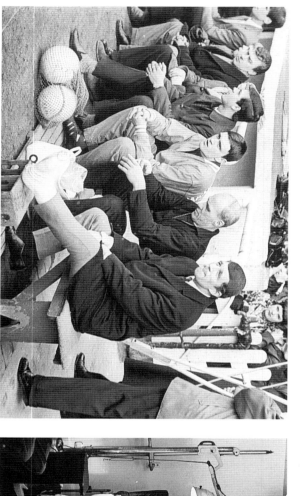

Herd sits it out with the United bench after breaking his leg.

Kidd treatment. United physio Ted Dalton treats the star.

A critical moment for United as hot-shot David Herd breaks his leg against Leicester in 1967. It effectively ended his career with The Reds.

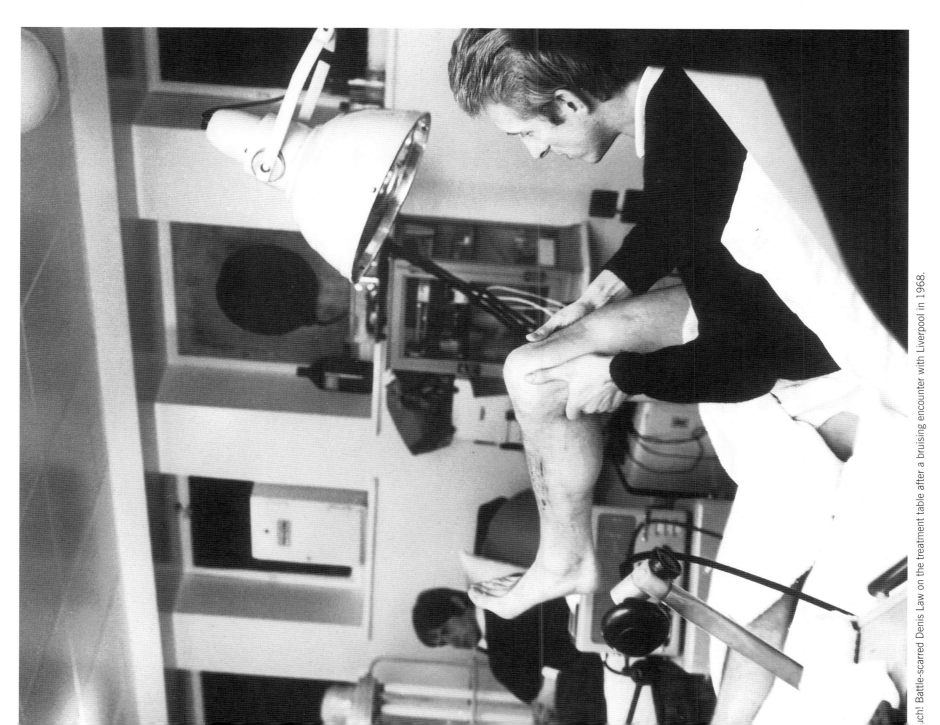

uch! Battle-scarred Denis Law on the treatment table after a bruising encounter with Liverpool in 1968.

From hit man to bat man. Best walks out to play in a cricket match between United as European champs and City the League title holders in 1968.

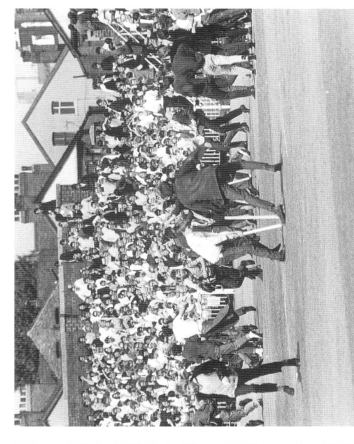

...bby Stiles in spec-ulative boundary mood...

It was supposed to be a "friendly", but fans battled each other for trophies.

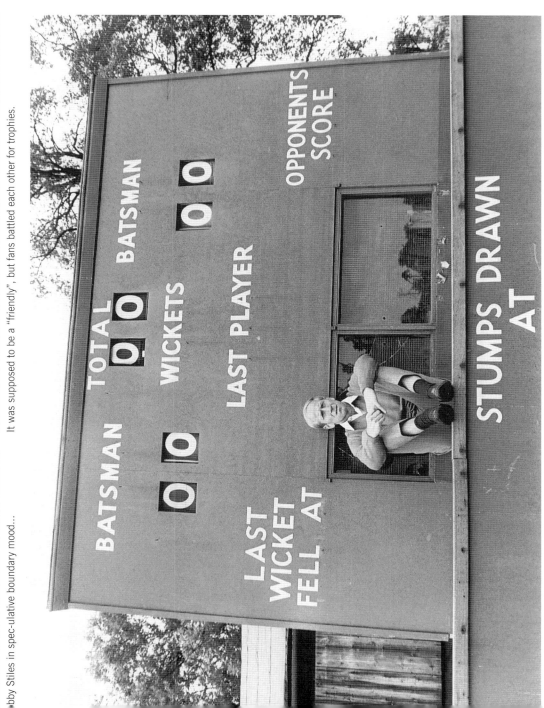

...bby loved cricket and relaxes at a match before England's World Cup Final game in 1966.

Strip show... models show off the new Manchester United all-blue strip in 1968 and right, United started to move heavily into merchandising the club colours

Alan Gowling (8) scores a fine debut goal for United against Stoke in 1968. He once scored four against Southampton in 1971.

Leicester 'keeper Peter Shilton shakes hands with Rimmer after United condemned the midlanders to relegation in 1968.

The sweet smile of success. Busby had steered United from the tragedy of Munich to the glory of The European Cup trophy.

# Europe Conquered

The night of May 29, 1968 was a mild one, full of the promise of summer when the streets and parks of Manchester would normally be full of youngsters acting out their hopes and dreams as budding footballers. The Beatles and The Rolling Stones were in full flow, but nobody would be indoors listening to records. On nights like these in the half of the City that was Red, kids could be heard saying: "I'm Best, you be Charlton". "OK, I'll be Law", would say another; and the immense grip the club Manchester United had on young hearts would tighten once more. But this night was different. The streets were deserted. Not a soul ventured out, the shops were empty, some even closed. This was a night when history could be made and even policemen gave up pounding the beat in the belief that anyone committing a crime was welcome to it – so long as United won. The Busby Babes had just 90 minutes to clasp what was known as the Holy Grail, the European Cup, to the bosom of a club, and a city, which had known such grief through Munich. We had waited a long, long time for this moment and finally it had arrived. It was our time.

But could United overcome the power, the technique and the panache of Portuguese giants Benfica, a name feared in Englis football then as much as Juventus today? They boasted a play of supreme grace and quality in Eusebio, a man who could destr teams and dreams in a matter of seconds when given the chanc United fans respected him – and feared what he might do to gai revenge for his team's 5-1 destruction by The Reds in the 19 quarter final of the same competition. But then United were at th peak of their power in English football. We had nothing to fe with the likes of Charlton, Best, Kidd, Foulkes, Stiles, Creran Stepney and David Herd. Denis Law was injured and would mi the biggest game in United's history. That was a worry. The poach par excellence would not be around to grab that last-minute winn should we be up against it as he had done so often in the past.

As the game got under way it was clear what Benfica's tacti were – close down the marauding Best, who had so dazzled the two years earlier, and you take the sting out of the Engli Champions. They clattered him, the Irishman needing every oun of this instinctive balance to stay on his feet and take United forwar But in concentrating on Best they left Charlton a free agent an rising to a cross from defender Tony Dunne he headed in the to

...e moment we'd all waited for. Best in a Benfica shirt and Johnny Aston with the European Cup in 1968. The duo ran the Benfica defence ragged.

...ner: United 1, Benfica 0. Manchester went crazy, screams that ...se days would have the emergency services rushing into houses ...e heard from living rooms crowded with ecstatic but nervously ...hausted fans. United took the initiative with Aston and Best ...king in movements which had the Benfica defence on the back ...ot like tango dancers.

Then, disaster. The experienced Benfica rallied, knowing that ...re last hope was to attack. With ten minutes to go and United ...king ragged through sheer physical effort, Benfica swept forward. ...was all over in a flash. Torres headed a crossed ball down to the ...t of Graca and it was in the back of the net. How many times ...r the years have United fans endured such agony? How many ...es has the team given such hope and then leaked a simple goal ...put themselves and the fans through it all again.

It was extra time, and as the exhausted United players squatted ...the pitch, drenched in sweat, thousands of United fans sat on ...ors in front of televisions feeling exactly the same way. As the ...ne resumed, Benfica sensed they had knocked the heart out of ...ited, sweeping forward for the killer punch. Their chance came ...m Eusebio who, skipping past Stiles was clear on goal with only

Stepney to beat. He blasted the shot from point blank range – and that was his big mistake. Stepney became the everlasting hero of devoted United fans that night as the ball thumped into his chest and he held on for dear life. Eusebio – and the millions watching – couldn't believe it, and the striker had the grace to pat the keeper on the back as a token of total respect. It was the turning point of the game, a classic moment never to be forgotten. United now rallied, knowing the opposition's big chance had gone. Best received a ball headed forward by Kidd and took it all the way, rounding the goalkeeper and slotting into the net. Kidd was then on the end of a Charlton corner and took the rebound off the bar to place it firmly in goal. Then The Master, Charlton, added the final flourish, connecting with Kidd's cross to flick the ball home with a glorious flourish. It was all over. Manchester street's erupted with celebration – and relief – and immediately youngsters took to the streets to play out the game for themselves. United were back. Champions of Europe.

As the decade was drawing to a close, United had proved the dominance of English football. A dream nurtured for 50 years had been realised. Matt Busby and his Babes had promised ecstasy after the agony of Munich – and delivered.

United's John Connelly attacks Partizan Belgrade's goal in the 1966 battle.

Denis Law and David Herd launch another assault on the Partizan goal.

"A gift from God" they cried as Stiles scored this goal against Partizan.

Benfica's master Eusebio leaves Stiles and keeper Harry Gregg lost as he scores in United's 3-2 win at Old Trafford in 1966.

Malta's Hibernians arrive in Manchester for their European clash with United.

It's there. The Gornik keeper is distraught as United hit the net in 1968.

Charlton (left) can't contain himself after Kidd's late goal against Gornik Zabrze in '68.

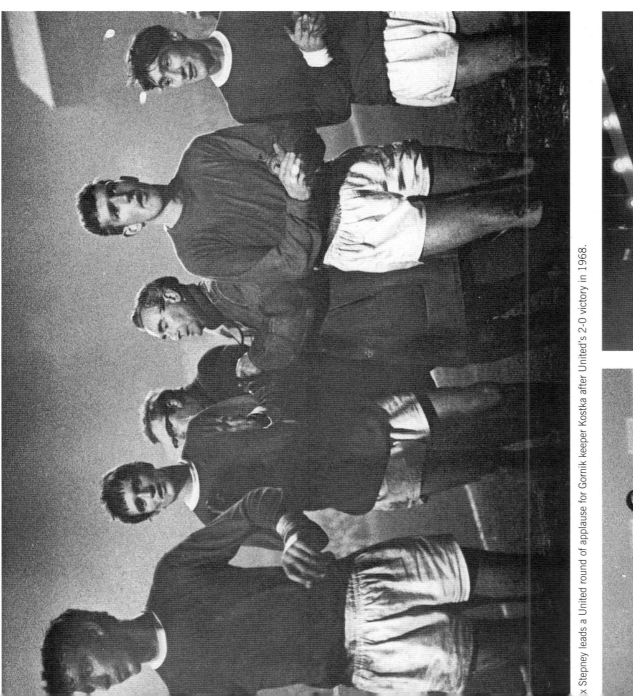

Alex Stepney leads a United round of applause for Gornik keeper Kostka after United's 2-0 victory in 1968.

Brian Kidd (left) wins the race for the ball in United's 1968 10-0 demolition of Anderlecht, and (right) The Reds pile on the pressure.

Magic. United players celebrate after Best's winner against Real Madrid.

Law and Kidd look on as Best stuns Real Madrid with a goal in 1968.

High fliers. Law and Aston in balletic mood against Real Madrid in 1968.

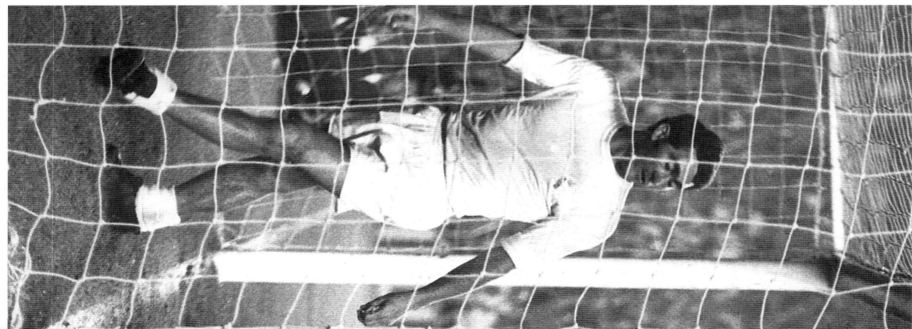

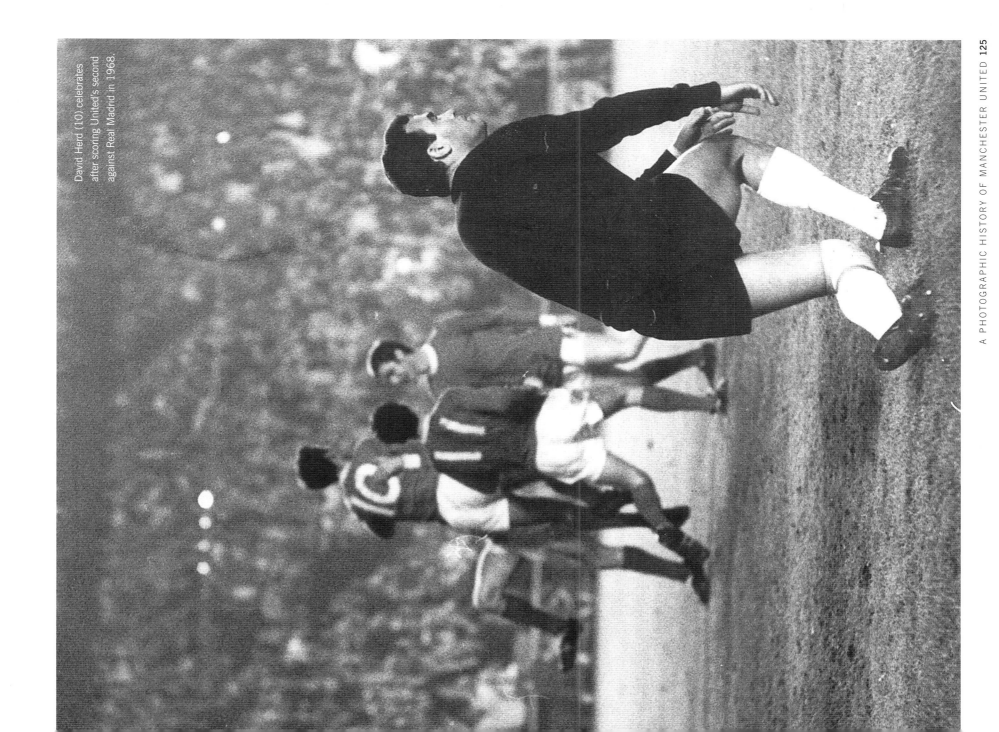

David Herd (10) celebrates after scoring United's second against Real Madrid in 1968.

Here's how you do it. Busby schools his subjects before the 1968 European Cup Final.

The Godfather. Matt Busby before the '68 European Cup Final. He never lost his hands-on approach to team preparations.

Paddy Crerand gives his all against Benfica in the 1968 European Cup Final. He epitomised the effort United's players put into the victory.

Pure joy. Charlton's on cloud nine after scoring a stunner in the European Cup Final against Benfica.

aven sent. Denis Law in a typical victory pose as he scores in United's 1969 European Cup semi-final against AC Milan. Charlton also scored in the 2-0 win.

e Milan goalkeeper is injured after a bottle is thrown on the pitch.

Matt Busby displays the Estudiantes club pennant before the infamous duel with the Argentinians in the 1968 World Club Championship.

The Un

A scarre

Bobby Charlton explains to the press what went wrong.

...rns with the team after a bruising defeat by Estudiantes in the World Club match.

...plane for Agentina. It was to be a severe test of their strength.

Kidd and Tony Dunne can only watch as Veron of Estudiantes scores in the 1969 encounter.

Willie Morgan slides home a late equalizer ...

... and Charlton does the honourable thing.

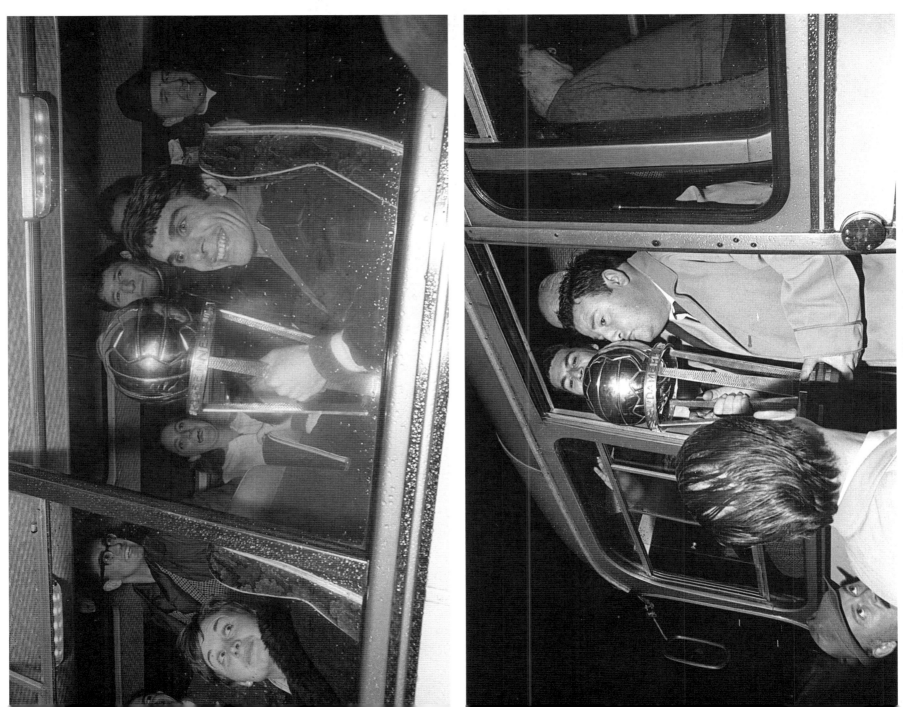

e Estudiantes team took the World Club Championship trophy over two legs in 1969 – and enjoyed every minute.

# Football's Gentleman Giant

P ick the remotest bar in the wildest part of the world, where no English is spoken, and utter the magic mantra: "Manchester United." It's a safe bet the response will involve a thumbs-up and the sacred words: "Bobby Charlton." If you are really lucky it may also involve a free drink. It is impossible to overestimate the global respect and affection for the game's true gentleman. To most fans abroad he IS English soccer. In over four decades of first class football the great man was only booked once – and that was by mistake. A tireless ambassador for the game, he deservedly became Sir Bobby in 1974. The down-to-earth miner's son from Northumberland still stands head and shoulders above other sportsmen when it comes to setting an example to young people. Impeccable manners and incredible patience have carried him through some of United's most traumatic moments. A living legend, his talent, fearsome right foot and sheer guts took him to the very top. He survived Munich to help bring England it's most prestigious trophy. There was jubilation throughout the land the day he held the World Cup aloft, after beating old rivals Germany.

Thanks to Sir Bobby bald really is beautiful to millions of soccer fans too. When his distinctive dome, with the trademark three strands slicked down across the top, loomed up in front of opposing players it was a sign of manliness. It beamed the message: "Get out of the way son, I'm coming through." Being bald also gave

him the air of an elder statesman, useful when galvanising a ragg team. He came across as a mature man surrounded by youngsto during the World Cup, even though he was still in his early 30 That's the way it's always been for Sir Bobby. He's exhibited wisdo beyond his years and soccer has been the better for it. A man his word, he has always believed in fair play. To find the source his basic no-nonsense decency you need look no further than l beloved mother Cissie. She came from top quality soccer stoc rooted firmly in the North East of England. The Milburn fam has produced a dynasty of firm, but fair, footballers. Her brothe were legends in their own time. George, Jack and Jim gave Lee United backbone and Stan was a Leicester City stalwart. Cous "Wor" Jackie Milburn struck fear into the heart of the oppositi as one of Newcastle United's most famous strikers. It's alwa been a family affair. When Bobby tasted the sweetest success Wembley in 1966, his big brother Jack was there on the pitch savour it too.

He's always done the right thing. As a brilliant England Schoolb he was headhunted by around 20 clubs. Many youngster's wou have been swayed by big promises from lesser teams, but Bob had already said "Yes" to United...and that was that. From t very beginning of his time at the club he showed great fortitud When Busby finally asked him to join the first team in October 19 the youngster pretended he was fully fit, even though he was sufferi

om an ankle injury. Bobby ignored the pain and scored twice. The
mpetition for places in the squad was just as fierce in those
ays as it is today and it was hard to say no. To start with his
rvices were only required when Babes like Tommy Taylor were
t of action, but he soon became an important part of the team.
hen United won the league in May 1957 he had contributed 10
als. The following season he made sure of a permanent place
the first 11 when he scored a hat-trick during United's 7-2 win
ainst Bolton. European clubs were also beginning to respect
s powerful shooting. He put two in the back of the net when United
ew 3-3 with Red Star Belgrade during that fateful second leg Cup
e in February 1958, which earned the team a place in the semi-
als and years of sorrow.

ncredibly Bobby escaped from the Munich Air Disaster with
only minor injuries. Although knocked cold by the impact,
he was pulled free from the fuel-soaked wreckage by
goalkeeper Harry Gregg and spent a short time in hospital
recovering from a bang on the head, shock and cuts. During
e club's darkest season he was an inspiration. Instead of taking
ne off, he went straight back to work in 1958-59, scoring 28
als in 38 league games. He was a key figure in the reconstruction
the side after Munich and in January 1962 netted his 100th
ague and cup goal for the club during a match against Tottenham.

Bobby was settling down off the pitch too. He married wife Norma
in July 1961. One of their two daughters, Suzanne, is a well known
TV weather forecaster. As well as being a United stalwart, Bobby
became a permanent fixture in the England squad during the
sixties. In over a decade he won 106 caps and hammered home
49 goals – a record. The Portuguese will never forget the two
goals he put past their keeper in 1966, which gained England a
place in the World Cup final and the ultimate soccer victory.

He made sure United didn't miss out on the international
stage either. Bobby was the captain of the team when they won
the European Cup by beating Benfica 4-1 in May 1968. He scored
the first and last goals. It cost him almost every ounce of energy.
The dedicated professional was so tired he couldn't even leave
his room to join the party. Having won everything in sight, it seemed
that he could go on forever. But age was taking its toll and new
manager Tommy Docherty was desperate for fresh talent. Gallant
as ever, Bobby took the gentleman's way out and retired gracefully.
His last league match for United was against Chelsea in April
1973 but 60,000 had turned up for his last Old Trafford appearance
the week before. The United faithful gave him a send off few players
would ever experience. A great player, he was not cut out for
management and, after a spell in charge of Preston became a roving
ambassador for the game. He's now a director of the club and barely
misses a game.

Charlton in full flow against Coventry in 1970. His was an unmistakable style.

Dream maker: Bobby visits a young fan in hospital with the FA Cup in 1963.

...rlton rises to meet a cross as Law waits to poach in the Chelsea goalmouth in 1965. Bobby was as good with his head as his feet.

...stoppable. Blackpool's goalkeeper is left floundering by a typical Charlton dummy as the striker slides home the second in a 2-1 win in 1966.

Bobby – with cigarette! –
before flying to Belfast for
an England game in 1964

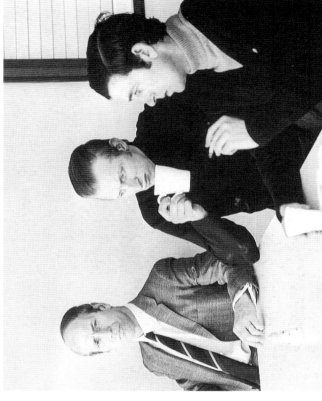

e work ethic. Bobby rests with Denis Law and David Herd after a punishing training session and (right) with Shay Brennan in the United canteen.

oung George Best shares high tea with Charlton before flying out to the Estudiantes World Club Championship game.

The look of love. Bobby and wife Norma shunned the limelight. This is a rare shot of his private life, taken at their Cheshire home in 1959.

Hero dad. Bobby and wife Norma show off his trophies to his children Andrea and Suzanne. He was a devoted family man.

Now remember our kid, shoot! Bobby and Jackie on England duty in 1965.

Avenger. He may be United's quiet man – but Bobby cut a dash at times

...therly rivals. The Charlton brothers were a legend across the Pennines as Jackie backed up Leeds and Bobby took them on for United.

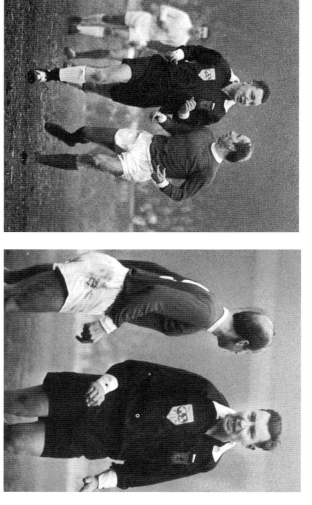

A gentleman he may have been, but Charlton had passion and could give a ref a bit of stick at times.

Bobby was always the first for autographs... especially after the FA Cup victory over Leicester in 1963, when the team emerged from their hotel.

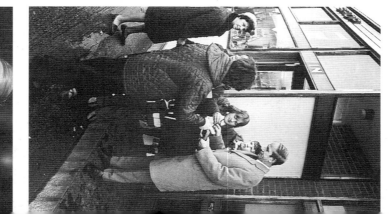

Bobby the peacemaker.

Charlton got his only booking in the '6 World Cup game with Argentina.

sweat. He was the pivot of the England side in 1966 and even the great Gordon Banks got the treatment on the training pitch.

A Stoke pottery honours Bobby's 100 caps with a special plate.

...bby in 1970 with his 100 England caps – a great achievement.

...arlton was the epitome of manners on ...pitch - and was rewarded well.

Receiving the 1969 Gillette Sportsmanship Award from United boss Louis Edwards.

Charlton takes on West Ham's Martin Peters in 1966.

Skipping over a lunge from a Newcastle defender in 1968.

Sheer power. Against Derby in the 1970 Cup Final.

A deadly dead ball as the United squad wince.

Classic style from Charlton as he fires past the Leeds defence in a hard fought game in 1968.

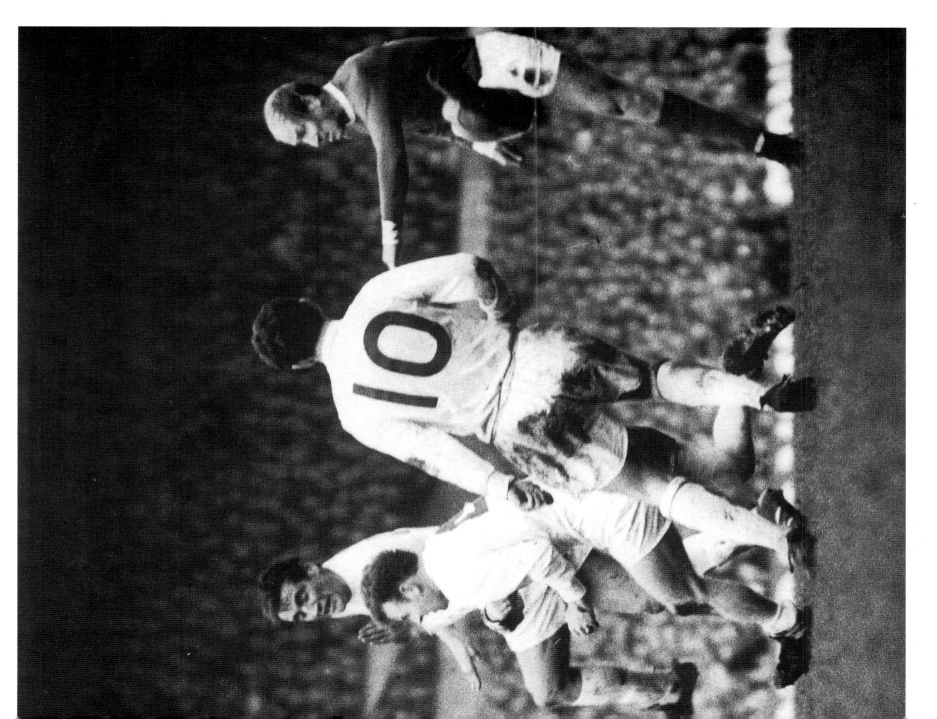

A defender's nightmare. Bobby nutmegs Chelsea's Charlie Cook in 1971.

Even the great Gordon Banks can't stop him in the 1972 FA Cup against Stoke in 1972.

...th United Chairman James Gibson in London for his final game for United against Chelsea in 1973, and (right) announcing his decision to retire.

A well-deserved retirement pint in the Old Trafford bar.

...d of an era as Bobby makes his final exit from Old Trafford.

Sir Bobby Charlton can't resist a touch of the ball.

# The Blond Bomber

I f ever there was a player who summed up the sheer joy of being a top footballer it was Denis Law. Week in, week out, Law ran his socks off for the team and his celebration after scoring became legendary. Poaching in the six yard box, he would plant the ball in the net, wheel away with one arm raised, finger pointing to the heavens and a look of ecstasy on his face. Youngsters everywhere copied his style for years, clutching their sleeve cuffs as Law did instinctively. Nobody haunted the opposition's penalty area like Law, dubbed "The King" by thousands of adoring Stretford End fans. He was a master of his craft, at the right team, at the right time. He was the viper who so often snatched a vital goal to retrieve the team's fortunes.

But in his early days, Law hardly seemed built for the task. A skinny, though supremely fit kid from Aberdeen, he was looked upon as a lightweight early in his career with Huddersfield Town in 1955. He suffered from an eye defect, forcing him to wear glasses throughout his childhood. An operation that year put it right but the experience of ridicule gave him added steel. Little did that team know what he would go on to achieve, both abroad and with the biggest club in Britain. United spotted his potential early – Matt Busby, who else, offered Huddersfield £10,000 for the 16-year-old player in 1956 and was rebuffed by none other than Bill Shankly, then manager of the Yorkshire club. Both he and Busby

knew a talent when they saw one, and United would have to w to get their man. After signing professional forms for Huddersfie Law was sucked straight into the Scotland international squad 18 years of age to play against Wales in October, 1958. Again th figure of Busby loomed large in his life – Busby was the Scotla manager. Law scored in a 3-0 victory and assured his future wi the Boss.

L aw did eventually come to Manchester – but not to Unite He signed for City in 1960 for a record fee of £55,00 It was not a happy marriage. City were struggling a Law could not find his mark. Just a year later Italia giants Torino moved in and offered the player rich and perks beyond his dreams. He moved – but was unhappy. T Italian style of football – defensive, the slow build-up which is prevale even today – was not for this dynamic striker and within a year was desperate to leave. United came to the rescue, bringing hi to Old Trafford in 1962. He made his mark straight away, scori in the FA Cup victory over Leicester City and leading the tea with an emphatic style rarely seen before. Law was The Man f thousands of fans. He was part of what, in Manchester pubs at t time, was referred to as 'The Holy Trinity' along with Best and Charlt Law, though, was to be robbed of the ultimate glory of Unite

ropean triumph by injury. He admits that sitting on the sidelines
 such a night was "agony", though he had played his part to the
 l the previous season when United trounced Benfica 5-1. The
jury was to signal the end of his time at Old Trafford and when
 ocherty arrived in the early seventies, Law was one of the first to
, transferred back to Manchester City in 1974 on a free. United
ns everywhere know just how fateful that move would prove to
. His infamous back-heeled goal in the dying minutes of the vital
rby sent United into the Second Division. Stretford end's favourite
d destroyed their hopes, but to this day Denis Law remains a
n of Old Trafford.

His record for The Reds shows why. He made 393 appearances
d scored 236 goals. He was a striker of the old school but his
ve for United has never waned. Though he is guarded today
out his relationship with Docherty, Law has always remained
al to the ethos of the club that thrust him into the limelight .

He is seen on TV as an authoritative pundit, mixing his football
owledge with a wicked Scottish wit but Law prefers the quiet life
ese days. His love of United remains fierce and he remains friends
th the greats he played alongside – Bobby Charlton especially.
t the last word on this consummate footballer should go to
eorge Best, who turned to Law as a confidante many times during
s own troubles.

Netted. Law's instinctive reaction to the joy of scoring was the raised right arm. If fans missed the goal, all they looked for was the Denis salute.

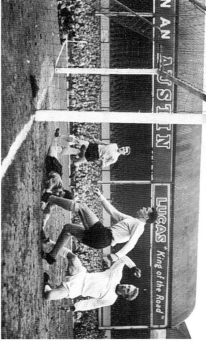

Scoring the first goal in the '63 Cup semi-final against Southampton.

Law grabbed three in the '63 Cup Winner's Cup against Willem II.

Just making sure as he nets against Everton in 1966.

Mr Cool. Law slots home a penalty against West Ham in 1967.

ectacular overhead kicks were a Law speciality. This was in a 3-1 defeat of Spurs in 1967 and he was unstoppable.

urs 'keeper Pat Jennings stood no chance when one-on-one with Law.

He blasts a shot past the West Ham defence in 1963.

He loved the battles against Liverpool and scores here in 1963.

bacher par excellence. Against City in the '69 League Cup semi-final.

The secret of Denis Law's success was his amazing balance on the ball. Here he wrong-foots the Blackburn defence in the 1965 2-2 draw.

Respect. Leeds hard man Billy Bremner tries to stop Law in 1968.

He rounds Villa 'keeper Wilson on the way to four goals in October 1964.

King of his world. Against Nottingham Forest in 1965.

He was just as good with his head. Here he lets the ball skim off his forehead to loop into the net against West Bromwich Albion in 1966.

The flying Scotsman – Law scores a stunning header against a bewildered Spurs in 1967.

The 'keeper's beaten and Law heads past the post against Forest in 1965.

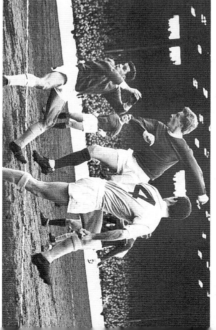

Four up! He heads home in United's 4-1 win over Manchester City in 1964.

The Lawman! Denis is there to grab a great goal against The Gunners in 1966.

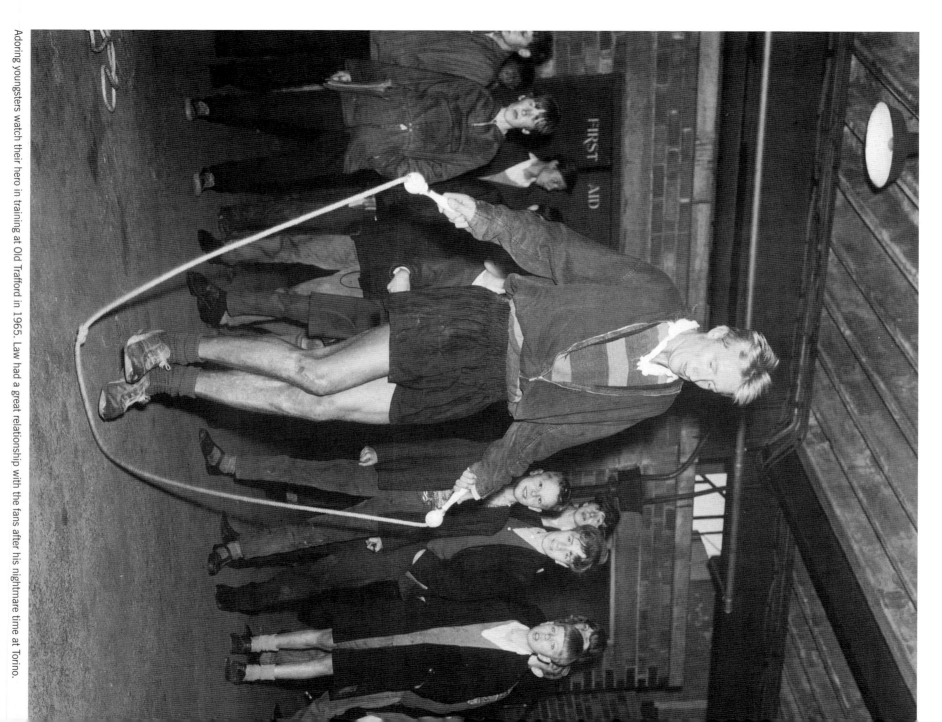

Adoring youngsters watch their hero in training at Old Trafford in 1965. Law had a great relationship with the fans after his nightmare time at Torino.

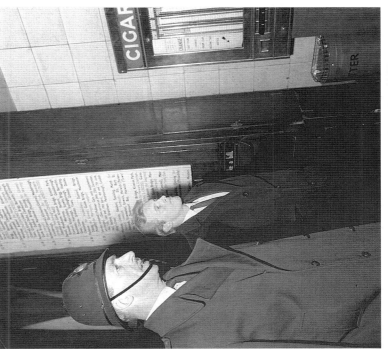

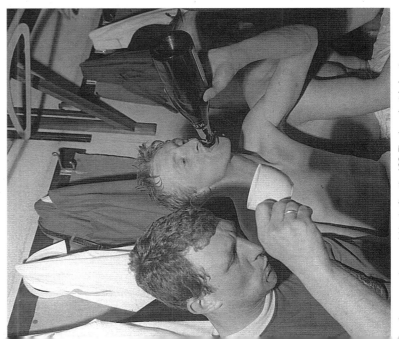

eupational hazard. Sometimes the only way defenders could stop him was to bring him down. This was in a game against Sunderland in 1964.

Law in Sheffield for an FA disciplinary hearing in December 1967.

te of success. Law and Herd after the '63 Final against Leicester.

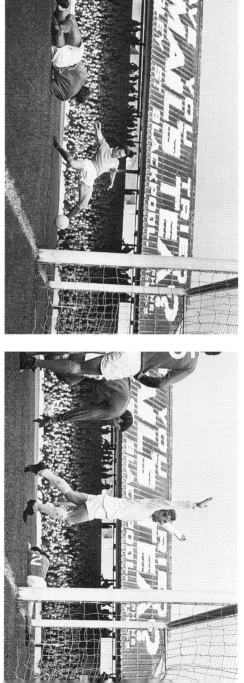

My ball! Law's shot beats the Blackpool defence, and while the opposition collects itself Denis collects the ball from the net. Then Best rushes in to congrat...

Law had tremendous respect for the boss. Here they shake hands after the player signed a new two-year contract with United in 1966.

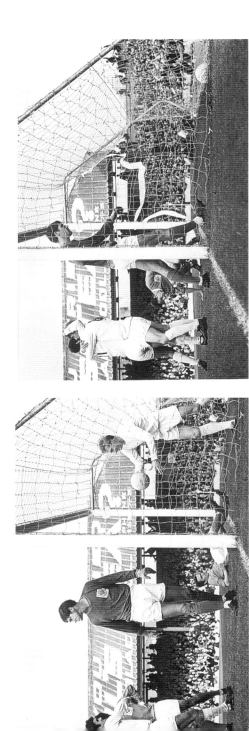

...ent on to win 3-1.

Scotsman discusses his case with Busby, David Herd and Pat Crerand in Sheffield before his FA disciplinary hearing in 1967.

A black day for fans as Law gives his reaction to being transfer-listed in 1970.

He gets in the spirit with wife Diana, Christmas 1964.

, Crerand and their wives as Busby is made a Freeman of Manchester.

is arrives at the funeral of another great Scottish football figure, Liverpool manager Bill Shankly, in 1981.

Three United heroes. Best, Law and Crerand during training in 1969 – on the day Wilf McGuiness took over.

And it's there! Thanks Denis, you were brilliant.

Missed me...

In full flight...

# The First Superstar

H e was the ultimate pin-up of the sixties – "the James Bond of football" as team-mate Willie Morgan once dubbed him. George Best had everything a player could wish for, blessed with unbelievable ball control, uncanny football imagination and a physical strength and determination which belied his meagre frame. One thing was for sure, as his talent developed he left defenders totally shaken and adoring fans stirred by his skills. But the boy from Belfast had something else which shot him into the category of Britain's first soccer superstar – pop star looks and a sex appeal never before associated with footballers. All these elements combined to produce a media dream machine at a time when Britain was desperate to break out of the fifties post-war strait-jacket. A working class boy really could become a hero to millions and "Georgie" was the one. The public appetite for this genius was phenomenal, bringing him unparalleled wealth and everything that went with it – fast cars, expensive clothes, fabulous homes and his choice of the most beautiful women of the time. They were always at his side.

But the pressures of performing both on and off the pitch were fierce and there are those who believe his ultimate downfall was inevitable: you would have to be superhuman not to succumb to the temptations George Best had thrown his way at such a tender age. True United fans, however, remember him for what he did on the pitch as the team grew in stature after Munich and marched towards greatness in Europe. The young Best was spotted playing football with his mates on the depressed, windswept Craigie Estate in Belfast by legendary United scout Bob Bishop, who could not believe that a skinny kid could possess such talent. A few phone calls back to Busby at United's Old Trafford base and the youngster was on his way to Manchester, only to return home a few weeks later

homesick and depressed. Busby persuaded him back – and a legend was born. Best made his debut at the age of 17 in 1 against West Bromwich Albion, and after a spell back in the reserv he returned with a stunning goal in United's 5-1 demolitio Nottingham Forest. A career with the Reds spanning 466 Leag Cup and European games and 176 goals brought justifia comparisons with the great Brazilian Pele and he proved he worthy of the tag in the greatest game of his life, when Un took on the might of Benfica in the 1968 European Cup Fina Wembley. He simply dazzled the Portuguese, mesmerizing defence with mazy runs. Whenever he had the ball, the crowd knew something was about to happen. Even the senior play like Charlton, Law and Stiles bowed to his prowess. Denis I recalls: "When George was on the ball, it was a sight to behold was superb. Mind you at times you would never get the ball fi him."

T he glory of that victory just added to the aura a the public adulation foisted on the young Best, soon the cracks began to show as life outside of foot started to take hold. He was photographed everyw he went – with a different girl on his arm – advertis companies clamoured for his signature and he seemed to ha new car every day. While other players like Charlton and commanded £500 a week from football, Best was banking £5, a week from a myriad activities. Inevitably, his champagne lifes clashed with the strict management of Busby. By 1972 he was fai to turn up for training. Though Busby tried to control the wayw genius, heavy fines were imposed and he was ordered out of luxury house in Manchester and sent to live with Pat Crerar family "for safekeeping". Pictures of Best in yet another c

...tching yet another glass of champagne and surrounded by yet another bevy of beauties would appear in the papers and, increasingly, his relationship with team-mates, and the club as employer, reached breaking point. It snapped in 1974 when United, then under Tommy Docherty, realised he was beyond control. He played his last game for the club on New Year's Day.

When he left United, he could have moved to any club in the world but not George Best. He astonished everyone by signing to play non-League team Dunstable as if in a fit of pique. The team used attendances of 200 were suddenly entertaining 12,000. Fulham finally brought him back into the fold to play alongside his buddy Rodney Marsh, again boosting attendances four-fold, but Best then decided America was the place for him. He moved to the sunshine and non-stop beach life with the Los Angeles Aztecs before returning for his final stint in English football at Bournemouth.

His private life since finishing with football has given headline writers a field day – culminating in his arrest for drink driving and subsequent prison sentence in 1984 after assaulting a police officer. These days he has found some peace, working as a radio and TV commentator, and he admits himself that his marriage to a year old model Alex Pursey has brought stability he has never known since his younger days. His son Callum, by former wife Angie, lives with his mother in America but plays football like his dad. George meanwhile looks back on his amazing years with a refreshing honesty. When asked once why he went to play football in North America he replied: "I was driving through London and saw an advert saying 'Drink Canada Dry'". United fans have followed George Best's mercurial rise and fall from grace at their beloved club with dismay, envy and wonderment – but always with a tinge of gratitude that the man many still believe to be "The Best there ever was" played in the glorious Red and White.

Best charges in on the Liverpool 'keeper in 1965.

George was also a deadly penalty taker. Here he beats Liverpool 'keeper Tommy Lawrence in 1965.

In full flight, there was no sight to match him. The t

his foot. Here, Wolves 'keeper Parkes is beaten by the classic 'drop of the shoulder' from Best.

Once past the defence, he was a clear favourite to score here against Spurs in 1968 but the 'keeper gets a foot to the ball. It was a case of throwing yourse

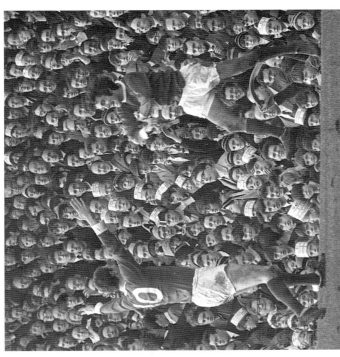

You beauty. Herd races to greet Best after his goal against Spurs in 1966.

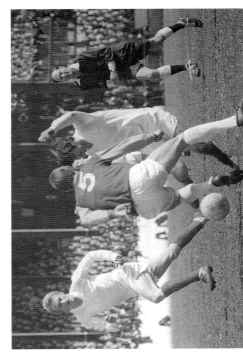

That shimmy again. He beats Arsenal's defender Heffer in 1967.

He often taunted the opposition, here taking on Spurs' Terry Venables in 1968.

A PHOTOGRAPHIC HISTORY OF MANCHESTER UNITED **175**

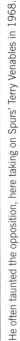

e only way to stop him.

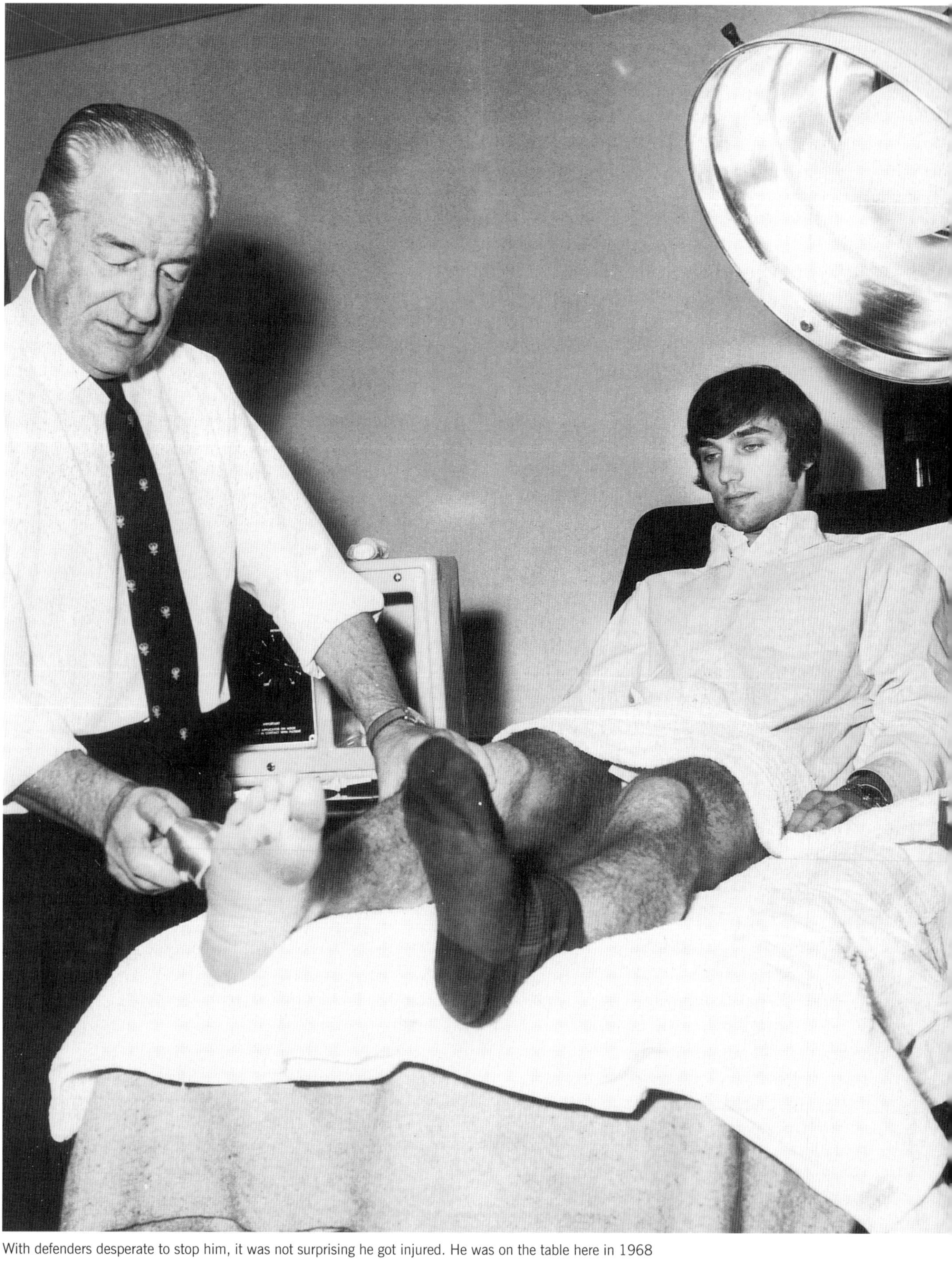

With defenders desperate to stop him, it was not surprising he got injured. He was on the table here in 1968

soon got a taste for the sunshine, often disappearing for a break in Spain. In later years it would prove a problem for United.

Mobbed as he leaves a training session in 1968.

Despite his pop star image, fans could still get close to the hero.

He obliges fans again before an England v. Russia game in 1969.

He got the superstar treatment when he visited Dublin in 1970.

They all wanted pictures after the '68 European Cup Final performance.

Returning from the 1966 match against Benfica where the Portuguese press dubbed him "El Beatle", a tag which stuck for good.

David Sadler takes on Best during a training session in 1970.

He had to race for the tunnel after a game against Ipswich in 1970.

his early years Best was supremely fit and a trainer's dream.

hero! George is greeted by a fan as he leaves the pitch in 1971.

Busby with his discovery after Best was sent off against Chelsea in 1971.

He returns from United's tour of Europe in 1969 looking battle-scarred.

His lowest moment came in 1984 when he was jailed for assaulting a police officer.

Leaving for another FA grilling with O'Farrell.

Surrounded by guards after receiving death threats before a game at Newcastle in 1971.

As his problems mounted in 1971, Busby helped him face the press.

In 1970, he and Busby went to London to defend Crerand at an FA hearing.

listen son. Best adored Matt
by and the boss kept a close
on his young protege.

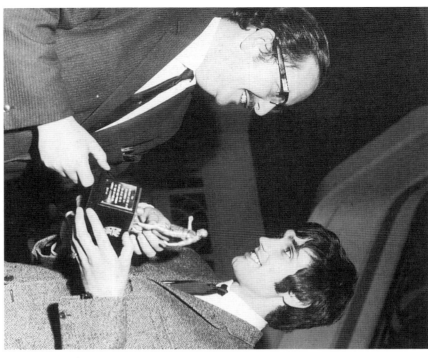

Just rewards... receiving the Player Of The Year Award in 1968.

Nice one, George. Bobby congratulates him on his Award.

United's greats honour him on the pitch as Footballer Of The Year in 1969.

George for PM! Arriving at a Downing Street party for The Reds in 1970.

t for dead. George dances through the Burnley defence in 1969...

nd takes them on again. He could mesmerize – and infuriate the opposition with his skills.

The idol of millions. He had the looks, the hair and the sex appeal.

His trickery leaves a Wolves defender tripping over himself in 1969.

Giving everything against Leeds again in 1970.

He's off... against Leeds in 1972.

Denis Law and Brian Kidd turn to the United genius while QPR's defence picks itse

1972.

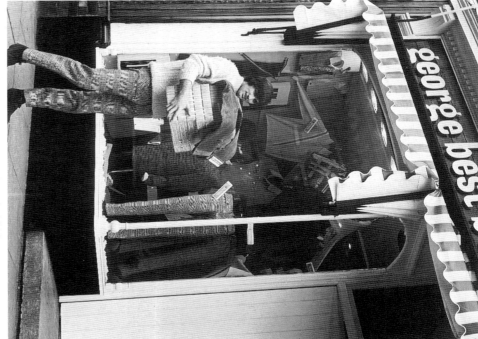

His business interests boomed with boutiques in 1966.

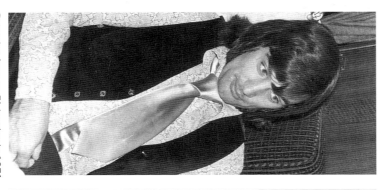

Returning from an FA hearing in 1971 after swearing at the referee.

Leaving Sinead Cusack's flat as his problems began to mount.

Have a drink! At the door of his Manchester nightclub in 1973.

Arriving back from the World Cup in 1972.

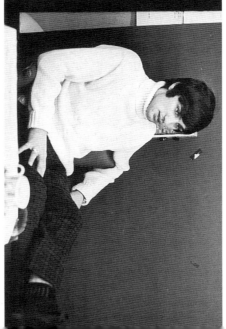

By 1966, Best needed an office to handle his career – and fan mail.

Champagne and kisses on his 21st birthday

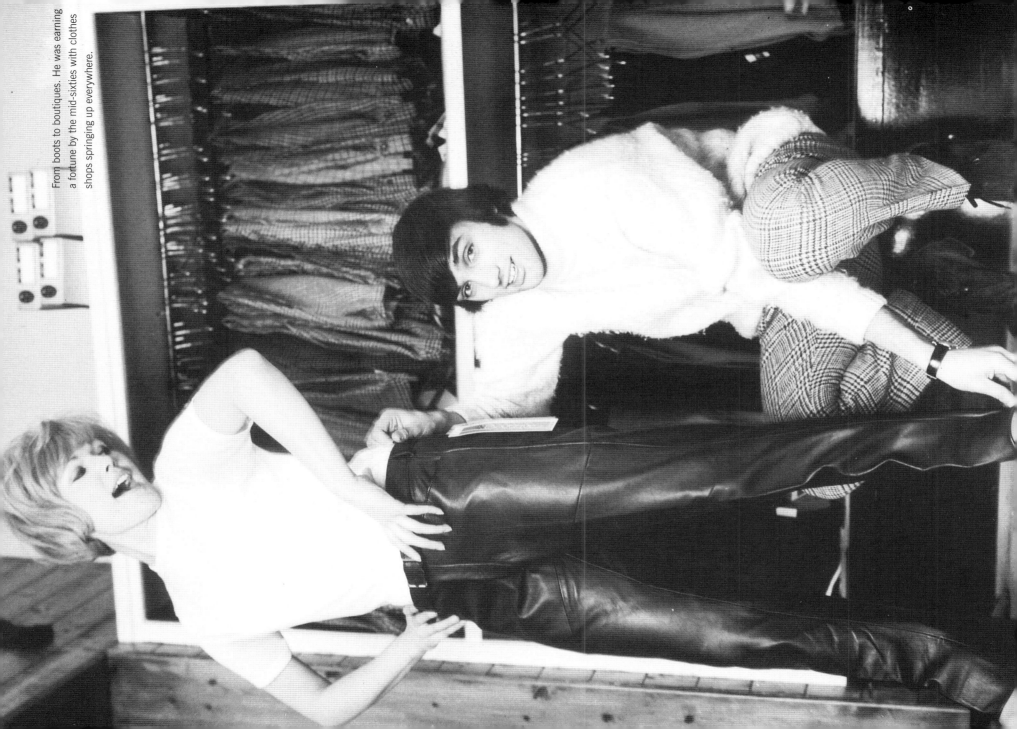

International playboy – Best relaxes in a bar while on holiday in Majorca with actress Susan George in 1969

Fun in the sun. The star brushes up his skills with Susan George and then its champagne time for the couple

With ex-Bunny girl Linda Joinett in Palm Springs.

With model Heidi Stillians in California.

George's girl: Miss Great Britain Carolyn Moore in 1972.

Sixties swingers. The couple's relationship was making headlines back in Britain, but Best seems to be at his happiest.

Golden couple. George with Swedish teacher Elisabeth Bengson in Spain in 1972

The look says it all. Best and Eva Haraldsted announced in August 1969 that they were to marry.

Dandies: George and models joined by Law and Charlton.

The centre of attention again during a fashion shoot in 1967.

Girls flocked to George's side – even when he was trying on a new pair of boots!

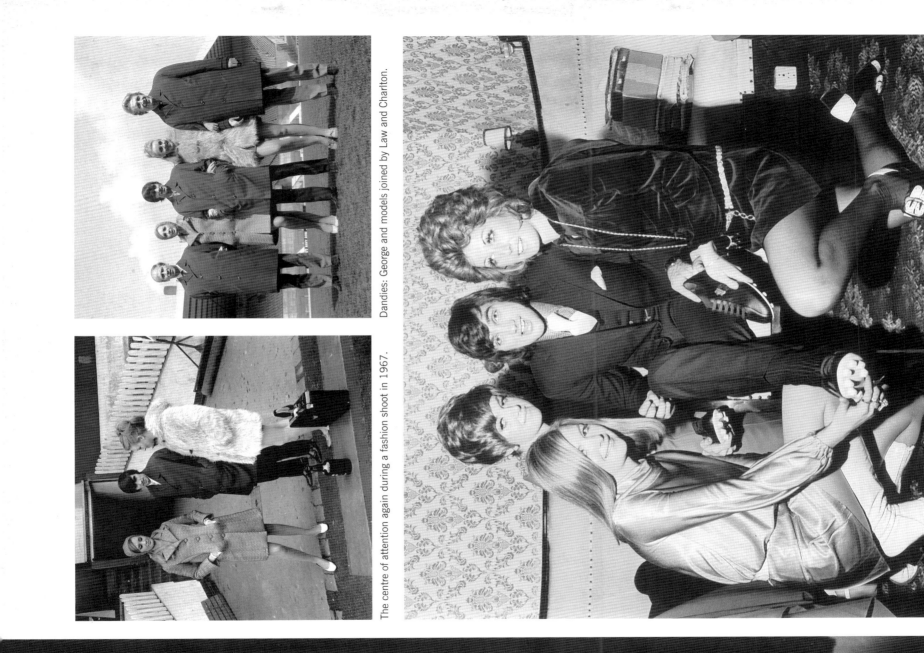

Dandies: George and models joined by Law and Charlton.

The centre of attention again during a fashion shoot in 1967.

Girls flocked to George's side – even when he was trying on a new pair of boots!

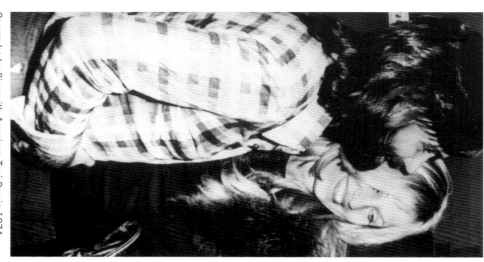

George had a fling with American Toni Ceo in 1974.

Top mop: Making an advert for men's hairspray in 1969.

George and Eva Haraldsted (back row, centre) at a 1969 charity bash.

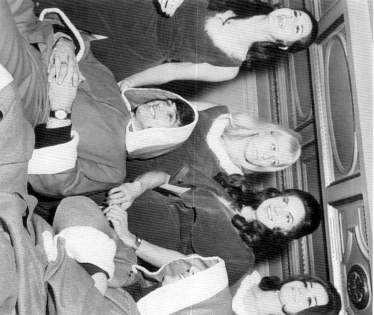

George and girlfriend, ex-Miss World Mary Stavin in 1982.

Best with singer "L

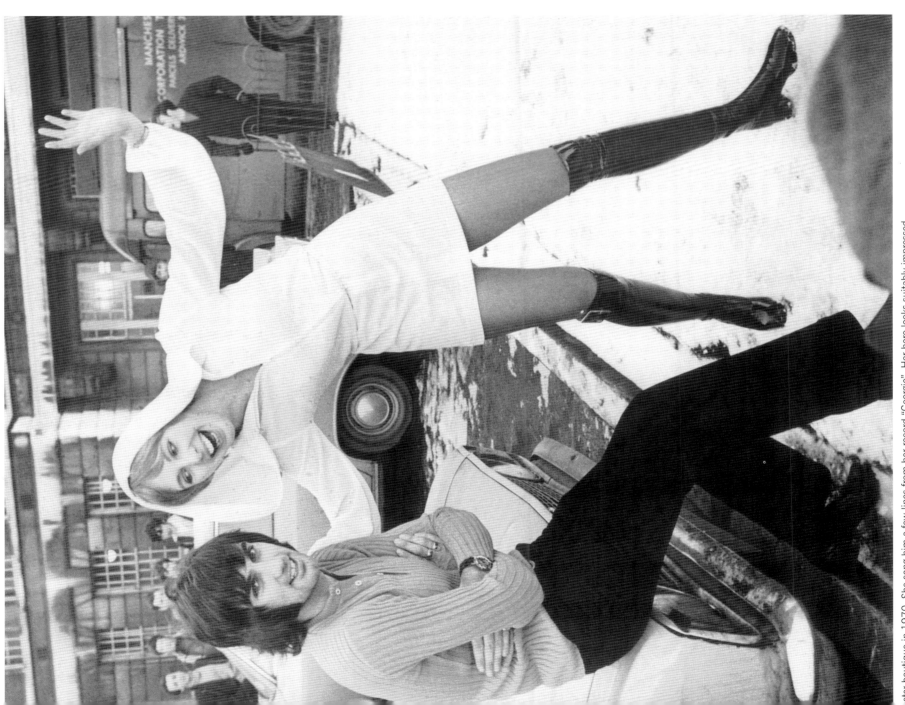

...ster boutique in 1970. She sang him a few lines from her record "Georgie". Her hero looks suitably impressed.

Photographers followed him everywhere. Best and girlfriend Jackie Glass at a reception to honour United's 1968 European Cup triumph.

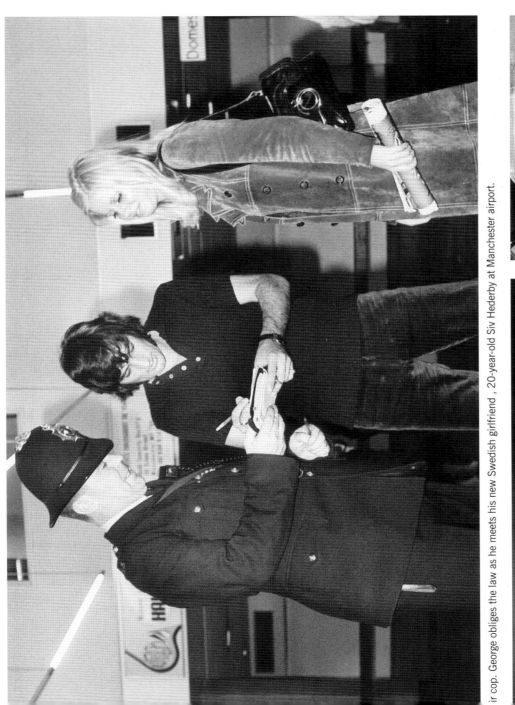

The law as he meets his new Swedish girlfriend, 20-year-old Siv Hederby at Manchester airport.

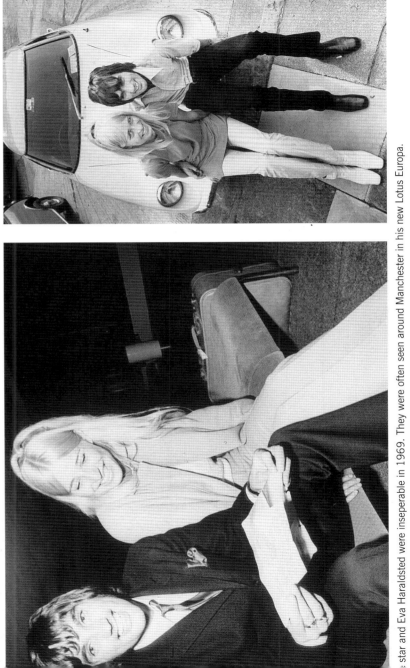

e star and Eva Haraldsted were inseperable in 1969. They were often seen around Manchester in his new Lotus Europa.

# Ram-Raid Footballer

Norbert Peter Stiles was probably the unlikeliest player ever to achieve greatness in football, but that is exactly what he did for both United and his country. The diminutive defender became a household name through his exploits. Tireless on the pitch, relentless in his pursuit of victory, Manchester United fans recognised the terrier in him and took the man to their hearts from the start. He was also one of the first products of the club's successful youth policy – United signed him as a schoolboy in 1957 and then made him professional two years later. But fate was to make its play for Stiles. The disaster of 1958 at Munich robbed United of its greatest talents – Duncan Edwards, David Pegg and Tommy Taylor – men who promised to give United the dominance the club expected under Matt Busby's guidance. As the club desperately tried to recover it turned to the talent back home. Stiles was thrown into the defence, making his debut at the age of 18 against Bolton Wanderers in 1960. He soon proved his worth, many strikers twice the size of Stiles were stopped short and left wondering what had hit them. Stiles quickly assumed a pivotal role in the United side and his name was always one of the first on the team sheet.

His fitness was phenomenal. He was a player who could defend, take over the midfield and even get up front to score, as he did memorably in the European Cup semi-final against Partisan Belgrade at Old Trafford in March 1966. United the champions were up against it without the injured Best and went down 1-0 in the first half. The tension at the game was unbearable, United needing two goals to secure a place in the final. Hope came when Stiles, marauding down the left flank, let fly a hopeful shot, a real

"grasscutter" which shot through the bewildered Partisan defen[ce] and under the goalkeeper's flailing body into the net. The Uni[ted] faithful erupted with cries of "a gift from God", which gives so[me] idea of the esteem they held for Stiles. It was not enough for Uni[ted] to go through, but Stiles' was forever loved for his display of pass[ion] and diligence that night.

It was not long before the local lad was sought out for natio[nal] honours, winning nine caps for his country before that histo[ric] World Cup victory over Germany in 1966 and the unforgetta[ble] scenes of the gap-toothed defender conducting a victory da[nce] around Wembley. The whole nation fell in love with the little m[an] then – he epitomised the bulldog spirit of the English ga[me] against the technique of the continental teams. Like all the te[am] on that day in 1966, he has never looked back, but greater c[lub] honours were waiting in the wings for Nobby. Two years af[ter] lifting the World Cup, he strode onto the pitch at Wembley [to] face Benfica in the European Cup Final, a match United w[ere] desperate to win. The team were victorious and Stiles once m[ore] was at the centre of the celebrations, hugging Bobby Charlt[on] for the world to see.

The player stayed at United until 1971 when he join[ed] Middlesbrough as the European championship team began[to] break up. He tried his hand at management with Preston and W[est] Ham before returning to Old Trafford to work with the youth te[am] in 1989. His place in United's hall of fame is assured after [his] exploits and the now pinpoints Nicky Butt as the player in t[he] current United squad who compares in the style and tenaci[ty] brought to his game.

Letting his feelings be known as the ref refuses a penalty against West Ham in 1967.

Stiles was a fitness fanatic and it paid off on the pitch. He even continued the workouts in the dressing room.

y could score goals
ll as stop them, as
d with this flyer
nst Arsenal in 1966.

Nobby loved to get the most from his shirt.

He gets an earfull from the ref in United's game against Everton in 1966.

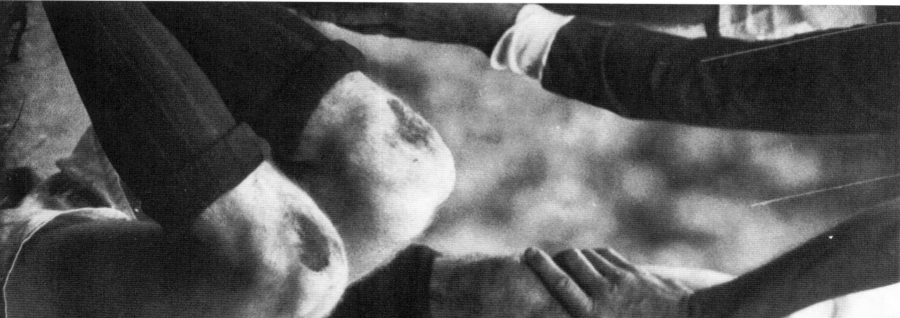

Stiles never shirked a challenge, even when it was painful as in the 1966 Everton game.

His United team-mates dubbed him "Happy" – and here's the proof.

Denis Law wins hands down in a knobbly knees contest against Stiles.

Ahead of his time, Nobby Stiles makes an early grunge fashion statement.

Nobby and Harry Gregg face the taunts of an Everton fan after United's defeat in the FA Cup semi-final.

Nobby's passing improved dramatically when United got him contact lenses.

Happy again as he relaxes at home in Manchester in 1966. The teeth would come out for a game though!

Returning from Milan with Wilf McGuinness in 1969.

...went a long way after leaving school. On returning, he remembered getting "a few leatherings"

Rivals still. Nobby and City's Mike Summerbee tee off.

...mily man. Nobby gets some gardening done watched by wife Kay and son John.

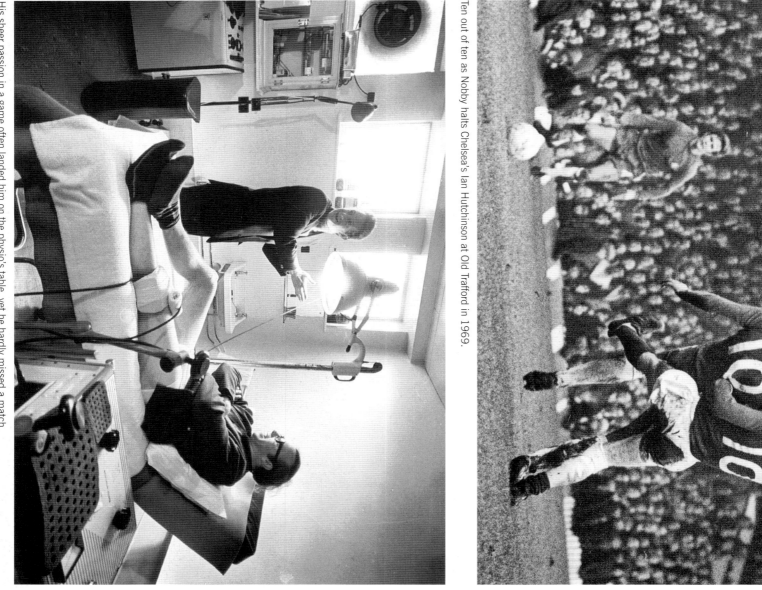

Ten out of ten as Nobby halts Chelsea's Ian Hutchinson at Old Trafford in 1969.

His sheer passion in a game often landed him on the physio's table, yet he hardly missed a match.

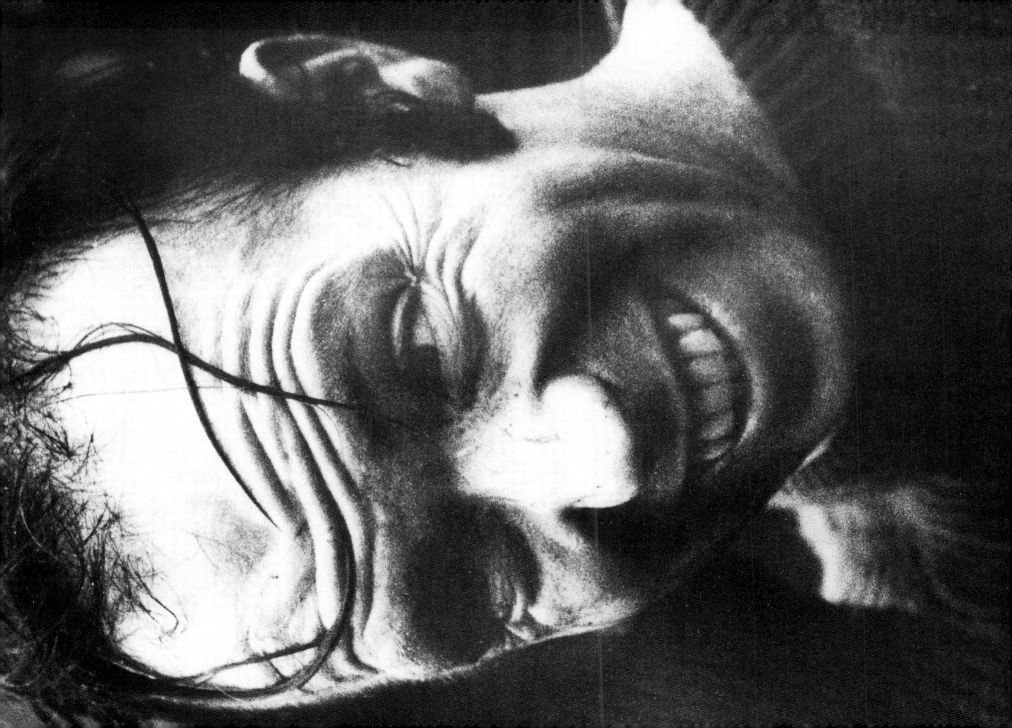

## 1968-1969

An ugly season that started badly with the infamous World Club Championship matches against the Argentinian side Estudiantes. They were marked by violence on the pitch, sending-offs and injuries. Although the South American champions carried off the Inter-Continental Cup, after a Buenos Aires win and Old Trafford draw, there were no real winners from the debacle. Busby, about to give up being team manager, watched United surrender his precious European Cup too. They were knocked out in the semi-finals by AC Milan. The Italian keeper Cudicini was felled by a brick when Old Trafford crowd trouble erupted. United also finished 11th in the League and dropped out of the FA Cup in the sixth round.

### League (Division 1)

| Date | Opponent | | | Score |
|---|---|---|---|---|
| Aug 10 | Everton | H | W | 2-1 |
| Aug 14 | WBA | A | L | 1-3 |
| Aug 17 | Manchester C | A | D | 0-0 |
| Aug 21 | Coventry C | H | W | 1-0 |
| Aug 24 | Chelsea | H | L | 0-4 |
| Aug 28 | Tottenham H | H | W | 3-1 |
| Aug 31 | Sheffield W | A | L | 4-5 |
| Sep 7 | West Ham U | H | D | 1-1 |
| Sep 14 | Burnley | A | L | 0-1 |
| Sep 21 | Newcastle U | H | W | 3-1 |
| Oct 5 | Arsenal | H | D | 0-0 |
| Oct 9 | Tottenham H | A | D | 2-2 |
| Oct 12 | Liverpool | A | L | 0-2 |
| Oct 19 | Southampton | H | L | 1-2 |
| Oct 26 | QPR | H | W | 3-2 |
| Nov 2 | Leeds U | A | D | 0-0 |
| Nov 9 | Sunderland | A | D | 1-1 |
| Nov 16 | Ipswich T | H | D | 0-0 |
| Nov 23 | Stoke C | A | D | 0-0 |
| Nov 30 | Wolverhampton W | H | W | 2-0 |
| Dec 7 | Leicester C | A | L | 1-2 |
| Dec 14 | Liverpool | H | W | 1-0 |
| Dec 21 | Southampton | A | L | 0-2 |
| Dec 26 | Arsenal | A | L | 0-3 |
| Jan 11 | Leeds U | A | L | 1-2 |
| Jan 18 | Sunderland | H | W | 4-1 |
| Feb 1 | Ipswich T | A | L | 0-1 |
| Feb 15 | Wolverhampton W | A | D | 2-2 |
| Mar 8 | Manchester C | H | L | 0-1 |
| Mar 10 | Everton | A | D | 0-0 |
| Mar 15 | Chelsea | A | L | 2-3 |
| Mar 19 | QPR | H | W | 8-1 |
| Mar 22 | Sheffield W | H | W | 1-0 |
| Mar 24 | Stoke C | H | D | 1-1 |
| Mar 29 | West Ham U | A | D | 0-0 |
| Mar 31 | Nottingham F | A | W | 1-0 |
| Apr 2 | WBA | H | W | 2-1 |
| Apr 5 | Nottingham F | H | W | 3-1 |
| Apr 8 | Coventry C | A | L | 1-2 |
| Apr 12 | Newcastle U | A | L | 0-2 |
| Apr 19 | Burnley | H | W | 2-0 |
| May 17 | Leicester C | A | W | 3-2 |

# The Dark Ages

One thing was clear after the European Cup victory of 1968 – the club's supremo Matt Busby was now ready to relinquish control of the club he had built from nothing after Munich to become the European Champions. He had achieved his own personal dreams and fulfilled the promise that just 10 years earlier had seemed such an impossibility. To United fans, his place in history was assured. It was time for him to step aside and in 1969 he resigned as manager. What he, nor the fans still flushed with European success, could have envisaged was that such an intuitive decision that his time was over would usher in a period of instability and a truly dark time in United's history.

Of course, any manager with an ounce of ambition would want to manage Manchester United, but where was the man who could fill Busby's boots, build on the bedrock of European glory and take the club forward to anticipated total domination for the next decade? To say Busby was a hard act to follow is a monumental understatement – it would become an impossible job for a succession of men whose intentions were always honourable, but whose abilities never quite matched the magic Busby had instilled in the hearts and minds of players and fans alike. Whoever came in had one big problem to face – the team that brought home the European chalice in 1968 was now an ageing force. They had made their mark, but as the seventies broke they were no longer equipped to continue the success the club had previously enjoyed. That left any incoming manager with the unenviable task of clearing out men who had become national heroes – and to do so with Busby looking over his shoulder from his new position as General Manager. Over the next decade, The Godfather gave way to a string of stepfathers – and any

amateur psychologist can pinpoint the problems that creates in a family as tightly bonded as this United team

There was no end of credible candidates available – Ron Greenwood, Don Revie, former United stalwarts Johnny Carey and Brian Clough were being touted as successors, but as usual, United surprised everybody by looking within itself for a new leader. Wilf McGuinness, then a junior member of the training staff and just 31 years of age, was selected and found himself having to guide players of his own age on the training pitch. He was United through and through but the task ahead was an unenviable one. He was even the manager – the board decided he should be Chief Coach, which gave the immediate impression that, in fact, Busby was still in charge as "General Manager". It was precisely this clouding of his status that was unfair on the youthful McGuinness and created an air of instability at the club when it should, crucially, have been laying the foundations for the next decade and building on the success of the previous season.

His start was not good. United drew the first game of the 1969 season 2-2 away to Crystal Palace, then followed sound beatings by Everton, home and away, and Southampton. Worse, United were thrashed 4-0 by Manchester City and then 5-1 by Newcastle. McGuinness responded by starting a clear-out of the older player. Foulkes was replaced by Ian Ure, Law was transfer-listed at £60,000, Given at £15,000 and Shay Brennan, who had joined the club with new boss 16 years earlier, was given a free transfer. The team reached the semi-final of the League Cup, only to lose to Third Division Aston Villa. United were looking mediocre and that was not acceptable at Old Trafford with the board or the fans. At Christmas, McGuinness was demoted to trainer of the reserve team matters

Matt Busby stepped in "to take over team matters

**FA Cup**

| Jan 4 | Exeter C (3) | A | W | 3-1 |
|---|---|---|---|---|
| Jan 25 | Watford (4) | H | D | 1-1 |
| Feb 3 | Watford (4R) | A | W | 2-0 |
| Feb 8 | Birmingham C (5) | A | D | 2-2 |
| Feb 24 | Birmingham C (5R) | H | W | 6-2 |
| Mar 1 | Everton (6) | A | L | 0-1 |

**European Cup**

| Sep 18 | Waterford (1) | H | W | 3-1 |
|---|---|---|---|---|
| Oct 2 | Waterford (1) | H | W | 7-1 |
| Nov 13 | Anderlecht (2) | H | W | 3-0 |
| Nov 27 | Anderlecht (2) | A | L | 1-3 |
| Feb 26 | Rapid Vienna (3) | H | W | 3-0 |
| Mar 5 | Rapid Vienna (3) | A | D | 0-0 |
| Apr 23 | AC Milan (SF) | A | L | 0-2 |
| May 15 | AC Milan (SF) | H | W | 1-0 |

# 1969-1970

Following Busby's promotion to general manager, United's reserve trainer Wilf McGuinness was given the title chief coach and the awesome task of looking after the first squad in April 1969. Although he was enthusiastic, it was never going to be easy. The season started with a draw and three defeats in a row. United were an ageing side in need of refreshment. Busby made his presence felt by buying Arsenal's Ian Ure for £80,000 to replace veteran centre-half Bill Foulkes. There were good games, notably a 7-0 victory over West Bromwich at Old Trafford and bad, particularly a 4-0 defeat by Manchester City. The team finished 8th and, despite reaching FA and League Cup semi-finals, were ready for a shake-up. Law and Givens were put up for sale and nine other players given free transfers.

**League (Division 1)**

| Aug 9 | Crystal Palace | A | D | 2-2 |
|---|---|---|---|---|
| Aug 13 | Everton | H | L | 0-2 |
| Aug 16 | Southampton | H | L | 1-4 |
| Aug 19 | Everton | A | L | 0-3 |
| Aug 23 | Wolverhampton W | A | D | 0-0 |
| Aug 27 | Newcastle U | H | D | 0-0 |
| Aug 30 | Sunderland | H | W | 3-1 |
| Sep 6 | Leeds U | A | D | 2-2 |
| Sep 13 | Liverpool | H | H | 1-0 |
| Sep 17 | Sheffield W | A | W | 3-1 |
| Sep 20 | Arsenal | A | D | 2-2 |
| Sep 27 | West Ham U | H | W | 5-2 |
| Oct 4 | Derby C | A | L | 0-2 |
| Oct 8 | Southampton | A | W | 3-0 |
| Oct 11 | Ipswich T | H | W | 2-1 |
| Oct 18 | Nottingham F | H | D | 1-1 |
| Oct 25 | WBA | A | L | 1-2 |

d he ever really given them up?

The whole episode was unsavoury and McGuinness the victim, not the culprit. Many of the players were living on the past glory of the European Cup and found it difficult to relate to a man of their own generation who had achieved no such honour in his own right – on the pitch. There is a cliché in football that things have to get worse before they get better" and it was a period when United had to dig deep to survive. The biggest test came in its handling of an increasingly wayward George Best. The darling of the fans for the past decade was becoming unmanageable, even for Busby. He failed to turn up for training, arriving at games minutes before the start and even not appearing before a disciplinary hearing, leaving Matt Busby to argue his case in London alone. His non-appearance for a game against Chelsea at Stamford Bridge was the final straw for Matt. He told Best to stay away, not realising until the media circus started that his protege was already in the capital – holed up in the London flat of his latest girlfriend Sinead Cusack. The Best saga is detailed elsewhere, but that had become inevitable started. But before the axe could be improved with new blood, a new manager had to be found. United landed the mild-mannered Frank O'Farrell from Leicester in 1971, a manager of credibility but, as it turned out, neither the authority or the charisma to deal with a team laden with superstars advancing in years.

A

t first, it seemed O'Farrell had the Midas touch. The team got off to a flyer, losing only one of their first 14 games, shooting to the top of the First Division. United even weathered the closure of Old Trafford after a knife was thrown on the pitch – these were the days when hooliganism blighted football throughout Britain – having to play their games at other grounds. But O'Farrell's honeymoon period was short. By December the team was sliding down the league following a string of defeats and an ignominious exit from the League Cup at Stoke in fourth round.

Something had to be done and O'Farrell raided the market, bringing in one of United's best-loved sons – Martin Buchan, a quiet, stout defender from Aberdeen. His managerial acumen was sound. A team that needs not so much on the goals it scores as the goals it concedes not to concede (For years Arsenal have operated on the basis that a 1-0 win will always do).

United were leaking badly at the back and Buchan came in to stem the tide, much the same way as Ferguson has brought in Jaap Stam to shore up the central defence after the departure of Bruce and Pallister. Buchan's impact was immediate, United winning eight of the last 12 games with the big man at the back. He would go on to play over 450 games for The Reds. O'Farrell also brought in Ian Storey-Moore from Nottingham Forest, though his impact was marred by injury. United finished eighth in the League. The fans expected more. To add to O'Farrell's problems Best was misbehaving again. He was unreliable, sometimes cavalier in his attitude to the club. He was fined again, dropped from the squad – all in an effort to make the wild man of football calm down. It didn't work and the episode sapped morale at the club. O'Farrell did what he knew best by bringing in another United favourite Sammy McIlroy, then just 17, to cover for crazy George. He was an instant success, scoring freely and in style. For a while, United fans forgot about Best and hailed the new Irish wonder. With United languishing near the bottom of the league, O'Farrell brought in Ted McDougall from lowly Bournemouth to bolster the strike force.

Whatever history decides about Frank O'Farrell's reign at Old Trafford, he stabilised a dangerously fragile team and blooded new players who have become firm favourites with fans of that generation. But his time was drawing to a close. Defeats at Manchester City and a 4-1 mauling by Spurs sealed his fate. He was sacked on December 19, 1972 because of "poor results". It emerged later that Busby had already lined up fellow Scot Tommy "The Doc" Docherty to take over . At the same time George Best was sacked from the club, though he maintained then that he had resigned before the axe fell. The clouds were gathering. Bobby Charlton retired in 1973 after Docherty's arrival with over 60,000 fans turning up for his last game at Old Trafford against Sheffield United. The famous Busby Babes were splintered and Docherty was in charge. But the first year was to be a disaster for the Scot. United slipped lower and lower in the First Division until the final seconds of the season. United were playing for their lives against Manchester City who fielded Denis Law, transferred by Docherty earlier in the year. They needed a win to stay up. With eight minutes to go, a scramble in the goalmouth left Law in the sky blue shirt facing the wrong way but with the ball at his feet. His simple back heel relegated The Reds. It was a moment Law has never been allowed to forget and one that condemned United to the unthinkable. Docherty shed tears as he felt the weight of the fans' disappointment and the memory of European glory was wiped out in an instant. United were officially a second class team.

It was down to The Doc to apply some radical surgery.

## 1970-71

Doubts about Busby's successor Wilf McGuinness grew. When United reached the semi-finals of the League Cup and were beaten by Aston Villa from the Third Division, his days were numbered. Shortly after Christmas he was replaced by Sir Matt and returned to coaching the reserves. The stress suffered by McGuinness must have been immense. When he left the club, soon after being demoted, all his hair fell out. George Best was behaving badly during this period, too, which made matters worse. With Sir Matt back in charge the

### Final League position: 8th

| P | W | L | F/A | Pts |
|---|---|---|-----|-----|
| 42 | 14 | 17 | 66/66 | 45 |

| | | | |
|---|---|---|---|
| Oct 31 | Stoke C | H | D 1-1 |
| Nov 8 | Coventry C | A | W 2-1 |
| Nov 15 | Manchester C | A | L 0-4 |
| Nov 22 | Tottenham H | H | W 3-1 |
| Nov 29 | Burnley | A | D 1-1 |
| Dec 6 | Chelsea | H | L 0-2 |
| Dec 13 | Liverpool | A | W 4-1 |
| Dec 26 | Wolverhampton W | H | D 0-0 |
| Dec 27 | Sunderland | A | D 1-1 |
| Jan 10 | Arsenal | H | W 2-1 |
| Jan 17 | West Ham U | A | D 0-0 |
| Jan 26 | Leeds U | H | D 2-2 |
| Jan 31 | Derby C | H | W 1-0 |
| Feb 10 | Ipswich T | A | W 1-0 |
| Feb 14 | Crystal Palace | H | D 1-1 |
| Feb 28 | Stoke C | A | D 2-2 |
| Mar 17 | Burnley | H | D 3-3 |
| Mar 21 | Chelsea | A | L 1-2 |
| Mar 28 | Manchester C | H | L 1-2 |
| Mar 30 | Coventry C | H | D 1-1 |
| Mar 31 | Nottingham F | A | W 2-2 |
| Apr 4 | Newcastle U | A | L 1-5 |
| Apr 8 | WBA | H | W 7-0 |
| Apr 13 | Tottenham H | A | L 1-2 |
| Apr 15 | Sheffield W | H | D 2-2 |

### League Cup

| | | | |
|---|---|---|---|
| Sep 3 | Middlesbrough (2) | H | W 1-0 |
| Sep 23 | Wrexham (3) | H | W 2-0 |
| Oct 14 | Burnley (4) | A | D 0-0 |
| Oct 20 | Burnley (4R) | H | W 1-0 |
| Nov 12 | Derby C (5) | A | D 0-0 |
| Nov 19 | Derby C (5R) | H | W 1-0 |
| Dec 3 | Manchester C (SF) | A | L 1-2 |
| Dec 17 | Manchester C (SF) | H | D 2-2 |

### FA Cup

| | | | |
|---|---|---|---|
| Jan 3 | Ipswich T (3) | A | W 1-0 |
| Jan 24 | Manchester C (4) | H | W 3-0 |
| Feb 17 | Northampton T (5) | A | W 8-2 |
| Feb 21 | Middlesbrough (6) | A | D 1-1 |
| Feb 25 | Middlesbrough (6R) | H | W 2-1 |
| Mar 14 | Leeds U (SF) | N | D 0-0 (at Hillsborough) |
| Mar 23 | Leeds U (SFR) | N | D 0-0 (at Villa Park) |
| Mar 26 | Leeds U (SFR2) | N | L 0-1 (at Burnden Park) |

It's over to you Frank. Matt Busby says farewell to management for good. He had resumed control after the McGuinness era

players pulled their socks up and finished 8th. After struggling with a knee injury Nobby Stiles left Old Trafford to play for Middlesbrough.

**League (Division 1)**

| | | | | |
|---|---|---|---|---|
| Aug 15 | Leeds U | H | I | 0-1 |
| AU 19 | Chelsea | H | D | 0-0 |
| AU 22 | Arsenal | A | L | 0-4 |
| AU 25 | Burnley | A | W | 2-0 |
| AU 29 | West Ham U | H | D | 1-1 |
| Sep 2 | Everton | H | W | 2-0 |
| Sep 5 | Liverpool | A | D | 1-1 |
| Sep 12 | Coventry C | H | W | 2-0 |
| Sep 19 | Ipswich T | A | L | 0-4 |
| Sep 26 | Blackpool | H | D | 1-1 |
| Sep 3 | Wolverhampton W | A | L | 2-3 |
| Sep 10 | Crystal Palace | H | L | 0-1 |
| Sep 17 | Leeds U | A | D | 2-2 |
| Sep 24 | WBA | H | W | 2-1 |
| Sep 31 | Newcastle U | A | L | 0-1 |
| Nov 7/ | Stoke C | H | D | 2-2 |
| Nov 14 | Nottingham F | A | W | 2-1 |
| Nov 21 | Southampton | A | L | 0-1 |
| Nov 28 | Huddersfield T | H | D | 1-1 |
| Dec 5 | Tottenham H | A | D | 2-2 |
| Dec 12 | Manchester C | H | L | 1-4 |
| Dec 19 | Arsenal | H | L | 1-3 |
| Dec 26 | Derby C | A | D | 4-4 |
| Jan 9 | Chelsea | A | W | 2-1 |
| Jan 16 | Burnley | H | D | 1-1 |
| Jan 30 | Huddersfield T | A | W | 2-1 |
| Feb 6/ | Tottenham H | H | W | 2-1 |
| Feb 20/ | Southampton | H | W | 5-1 |
| Feb 23/ | Everton | A | L | 0-1 |
| Feb 27/ | Newcastle U | H | W | 1-0 |
| Mar 6/ | WBA | A | L | 3-4 |
| Mar 13 | Nottingham F | H | W | 2-0 |
| Mar 20 | Stoke C | A | W | 2-1 |
| Mar 3/ | West Ham U | A | L | 1-2 |
| Mar 10 | Derby C | H | L | 1-2 |
| Apr 12 | Wolverhampton W | H | W | 1-0 |
| Apr 3 | Coventry City | A | L | 1-2 |
| Apr 17 | Crystal Palace | A | W | 5-3 |
| Apr 19 | Liverpool | H | L | 0-2 |
| Apr 24 | Ipswich T | H | W | 3-2 |
| May 1 | Blackpool | A | D | 1-1 |
| May 5 | Manchester City | A | W | 4-3 |

**Final League position: 8th**

| P | W | D | L | F/A | Pts |
|---|---|---|---|---|---|
| 42 | 16 | 11 | 15 | 65/66 | 43 |

**FA Cup**

| | | | | |
|---|---|---|---|---|
| Jan 2 | Middlesbrough (3) | H | D | 0-0 |
| Jan 5 | Middlesbrough (3R) | A | L | 1-2 |

**League Cup**

| | | | | |
|---|---|---|---|---|
| Sep 9 | Aldershot (2) | A | W | 3-1 |
| Oct 7 | Portsmouth (3) | H | W | 1-0 |
| Oct 28 | Chelsea (4) | H | W | 2-1 |
| Nov 18 | Crystal Palace (5) | H | W | 4-2 |
| Dec 16 | Aston Villa (SF) | H | D | 1-1 |
| Dec 23 | Aston Villa (SF) | A | L | 1-2 |

# 1971-1972

Irish railway worker turned soccer manager Frank O'Farrell seemed to be the answer to Sir Matt Busby's prayers. After making his mark at Leicester City he agreed to take over the hot seat from The Godfather and move the club forward. To make sure O'Farrell had

Busby acknowledges the fans at his final game as manager in 1969.

An emotional Busby announces his decision to step down from management.

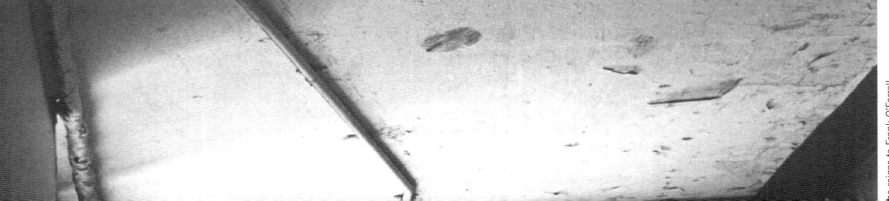

he reigns to Frank O'Farrell.

a free hand. Sir Matt gave up his job as general manager and joined the United board. O'Farrell certainly seemed to work wonders at the start of the season. By Christmas they were five points clear at the top of the First Division. However, the euphoria didn't last. From January 1 they suffered seven defeats in a row. The new manager realised it was time to buy some fresh talent and snapped up Martin Buchan from Aberdeen, plus Nottingham Forest's Ian Storey-Moore in February. O'Farrell had chosen well and the presence of the quality players helped stop the rot. United finished 8th.

## League (Division 1)

| Date | Opponent | Venue | Result | Score |
|---|---|---|---|---|
| Aug 14 | Derby C | A | D | 2-2 |
| Aug 18 | Chelsea | A | W | 3-2 |
| Aug 20 | Arsenal | A | W | 3-1 |
| Aug 23 | WBA | A | W | 3-1 |
| Aug 28 | Wolverhampton W | A | D | 1-1 |
| Aug 31 | Everton | A | L | 0-1 |
| Sep 4 | Ipswich T | H | W | 1-0 |
| Sep 11 | Crystal Palace | A | W | 3-1 |
| Sep 18 | West Ham U | H | W | 4-2 |
| Sep 25 | Liverpool | A | D | 2-2 |
| Oct 2 | Sheffield U | H | W | 2-0 |
| Oct 9 | Huddersfield T | A | W | 3-0 |
| Oct 16 | Derby C | H | W | 1-0 |
| Oct 23 | Newcastle U | A | W | 1-0 |
| Oct 30 | Leeds U | H | L | 0-1 |
| Nov 6 | Manchester C | A | D | 3-3 |
| Nov 13 | Tottenham H | H | W | 3-1 |
| Nov 20 | Leicester C | H | W | 3-2 |
| Nov 27 | Southampton | A | W | 5-2 |
| Dec 4 | Nottingham F | H | W | 3-2 |
| Dec 11 | Stoke C | A | D | 1-1 |
| Dec 18 | Ipswich T | A | D | 0-0 |
| Dec 27 | Coventry C | H | D | 2-2 |
| Jan 1 | West Ham U | A | L | 0-3 |
| Jan 8 | Wolverhampton W | H | L | 1-3 |
| Jan 22 | Chelsea | H | L | 0-1 |
| Jan 29 | WBA | A | L | 1-2 |
| Feb 12 | Newcastle U | H | L | 0-2 |
| Feb 19 | Leeds U | A | L | 1-5 |
| Mar 4 | Tottenham H | A | L | 0-2 |
| Mar 8 | Everton | H | D | 0-0 |
| Mar 11 | Huddersfield T | H | W | 2-0 |
| Mar 25 | Crystal Palace | H | W | 4-0 |
| Apr 1 | Coventry C | A | W | 3-2 |
| Apr 3 | Liverpool | H | L | 0-3 |
| Apr 4 | Sheffield U | A | D | 1-1 |
| Apr 8 | Leicester C | A | L | 0-2 |
| Apr 12 | Manchester C | H | L | 1-3 |
| Apr 15 | Southampton | H | W | 3-2 |
| Apr 22 | Nottingham F | A | D | 0-0 |
| Apr 25 | Arsenal | H | L | 0-3 |
| Apr 29 | Stoke C | H | W | 3-0 |

**Final League position: 8th**

| P | W | D | L | F/A | Pts |
|---|---|---|---|---|---|
| 42 | 19 | 10 | 13 | 69/61 | 48 |

## FA Cup

| Date | Opponent | Venue | Result | Score |
|---|---|---|---|---|
| Jan 15 | Southampton (3) | A | D | 1-1 |
| Jan 19 | Southampton (3R) | H | W | 4-1 |
| Feb 5 | Preston N E (4) | A | W | 2-0 |

Wilf McGuinness took over after Busby, but he was in for a torrid time as Chief Coach – Matt was always in the wings.

Feb 26 Middlesbrough (5) H D 0-0
Feb 29 Middlesbrough (5R) A W 3-0
Mar 18 Stoke C (6) H D 1-1
Mar 22 Stoke C (6R) A L 1-2

**League Cup**

Sep 7 Ipswich T (2) A W 3-1
Oct 6 Burnley (3) H D 1-1
Oct 18 Burnley (3R) A W 1-0
Oct 27 Stoke C (4) H D 1-1
Nov 8 Stoke C (4R) A D 0-0
Nov 15 Stoke C (4R2) A L 1-2

# 1972-1973

This disastrous season doomed manager Frank O'Farrell and opened the door for Tommy Docherty. When United failed to win in their first nine games it was obvious something had to be done. O'Farrell tried to buy his way out of trouble by signing Wyn Davies from Manchester City and Ted MacDougall from Bournemouth. But he was too late to save his job. The end came when United were beaten 5-0 by Crystal Palace in December. Tommy Docherty watched the defeat from the stands and was offered the post by Sir Matt Busby after the final whistle. O'Farrell was given his marching orders, along with bad boy George Best, on December 19. It was the end of an era for Bobby Charlton too. He retired after a record 604 League appearances.

**League (Division 1)**

Aug 12 Ipswich T H L 1-2
Aug 15 Liverpool A L 0-2
Aug 19 Everton A L 0-2
Aug 23 Leicester C H D 1-1
Aug 26 Arsenal H D 0-0
Aug 30 Chelsea H D 0-0
Sep 2 West Ham U A D 2-2
Sep 9 Coventry C H L 0-1
Sep 16 Wolverhampton W A L 0-2
Sep 23 Derby C H W 3-0
Sep 30 Sheffield U A L 0-1
Oct 7 WBA A D 2-2
Oct 14 Birmingham C H L 1-0
Oct 21 Newcastle U A L 1-2
Oct 28 Tottenham H H L 1-4
Nov 4 Leicester C A D 2-2
Nov 11 Liverpool H W 2-0
Nov 18 Manchester City A L 0-3
Nov 25 Southampton H W 2-1
Dec 2 Norwich C A W 2-0
Dec 9 Stoke C H L 0-2
Dec 16 Crystal Palace A L 0-5
Dec 23 Leeds U H D 1-1
Dec 26 Derby C A L 1-3
Jan 6 Arsenal A L 1-3
Jan 20 West Ham U H D 2-2
Jan 24 Everton H D 0-0
Jan 27 Coventry C A D 1-1
Feb 10 Wolverhampton W H W 2-1
Feb 17 Ipswich T A L 1-4

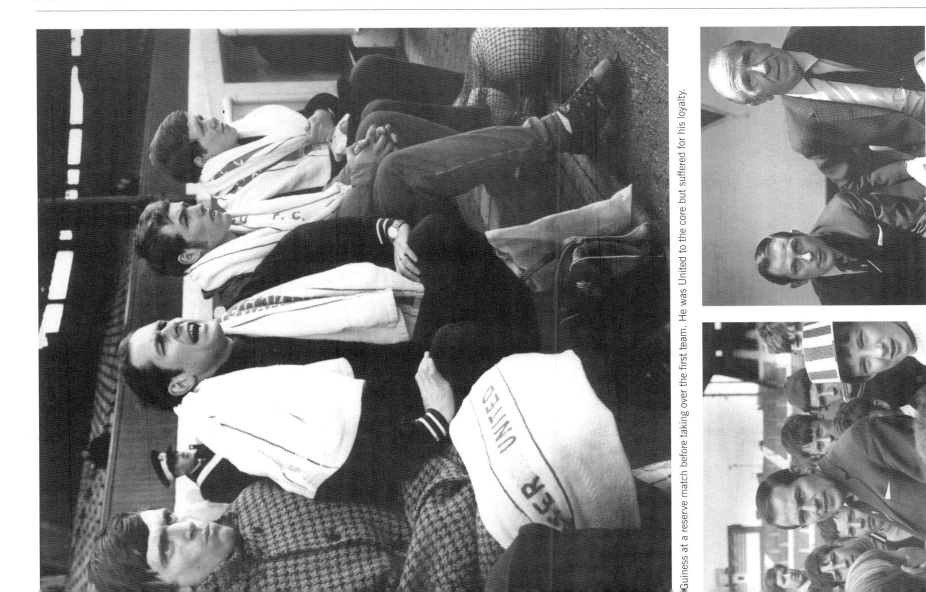

...Guiness at a reserve match before taking over the first team. He was United to the core but suffered for his loyalty.

...me position. McGuinness is the new boss, but the shadow of Busby always loomed large.

Let's get it together. McGuinness had to manage players who had become national heroes after the European Cup success.

## 1973-1974

Tommy Docherty's tartan spending spree had resulted in the arrival at Old Trafford of new players like George Graham from Arsenal and Lou Macari from Glasgow Celtic. The Doc's "wind of change" also blew rebel Best back into the squad and Law out of the club on a controversial free transfer. Despite all the new blood, United was heading for relegation. When they came up against old rivals Manchester City during a key end of season clash, a newly-signed player for the Blues sent The Reds down with a cheeky back-heeled goal. His name? Denis Law. The revenge was bitter sweet. While his team-mates celebrated, he just looked sad.

**Final League position: 18th**

| P | W | D | L | F/A | Pts |
|---|---|---|---|---|---|
| 42 | 12 | 13 | 17 | 44/60 | 37 |

**FA Cup**

| Jan 13 | Wolves (3) | A | L | 0-1 |
|---|---|---|---|---|

**League Cup**

| Sep 6 | Oxford U (3) | A | D | 2-2 |
|---|---|---|---|---|
| Sep 12 | Oxford U (3R) | H | W | 3-1 |
| Oct 3 | Bristol Rovers (4) | A | D | 1-1 |
| Oct 11 | Bristol Rovers (4R) | H | L | 1-2 |

**League (Division 1)**

| Aug 25 | Arsenal | A | L | 0-3 |
|---|---|---|---|---|
| Aug 29 | Stoke C | H | W | 1-0 |
| Sep 1 | QPR | H | W | 2-1 |
| Sep 5 | Leicester C | A | L | 0-1 |
| Sep 8 | Ipswich T | A | L | 1-2 |
| Sep 12 | Leicester C | H | L | 1-2 |
| Sep 15 | West Ham U | H | W | 3-1 |
| Sep 22 | Leeds U | A | D | 0-0 |
| Sep 29 | Liverpool | H | D | 0-0 |
| Oct 6 | Wolverhampton W | A | L | 1-2 |
| Oct 13 | Derby C | H | L | 0-1 |
| Oct 20 | Birmingham C | H | W | 1-0 |
| Oct 27 | Burnley | A | D | 0-0 |
| Nov 3 | Chelsea | H | D | 2-2 |
| Nov 10 | Tottenham H | A | L | 1-2 |
| Nov 17 | Newcastle U | A | L | 2-3 |
| Nov 24 | Norwich C | H | D | 0-0 |
| Dec 8 | Southampton | H | D | 0-0 |
| Dec 15 | Coventry C | H | L | 2-3 |
| Dec 22 | Liverpool | A | L | 0-2 |
| Dec 26 | Sheffield U | H | L | 1-2 |
| Mar 3 | WBA | H | W | 2-1 |
| Mar 10 | Birmingham C | A | L | 1-3 |
| Mar 17 | Newcastle U | H | W | 2-1 |
| Mar 24 | Tottenham H | A | D | 1-1 |
| Mar 31 | Southampton | A | W | 2-0 |
| Apr 7 | Norwich C | H | W | 1-0 |
| Apr 10 | Crystal Palace | H | W | 2-0 |
| Apr 14 | Stoke C | A | D | 2-2 |
| Apr 18 | Leeds U | A | W | 1-0 |
| Apr 21 | Manchester C | H | D | 0-0 |
| Apr 23 | Sheffield U | H | L | 1-2 |
| Apr 28 | Chelsea | A | L | 0-1 |

The new manager keeps an eye on his superstars during one of his first training sessions as boss in 1969.

| | | | | |
|---|---|---|---|---|
| Dec 29 | Ipswich T | H | W | 2-0 |
| Jan 1 | QPR | A | L | 0-3 |
| Jan 12 | West Ham U | A | L | 1-2 |
| Jan 19 | Arsenal | H | D | 1-1 |
| Feb 2 | Coventry C | A | L | 0-1 |
| Feb 9 | Leeds U | H | L | 0-2 |
| Feb 16 | Derby C | A | D | 2-2 |
| Feb 23 | Wolverhampton W | H | D | 0-0 |
| Mar 2 | Sheffield U | A | W | 1-0 |
| Mar 13 | Manchester C | A | D | 0-0 |
| Mar 16 | Birmingham C | A | L | 0-1 |
| Mar 23 | Tottenham H | H | L | 0-1 |
| Mar 30 | Chelsea | A | W | 3-1 |
| Apr 3 | Burnley | H | D | 3-3 |
| Apr 6 | Norwich C | A | W | 2-0 |
| Apr 13 | Newcastle U | H | W | 1-0 |
| Apr 15 | Everton | H | W | 3-0 |
| Apr 20 | Southampton | A | D | 1-1 |
| Apr 23 | Everton | A | L | 0-1 |
| Apr 27 | Manchester C | H | L | 0-1 |
| Apr 29 | Stoke C | A | L | 0-1 |

**Final League position: 21st**

| P | W | D | L | F/A | Pts |
|---|---|---|---|---|---|
| 42 | 10 | 12 | 20 | 38/48 | 32 |

**FA Cup**

| | | | | |
|---|---|---|---|---|
| Jan 5 | Plymouth A (3) | H | W | 1-0 |
| Jan 26 | Ipswich T (4) | H | L | 0-1 |

**League Cup**

| | | | | |
|---|---|---|---|---|
| Oct 8 | Middlesbrough (2) | H | L | 0-1 |

...ed 'keeper Jimmy Rimmer punches clear against Southampton in August 1969. But The Reds went down 4-1 at home.

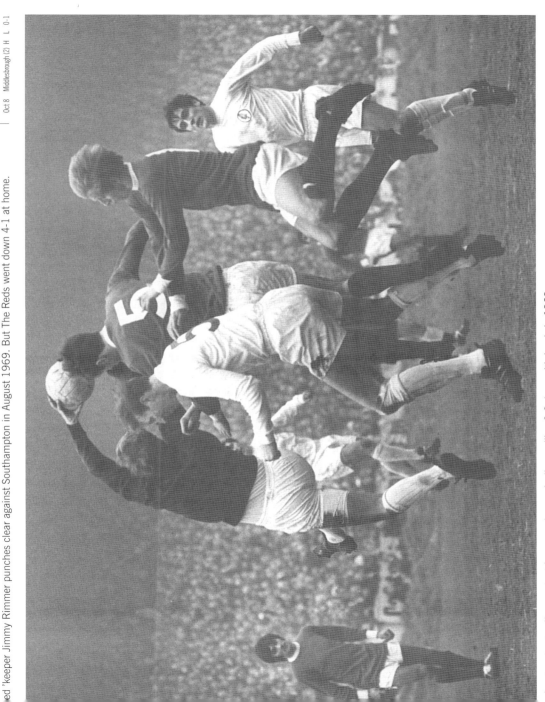

Charlton holds off the United front men in a typically gruelling 2-2 draw with Leeds in 1969.

Suited, booted – now Knighted. Busby outside Buckingham Palace after HM The Queen put the legend under the sword in 1968.

It's Sir to you son. Matt was a press reporter's dream.

The new Knight Of The Realm returns to his kingdom – Manchester.

Trafford's new Crown Prince. Young star Brian Kidd gets an unofficial coronation from a fan in 1970. He was to reign himself with Alex Ferguson one day.

Brian Kidd was a glimmer of hope in an ageing side in 1970. United were suffering but had a good Cup run and Kidd played a big part in the campaign.

United were leaking badly at the back in 1970. Right: United lost the first game of the season 1-0 to Leeds. It was an ominous sign for The Reds.

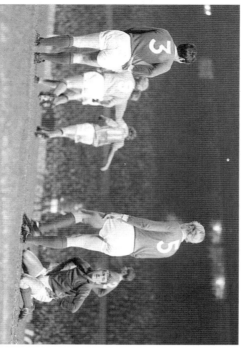

Stepney is down and United are put out of the Cup by City in 1969.

A dejected Brian Kidd after United lost out in the Cup to City in 1969.

Ure was a rugged Scots defender who stabilised United's fragile defence.

Ian Ure was signed in 1969 by McGuinness, costing £80,000 from Arsenal.

Not the most elegant of players, Ian Ure was a crucial stopgap for the side

ults were bad. After one season, he was fighting for his place.

My life in your hands. Matt is a This Is Your Life victim.

Bobby Charlton gets the This Is Your Life treatment in 1969.

"George, is it true you earn more than me?" Best and Prime Minister Wilson.

Best, Charlton
Stepney on the
Middlesbrough

The tension of the 1970 season reached fever pitch when United lost 4-1 to City in December.

Willie Morgan was a player of flair, but even this fan favourite could do little to stop the decline.

Bobby Charlton leads out United against City in 1971. The rivalry between the two clubs was intense as The Reds started to falter.

Busby gives Wilf McGuinness a few handy hints as General Manager. He was still the boss.

He stepped down, but Busby was always in the club spotlight. With United directors in 1971.

The O'Farrell's made every effort to fit in when

...uge task of guiding United back to success. Mrs O'Farrell at the club in 1971 with Law and Crerand and their sons.

Busby vacates his office on the arrival of Frank O'Farrell in 1971.

The new manager gets a welcome handshake from Busby on taking over.

Over to you Frank. O'Farrell knew the size of the job, but he could never a

cy of results to keep The Godfather of Old Trafford happy.

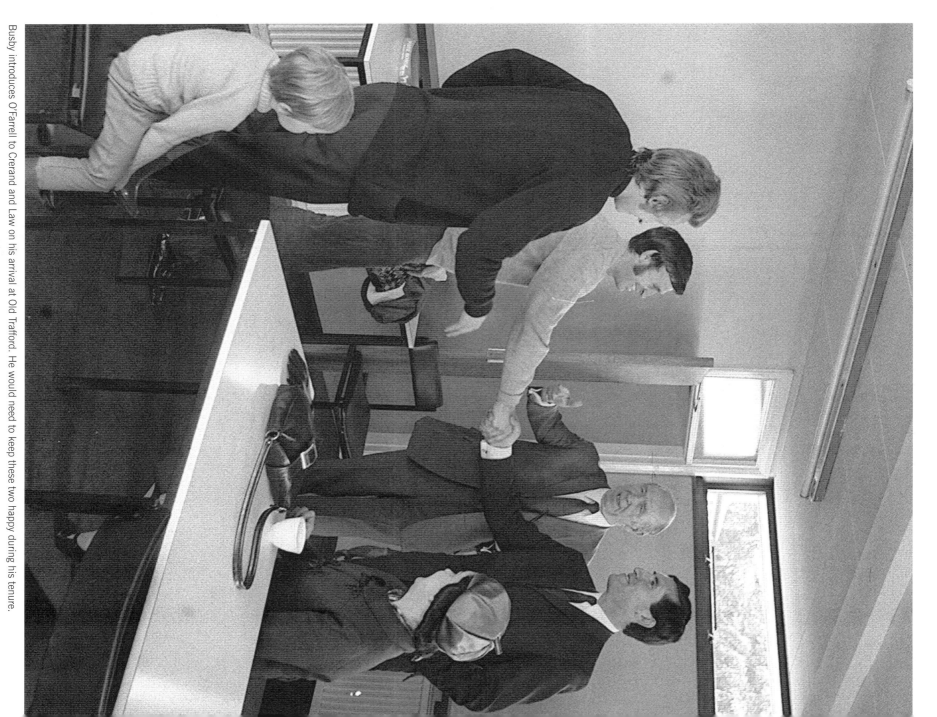

Busby introduces O'Farrell to Crerand and Law on his arrival at Old Trafford. He would need to keep these two happy during his tenure.

...arrell moved the elegant winger Willie Morgan to a midfield role – and it transformed his game in 1971.

Defender Tony Dunne, the Denis Irwin of the 1971 team.

...972 David Sadler was an old hand at United but invaluable to O'Farrell.

Martin Buchan was one
O'Farrell's best signings
1972 from Aberdeen.

elegant player, Buchan was a loyal servant for O'Farrell.

Best was to prove a sticky problem for the mild-mannered O'Farrell.

manager signs Ted McDougall from Bournemouth. He wanted the prolific striker to help United survive a League plunge. The player couldn't and left.

It was a case of Saturday Afternoon Fever when Sammy McIlroy arrived in 1971 aged 17

All sorted after a chat – but he's booked by Fr...

...as George avoids the gaze of his manager.

Stepney shields wayward Best from the boss...

...and McIlroy was the man to do it.

United hit back at Spurs in 1971...

All smiles on the training pitch with Law the joker this time.

Kidd gives Moore a hug after a goal. He scored in each of his first three games.

Storey-Moore came into the squad in 1972 to boost the strike force.

...re soars to score against Huddersfield in a 2-0 home win in February 1972. It kept United fans happy for a week.

Stepney is in despair as West Ham's Robson sinks United in 1972.

It was a dark period on and off the pitch as trouble erupted among the fans.

Police clear up the missiles.

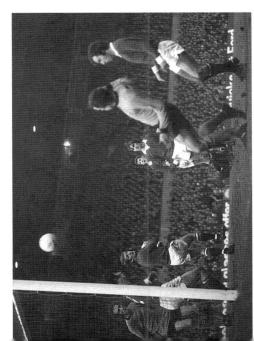

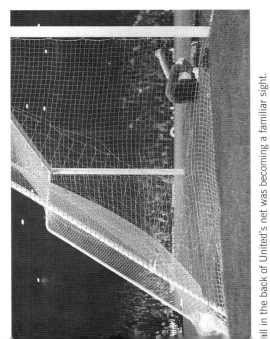

...chester City's Francis Lee piles on the agony for United in the 1972 season.

Leeds also made United pay.

then Wolves taunted the frail United defence.

A dejected Charlton after United are thrashed 5-1 by Leeds in 1972.

...all in the back of United's net was becoming a familiar sight.

Time's running out Frank. O'Farrell with Busby and Chairman Louis Edwards before the manager was chopped.

O'Farrell is besieged by the press as news breaks of his dismissal.

Tommy "The Doc" Docherty arrived in O'Farrell's wake and set about clearing out the ageing stars. But Bobby Charlton had his own retirement plans.

# 1974-1975

With newly-signed Stuart Pearson on board, United faced up to life in the Second Division for the first time since 1938. Although the team went down, crowd figures shot up as fans flocked to see Tommy Docherty bring the ailing club back to life. His new-look side didn't disappoint. They started the season with four wins in a row, including a 4-0 defeat of Millwall. There was more excitement too when Steve Coppell joined United from Tranmere Rovers in March. It was a great season for The Doc, who proudly watched his post-Busby squad bounce right back into the First Division.

## League (Division 2)

| Date | Opponent | H/A | Result | Score |
|---|---|---|---|---|
| Aug 17 | Leyton Orient | A | W | 2-0 |
| Aug 24 | Millwall | H | W | 4-0 |
| Aug 28 | Portsmouth | H | W | 2-1 |
| Aug 31 | Cardiff City | A | W | 1-0 |
| Sep 7 | Nottingham F | H | D | 2-2 |
| Sep 14 | WBA | A | D | 1-1 |
| Sep 16 | Millwall | A | W | 1-0 |
| Sep 21 | Bristol R | H | W | 2-0 |
| Sep 25 | Bolton W | H | W | 3-0 |
| Sep 28 | Norwich C | A | L | 0-2 |
| Oct 5 | Fulham | A | W | 2-1 |
| Oct 12 | Notts C | H | W | 1-0 |
| Oct 15 | Portsmouth | A | D | 0-0 |
| Oct 19 | Blackpool | A | W | 3-0 |
| Oct 26 | Southampton | H | W | 1-0 |
| Nov 2 | Oxford U | H | W | 4-0 |
| Nov 9 | Bristol C | A | L | 0-1 |
| Nov 16 | Aston Villa | H | W | 2-1 |
| Nov 23 | Hull C | H | W | 2-0 |
| Nov 30 | Sunderland | H | W | 3-2 |
| Dec 7 | Sheffield W | A | D | 4-4 |
| Dec 14 | Leyton Orient | H | D | 0-0 |
| Dec 21 | York C | A | W | 1-0 |
| Dec 26 | WBA | H | W | 2-1 |
| Dec 28 | Oldham A | A | L | 0-1 |
| Jan 11 | Sheffield W | H | W | 2-0 |
| Jan 18 | Sunderland | A | D | 0-0 |
| Feb 1 | Bristol C | H | L | 0-1 |
| Feb 8 | Oxford U | A | D | 0-0 |
| Feb 15 | Hull C | A | W | 2-0 |
| Feb 22 | Aston Villa | A | L | 0-2 |
| Mar 1 | Cardiff C | H | W | 4-0 |
| Mar 8 | Bolton W | A | W | 1-0 |
| Mar 15 | Norwich C | H | D | 1-1 |
| Mar 22 | Nottingham F | A | D | 0-1 |
| Mar 28 | Bristol R | A | L | 0-1 |
| Mar 29 | York C | H | W | 2-1 |
| Mar 31 | Oldham A | H | W | 3-2 |
| Apr 5 | Southampton | A | W | 1-0 |
| Apr 12 | Fulham | H | W | 1-0 |
| Apr 19 | Notts C | A | D | 2-2 |
| Apr 26 | Blackpool | H | W | 4-0 |

**Final League position: 1st**

| P | W | D | L | F/A | Pts |
|---|---|---|---|---|---|
| 42 | 26 | 9 | 7 | 66/30 | 61 |

## FA Cup

| Date | Opponent | H/A | Result | Score |
|---|---|---|---|---|
| Jan 4 | Walsall (3) | H | D | 0-0 |
| Jan 7 | Walsall (3R) | A | L | 2-3 |

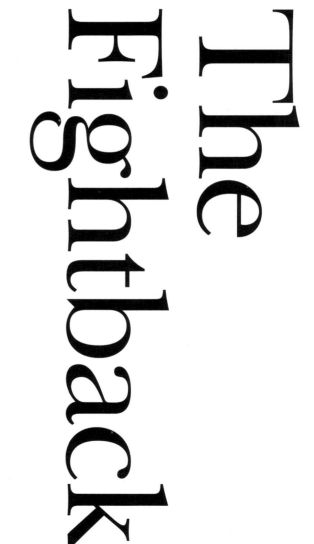

# The Fightback

To this day, Tommy Docherty is remembered with some affection in Manchester. Though he bears the unenviable reputation of the boss who presided over United's dreadful relegation after the Manchester City game in 1974, to many fans he was the man who eventually put the team back on the rails. Though the players he axed ruthlessly may tell a different story about the way they were levered out of the Old Trafford, he brought trophy success the fans craved and restored the dignity of a club that had achieved so much but was now floundering. But more important, it was Docherty who broke the managerial stranglehold of Matt Busby. The Doc was his own man, a tough Scot who had managed the national side and the set about restructuring the team with a certain relish when he arrived at Christmas, 1972. He knew what needed to be done. The team required a transfusion of fresh talent. Bobby Charlton inadvertently gave him a helping hand by announcing his retirement from the game, Denis Law was sold to Manchester City – a move which would come back to haunt The Doc – and Best, struggling with a heavy drink problem, had been dismissed by the club. As the new manager said at the time: "There are players here who are not up to Manchester United's standards". The message was clear and Docherty, with the full backing of chairman Louis Edwards, started to spend. The love affair between Scotland and Manchester United – a crucial element in the club's history even to this day – began in earnest.

His first move was to raid Arsenal's double-winning side, bringing George Graham north for £120,000 to bolster the midfield. An elegant player, he was dubbed "Stroller" by the vocal Stretford End clan because of his calm approach to the game. He was followed by a tough full-back – Alex Forsyth from Partick Thistle, Big Jim Holton, and then one of Docherty's best signings, Lou Macari, joined for a record fee of £200,000. A real

footballing dynamo, he would go on to become a f[…] favourite with the United followers. But despite the purchasing power, the team were still not challeng[…] for honours, finishing 18th. Docherty was not dishe[…]ened. Young bloods like Brian Greenhof and Ge[…] Daly were coming through the ranks and the mana[…] was still looking for talent. In came Stewart Hous[…] from Brentford, a solid if unromantic player. But th[…] The Doc stunned Manchester by announcing his la[…] acquisition – George Best was back from Spain a[…] eager to play for United again. His first appearan[…] in October 1973 against Stoke was greeted with rapt[…] by the fans who would forgive anything just to ha[…] "Georgie" back in the fold. Not exactly back to the fo[…] of his previous days, Best provided an interlude mu[…] enjoyed at Old Trafford which served to disguise [...] fear of relegation now staring United in the face. [...] inevitable came against Manchester City when Unit[…] now in dire need of the win, were thrown into Divis[…] Two by a Denis Law back heel. It was one of the grea[…] ironies in football history. The fans were crushed a[…] The Doc was at his lowest ebb.

As always in United's history, advers[ity] brings out the best in the team and [...] following season saw The Reds storm ba[ck] to winning ways. Crowds increased a[s] yet more new faces arrived. Stuart Pears[on] was bought from Hull City, Steve Coppell came in fr[om] Tranmere Rovers and Millwall winger Gordon H[ill] completed a formidable line-up the Second Divis[ion] teams found almost invincible. The Doc's youth po[licy] was paying off as well, with Jimmy Nicholl and Art[hur] Albiston forcing their way into the team. United w[ere] back in the top flight and Docherty's promise of hono[ur] started to ring true. The team was now flying in [the] FA Cup, meeting Southampton in the final of 19[76] The Reds lost to the Second Division side 1-0 but [...]

League Cup

Sep 11 Charlton A (2) H W 5-1
Oct 9 Manchester C (3)H W 1-0
Nov 13 Burnley (4) H W 3-2
Dec 4 Middlesbrough (5)A D 0-0
Dec 18 Middlesbrough (5R)H W 3-0
Jan 15 Norwich C H D 2-2
Jan 22 Norwich C A L 0-1

# 1975-1976

Tommy Docherty's revival was in full swing. United were back In the First Division and determined to stay there. They lost only nine games during the season and finished third. In one period between the end of November and middle of March they went 11 matches without a defeat. They had a great FA Cup run too, only losing in the final to Southampton. More names were added to the United team sheet, Tommy Jackson from Everton and Millwall's Gordon Hill. Youngsters like Jimmy Nicholl, Arthur Albiston and David McCreery were also starting to show first team promise.

League (Division 1)

Aug 16 Wolverhampton W A W 2-0
Aug 19 Birmingham C A W 2-0
Aug 23 Sheffield U H D 1-1
Aug 27 Coventry C H D 1-1
Aug 30 Stoke City A W 1-0
Sep 6 Tottenham H H W 3-2
Sep 13 QPR A L 0-1
Sep 20 Ipswich T H W 1-0
Sep 24 Derby C A L 1-2
Sep 27 Manchester C A D 2-2
Oct 4 Leicester C H D 0-0
Oct 11 Leeds U A W 2-1
Oct 18 Arsenal H W 3-1
Oct 25 West Ham U A L 1-2
Nov 1 Norwich C H W 1-0
Nov 8 Liverpool A L 1-3
Nov 15 Aston Villa H W 2-0
Nov 22 Arsenal A L 1-3
Nov 29 Newcastle U H W 1-0
Dec 6 Middlesbrough A D 0-0
Dec 13 Sheffield U A W 4-1
Dec 20 Wolverhampton W H W 2-1
Dec 23 Everton A D 1-1
Dec 27 Burnley H W 2-1
Jan 10 QPR H W 2-1
Jan 17 Tottenham H A D 1-1
Jan 31 Birmingham C H W 3-1
Feb 7 Coventry C A D 1-1
Feb 18 Liverpool H D 0-0
Feb 21 Aston Villa A L 1-2

Great Scots. Busby had Docherty in mind as O'Farrell's reign came to an end

ds were there and Docherty promised that United ld be back next year. He was right and United s loved him for that unswerving confidence and lty to the club. After winning revenge for the 76 Final defeat at Southampton and overcoming eds in the semi-final, United faced the mighty erpool at Wembley. The Merseyside team were a ssive side, League Champions and European Cup alists and had beaten United in the League 1-0. als from Pearson and the now famous deflection Macari's shot off Greenhoff's chest gave the nchester side a much-deserved 2-1 win. It was a eet victory. The rivalry between Manchester and erpool, just 30 miles from each other along the East ncashire Road, has always been intense and for ited fans this was a moment to savour. It was also cherty's finest hour. He had kept his promise. He ld do no wrong where the fans were concerned.

But as the team celebrated its first major trophy in rs, a time-bomb was ticking and Docherty knew he uld have to face the music soon. He had been nducting a secret affair with Mary Brown, the wife United's physio Laurie Brown. Nobody at the club ew of the matter, but it had become so serious that cherty was now ready to leave his wife for his new e. When the news broke, the fans and staff at the b were stunned. Docherty was called to a meeting h Louis Edwards and the directors and was sacked er he refused to resign. It was a difficult time for the b, fresh from the FA Cup victory and looking forward even greater success. His legacy was a strong team ich had a mix of youth and experience which put ited on a par with the best at the time. To this day The oc talks lovingly of the club he helped over the hurdle mediocrity. To him, United is still the best club in the ld.

With the departure of Docherty, United moved ickly to fill the void and brought in a surprise choice,

Dave Sexton from Queen's Park Rangers. He was the total opposite of the ebullient Docherty, a quiet, shy man but with a football brain nevertheless. His task was to continue the success The Doc had started, but to do it with the style United fans expected. He launched his own buying spree in 1978, signing the formidable Joe Jordan from Leeds – not the first time United would rob the Yorkshire club of a great striker – and then hit Leeds again to take defender Gordon McQueen. Gary Bailey made his debut in goal, going on to become a regular. Though challenging for title honours all the time, United's love affair with the FA Cup continued as they faced Arsenal at Wembley in 1979. In a game which will forever live in the memories of fans, United drew level at 2-2 with minutes to go, only for the Gunners to hit back immediately in the 90th. It was a heartbreaking moment. Had it gone to extra time United were confident of success but that last-gasp effort from the Londoners was a killer blow. It ended 3-2. In the aftermath of the defeat Sexton, conscious of the fact he would need new players, brought in one of the greats, Ray Butch Wilkins from Chelsea. Docherty signings such as McCreery and Brian Greenhof were sold, Gary Birtles was brought in up front for £1,250,000 but the striker never fulfilled his promise at a club with the highest expectations in British football. It was a strong squad but something was missing: the magic had gone out of United's game under Sexton and a mid-table position year on year was not good enough. In April 1980, after United had achieved seven wins on the trot, Sexton was sacked. Players have since said that they found Sexton boring and were unsure about what he wanted from them.

The next manager to take over the mantle at Old Trafford would leave them in no doubt. Goldfinger himself arrived in June 1981 in the larger-than-life form of Ron Atkinson.

# 1976-1977

A sweet season for United with a sour end for Tommy Docherty. While the team showed erratic form in the League they forged ahead in the FA Cup. The Doc tried to steady his side by buying Brian Greenhoff's big brother Jimmy from Stoke City. It worked and they finished 8th. The road to Wembley was hard. United narrowly defeated Southampton, then knocked out Aston Villa and Leeds before beating mighty Liverpool 2-1 in the final. It should have been The Doc's finest season, but he was sacked over his love for the club physiotherapist's wife Mary Brown and replaced by the more subdued Dave Sexton.

**Final League position: 3rd**

| P | W | D | L | F/A | Pts |
|---|---|---|---|-----|-----|
| 42 | 23 | 10 | 9 | 68/42 | 56 |

## FA Cup

| | | | | | |
|---|---|---|---|---|---|
| Jan 3 | Oxford U (3) | H | W | 2-1 |
| Jan 24 | Peterborough (4) | H | W | 3-1 |
| Feb 14 | Leicester C (5) | A | W | 2-1 |
| Mar 6 | Wolves (6) | H | D | 1-1 |
| Mar 9 | Wolves (6R) | A | W | 3-2 |
| Apr 3 | Derby C (SF) | N | W | 2-0 |
| | (at Hillsborough) | | | |
| May 1 | Southampton (F) | N | L | 0-1 |
| | (at Wembley) | | | |

## League Cup

| | | | | |
|---|---|---|---|---|
| Sep 10 | Brentford (2) | H | W | 2-1 |
| Oct 8 | Aston Villa (3) | A | W | 2-1 |
| Nov 12 | Manchester C (4) | A | L | 0-4 |

## League (Division 1)

| | | | | |
|---|---|---|---|---|
| Aug 21 | Birmingham C | H | D | 2-2 |
| Aug 24 | Coventry C | A | W | 2-0 |
| Aug 28 | Derby C | H | D | 0-0 |
| Sep 4 | Tottenham H | H | L | 2-3 |
| Sep 11 | Newcastle U | A | D | 2-2 |
| Sep 18 | Middlesbrough | H | W | 2-0 |
| Sep 25 | Manchester C | A | W | 3-1 |
| Oct 2 | Leeds U | A | W | 2-0 |
| Oct 16 | WBA | H | L | 0-4 |
| Oct 23 | Norwich C | H | D | 2-2 |
| Oct 30 | Ipswich T | A | L | 0-1 |
| Nov 6 | Aston Villa | A | L | 2-3 |
| Nov 10 | Sunderland | H | D | 3-3 |
| Nov 20 | Leicester C | A | L | 0-1 |
| Nov 27 | West Ham U | H | L | 0-2 |
| Feb 25 | Derby C | H | D | 1-1 |
| Feb 28 | West Ham U | H | W | 4-0 |
| Mar 13 | Leeds U | H | W | 3-2 |
| Mar 17 | Norwich C | A | D | 1-1 |
| Mar 20 | Newcastle U | A | W | 4-3 |
| Mar 27 | Middlesbrough | H | W | 3-0 |
| Apr 10 | Ipswich T | A | L | 0-3 |
| Apr 17 | Everton | H | W | 2-1 |
| Apr 19 | Burnley | A | W | 1-0 |
| Apr 21 | Stoke C | H | L | 0-1 |
| Apr 24 | Leicester C | A | L | 1-2 |
| May 4 | Manchester C | H | W | 2-0 |

| | | | | |
|---|---|---|---|---|
| Dec 18 | Arsenal | A | L | 1-3 |
| Dec 27 | Everton | H | W | 4-0 |
| Jan 1 | Aston Villa | A | L | 1-2 |
| Jan 3 | Ipswich T | H | W | 2-0 |
| Jan 15 | Coventry C | H | W | 2-1 |
| Jan 19 | Bristol C | H | W | 2-1 |
| Jan 22 | Birmingham C | A | W | 3-2 |
| Feb 5 | Derby C | H | W | 3-1 |
| Feb 12 | Tottenham H | A | W | 3-1 |
| Feb 16 | Liverpool | H | D | 0-0 |
| Feb 19 | Newcastle U | H | W | 3-1 |
| Mar 5 | Manchester C | H | W | 3-1 |
| Mar 12 | Leeds U | H | W | 1-0 |
| Mar 23 | WBA | H | D | 2-2 |
| Apr 2 | Norwich C | A | L | 1-2 |
| Apr 5 | Everton | A | W | 2-1 |
| Apr 9 | Stoke C | H | W | 3-0 |
| Apr 11 | Sunderland | A | L | 1-2 |
| Apr 16 | Leicester C | H | D | 1-1 |
| Apr 19 | QPR | A | L | 0-4 |
| Apr 26 | Middlesbrough | A | L | 0-3 |
| Apr 30 | QPR | H | W | 1-0 |
| May 3 | Liverpool | A | D | 0-1 |
| May 7 | Bristol C | A | D | 3-3 |
| May 11 | Stoke C | A | D | 3-3 |
| May 14 | Arsenal | H | W | 3-2 |
| May 16 | West Ham U | A | L | 2-4 |

**Final League position: 6th**

| P | W | D | L | F/A | Pts |
|---|---|---|---|-----|-----|
| 42 | 18 | 11 | 13 | 71/62 | 47 |

**FA Cup**

| | | | | |
|---|---|---|---|---|
| Jan 8 | Walsall (3) | H | W | 1-0 |
| Jan 29 | QPR (4) | H | W | 1-0 |
| Feb 26 | Southampton (5) | A | D | 2-2 |
| Mar 8 | Southampton (5R) | H | W | 2-1 |
| Mar 19 | Aston Villa (6) | H | W | 2-1 |
| Apr 23 | Leeds U (SF) | N | W | 2-1 |
| | (at Hillsborough) | | | |
| May 21 | Liverpool (F) | N | W | 2-1 |
| | (at Wembley) | | | |

**League Cup**

| | | | | |
|---|---|---|---|---|
| Sep 1 | Tranmere R (2) | H | W | 5-0 |
| Sep 22 | Sunderland (3) | H | D | 2-2 |
| Oct 4 | Sunderland (3) | A | D | 2-2 |
| Oct 6 | Sunderland (3R2) | H | W | 1-0 |
| Oct 27 | Newcastle U (4) | H | W | 7-2 |
| Dec 1 | Everton (5) | H | L | 0-3 |

**UEFA Cup**

| | | | | |
|---|---|---|---|---|
| Sep 15 | Ajax (1) | A | L | 0-1 |
| Sep 29 | Ajax (1) | H | W | 2-0 |
| Oct 20 | Juventus (2) | H | W | 1- |
| Nov 3 | Juventus (2) | A | L | 0-3 |

# 1977-1978

**League (Division 1)**

| | | | | |
|---|---|---|---|---|
| Aug 20 | Birmingham C | A | W | 4-1 |
| Aug 24 | Coventry C | H | W | 2-1 |
| Aug 27 | Ipswich T | H | D | 0-0 |
| Sep 3 | Derby C | A | W | 1-0 |
| Sep 10 | Manchester C | A | L | 1-3 |
| Sep 17 | Chelsea | H | L | 0-1 |
| Sep 24 | Leeds U | H | D | 1-1 |
| Oct 1 | Liverpool | H | W | 2-0 |
| Oct 8 | Middlesbrough | A | L | 1-2 |
| Oct 15 | Newcastle U | H | W | 3-2 |
| Oct 22 | WBA | A | L | 0-4 |
| Oct 29 | Aston Villa | H | L | 1-2 |
| Nov 5 | Arsenal | H | L | 1-2 |
| Nov 12 | Nottingham F | A | L | 1-2 |
| Nov 19 | Norwich City | H | W | 1-0 |
| Nov 26 | QPR | A | D | 2-2 |
| Dec 3 | Wolverhampton WH | H | W | 3-1 |
| Dec 10 | West Ham U | A | L | 1-2 |

Docherty was a steely manager, but he also liked the social life.

## 1978-1979

This was Dave Sexton's first season in charge. He had taken over from popular Tommy Docherty and needed to win the support of players and fans. It wasn't easy. He bought two players from Leeds, Joe Jordan and Gordon McQueen. Sexton also sold Gordon Hill to Tommy Docherty, who had taken over as manager at Derby County. A winning four match spurt at the end of the season helped the squad salvage some pride and 10th position. There was no joy in the FA Cup and crowd trouble at St Etienne marred their European Cup-Winners Cup campaign.

**Final League position: 10th**

| P | W | D | L | F/A | Pts |
|---|---|---|---|-----|-----|
| 42 | 16 | 10 | 16 | 67/63 | 42 |

### FA Cup
| | | | | |
|---|---|---|---|---|
| Jan 7 | Carlisle U (3) | A | D | 1-1 |
| Jan 11 | Carlisle U (3R) | H | W | 4-2 |
| Jan 28 | WBA (4) | H | D | 1-1 |
| Feb 1 | WBA (4R) | A | L | 2-3 |

### League Cup
| | | | | |
|---|---|---|---|---|
| Aug 30 | Arsenal (2) | A | L | 2-3 |

### European Cup Winners' Cup
| | | | | |
|---|---|---|---|---|
| Sep 14 | St Etienne (1) | A | D | 1-1 |
| Oct 5 | St Etienne (1) | H | W | 2-0 |
| Oct 19 | Porto (2) | A | L | 0-4 |
| Nov 2 | Porto (2) | H | W | 5-2 |

### League (Division 1)
| | | | | |
|---|---|---|---|---|
| Aug 19 | Birmingham C | H | W | 1-0 |
| Aug 23 | Leeds U | A | W | 3-2 |
| Aug 26 | Ipswich T | A | L | 0-3 |
| Sep 2 | Everton | H | D | 1-1 |
| Sep 9 | QPR | A | D | 1-1 |
| Dec 17 | Nottingham F | H | L | 0-4 |
| Dec 26 | Everton | A | W | 6-2 |
| Dec 27 | Leicester C | H | W | 3-1 |
| Dec 31 | Coventry C | A | L | 0-3 |
| Jan 2 | Birmingham C | H | L | 1-2 |
| Jan 14 | Ipswich T | A | W | 2-1 |
| Jan 21 | Derby C | H | W | 4-0 |
| Feb 8 | Bristol C | H | D | 1-1 |
| Feb 11 | Chelsea | A | D | 2-2 |
| Feb 25 | Liverpool | A | L | 1-3 |
| Mar 1 | Leeds U | H | L | 0-1 |
| Mar 4 | Middlesbrough | H | D | 0-0 |
| Mar 11 | Newcastle U | A | D | 2-2 |
| Mar 15 | Manchester C | H | D | 2-2 |
| Mar 18 | WBA | H | D | 1-1 |
| Mar 25 | Leicester C | A | W | 3-2 |
| Mar 27 | Everton | H | L | 1-2 |
| Mar 29 | Aston Villa | A | L | 1-3 |
| Apr 1 | Arsenal | H | D | 1-1 |
| Apr 8 | QPR | H | W | 3-1 |
| Apr 15 | Norwich C | A | W | 3-1 |
| Apr 22 | West Ham U | H | W | 3-0 |
| Apr 25 | Bristol City | A | W | 1-0 |
| Apr 29 | Wolverhampton W | A | L | 1-2 |

George "Stroller" Graham: tough but so relaxed.

Key line-up. George Graham, Willie Morgan and Alex Forsyth were the Scottish heart of Docherty's team.

Black-eyed boy. Willie Morgan in hospital in 1974 with an eye injury.

| | | | | |
|---|---|---|---|---|
| Sep 16 | Nottingham F | H | D | 1-1 |
| Sep 23 | Arsenal | A | D | 1-1 |
| Sep 30 | Manchester C | H | W | 1-0 |
| Oct 7 | Middlesbrough | H | W | 3-2 |
| Oct 14 | Aston Villa | A | D | 2-2 |
| Oct 21 | Bristol City | H | L | 1-3 |
| Oct 28 | Wolverhampton W | A | W | 4-2 |
| Nov 4 | Southampton | H | D | 1-1 |
| Nov 11 | Birmingham C | A | L | 1-5 |
| Nov 18 | Ipswich T | H | W | 2-0 |
| Nov 21 | Everton | A | L | 0-3 |
| Nov 25 | Chelsea | A | W | 3-1 |
| Dec 9 | Derby C | H | W | 2-0 |
| Dec 16 | Tottenham H | H | W | 2-0 |
| Dec 22 | Bolton W | A | L | 0-3 |
| Dec 26 | Liverpool | H | L | 0-3 |
| Dec 30 | WBA | H | L | 3-5 |
| Feb 3 | Arsenal | H | L | 0-2 |
| Feb 10 | Manchester C | A | W | 3-0 |
| Feb 24 | Aston Villa | H | D | 1-1 |
| Feb 28 | QPR | H | W | 2-0 |
| Mar 3 | Bristol C | A | W | 2-1 |
| Mar 20 | Coventry C | A | L | 3-4 |
| Mar 24 | Leeds U | H | W | 4-1 |
| Mar 27 | Middlesbrough | A | D | 2-2 |
| Apr 7 | Norwich C | A | D | 2-2 |
| Apr 11 | Bolton W | H | L | 1-2 |
| Apr 14 | Liverpool | A | L | 0-2 |
| Apr 16 | Coventry C | H | D | 0-0 |
| Apr 18 | Nottingham F | A | D | 1-1 |
| Apr 21 | Tottenham H | H | W | 1-0 |
| Apr 25 | Norwich C | H | W1=0 | |
| Apr 28 | Derby C | H | D | 0-0 |
| Apr 30 | Southampton | A | D | 1-1 |
| May 5 | WBA | A | L | 0-1 |
| May 7 | Wolverhampton W | H | W | 3-2 |
| May 16 | Chelsea | H | D | 1-1 |

**Final League position: 9th**

| P | W | D | L | F/A | Pts |
|---|---|---|---|---|---|
| 42 | 15 | 15 | 12 | 60/63 | 45 |

**FA Cup**

| | | | | |
|---|---|---|---|---|
| Jan 15 | Chelsea (3) | H | W | 3-0 |
| Jan 31 | Fulham (4) | A | D | 1-1 |
| Feb 12 | Fulham (4R) | H | W | 1-0 |
| Feb 20 | Colchester U (5) | A | W | 1-0 |
| Mar 10 | Tottenham H (6) | A | D | 1-1 |
| Mar 14 | Tottenham H (6R) | H | W | 2-0 |
| Mar 31 | Liverpool (SF) (at Maine Road) | N | D | 2-2 |
| Apr 4 | Liverpool (SFR) (at Goodison Park) | N | W | 1-0 |
| May 12 | Arsenal (F) (at Wembley) | N | L | 2-3 |

**League Cup**

| | | | | |
|---|---|---|---|---|
| Aug 30 | Stockport C (2) | H | W | 3-2 |
| Oct 4 | Watford (3) | H | L | 1-2 |

# 1979-1980

**League (Division 1)**

| | | | | |
|---|---|---|---|---|
| Aug 18 | Southampton | A | D | 1-1 |
| Aug 22 | WBA | H | W | 2-0 |
| Aug 25 | Arsenal | A | D | 0-0 |
| Sep 1 | Middlesbrough | H | W | 2-1 |
| Sep 8 | Aston Villa | A | W | 3-0 |
| Sep 15 | Derby C | H | W | 1-0 |
| Sep 22 | Wolverhampton W | A | L | 1-3 |
| Sep 29 | Stoke C | H | W | 4-0 |
| Oct 6 | Brighton & HA | H | W | 2-0 |
| Oct 10 | WBA | A | L | 0-2 |
| Oct 13 | Bristol C | A | D | 1-1 |
| Oct 20 | Ipswich T | H | W | 1-0 |
| Oct 27 | Everton | A | D | 0-0 |
| Nov 3 | Southampton | H | W | 1-0 |
| Nov 10 | Manchester C | A | L | 0-2 |

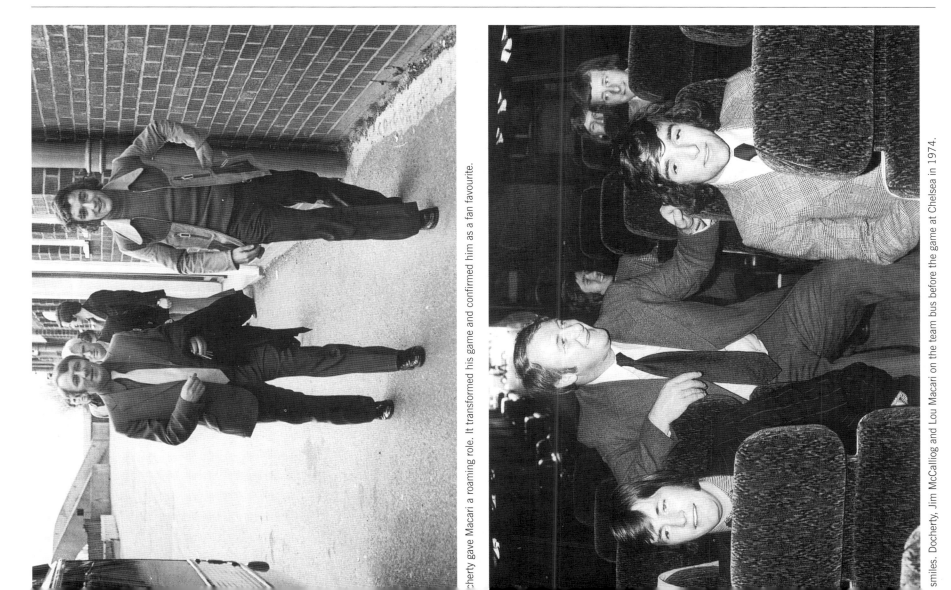

cherty gave Macari a roaming role. It transformed his game and confirmed him as a fan favourite.

smiles. Docherty, Jim McCalliog and Lou Macari on the team bus before the game at Chelsea in 1974.

| Nov 17 | Crystal Palace | H | D | 1-1 |
| Nov 24 | Norwich C | H | W | 5-0 |
| Dec 1 | Tottenham H | A | W | 2-1 |
| Dec 8 | Leeds U | H | D | 1-1 |
| Dec 15 | Coventry C | A | W | 2-1 |
| Dec 22 | Nottingham F | H | W | 3-0 |
| Dec 26 | Liverpool | A | L | 0-2 |
| Dec 29 | Arsenal | H | W | 3-0 |
| Jan 12 | Middlesbrough | A | D | 1-1 |
| Feb 2 | Derby C | A | W | 3-1 |
| Feb 9 | Wolverhampton WH | L | 0-1 |
| Feb 16 | Stoke C | A | D | 1-1 |
| Feb 23 | Bristol C | H | W | 4-0 |
| Feb 27 | Bolton W | H | W | 2-0 |
| Mar 1 | Ipswich T | A | L | 0-6 |
| Mar 12 | Everton | H | D | 0-0 |
| Mar 15 | Brighton & HA | A | D | 0-0 |
| Mar 22 | Manchester C | H | W | 1-0 |
| Mar 29 | Crystal Palace | A | W | 2-0 |
| Apr 2 | Nottingham F | A | L | 0-2 |
| Apr 5 | Liverpool | H | W | 2-1 |
| Apr 7 | Bolton W | A | W | 3-1 |
| Apr 12 | Tottenham H | H | W | 4-1 |
| Apr 19 | Norwich C | A | W | 2-0 |
| Apr 23 | Aston Villa | H | W | 2-1 |
| Apr 26 | Coventry C | H | W | 2-1 |
| May 3 | Leeds U | A | L | 0-2 |

**Final League position: 2nd**

| P | W | D | L | F/A | Pts |
|---|---|---|---|---|---|
| 42 | 24 | 10 | 8 | 65/53 | 58 |

## FA Cup

| Jan 5 | Tottenham H (3) | A | D | 1-1 |
| Jan 9 | Tottenham H (3R) | H | L | 0-1 |

## League Cup

| Aug 29 | Tottenham H (2) | A | L | 1-2 |
| Sep 5 | Tottenham H (2) | H | W | 3-1 |
| Sep 26 | Norwich C (3) | A | L | 1-4 |

Lou Macari and Ted McDougall before a training session at The Cliff in 1973.

A different world for United as they face the likes of Orient in Division Two, 1974, following relegation. They bounced straight back under The Doc.

ocherty celebrates the
rth of his grandchild with
ilk in January 1973

Docherty and Pat Crerand never got on – they were miles apart even in team photographs.

Against Orient in 1974. United bagged four straight wins, starting with this 2-0 victory.

Another step on the way back. United's Brian Greenhof slides in to score against Millwall in 1974.

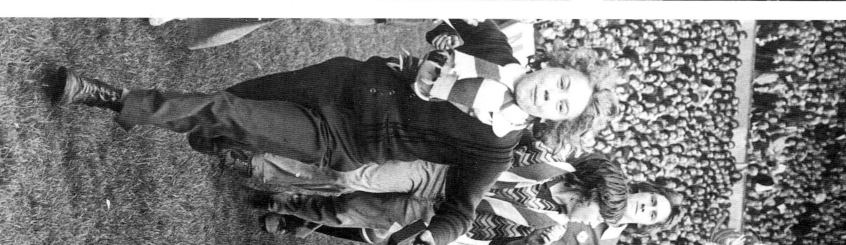

Docherty fulfilled his promise of restoring United to the

Martin Buchan and Alex Stepney parade the Division Two championship trophy after destroying Blackpool 4-0. The fans were happy now.

How did we miss that one! The rejuvenated United strike force can't believe this one didn't go in. They were normally on target in 1976.

Stuart Houston, a defensive rock for United when they needed it in 1975.

Jimmy Nicholl was a regular in the team under Sexton, but not Atkinson.

...rdon Hill was a wing wonder from Millwall – but Sexton eased him out.

Steve Coppell and Stuart Pearson in 1975 – they were good mates.

...cherty turns a blind eye to Pearson and Gordon Hill's photo-session with models before the 1977 Cup Final.

Back in Europe. United beat St Etienne 2-0 in 1977

Bet the one on the right is a City supporter. Police at the St Etienne victory.

Invading Europe. Back row: McGrath, Nicholl, Buchan, Stepney, Hill, Green

McCreery, McIlroy, Coppell, Albiston. Before the St Etienne match in 1977.

Blow me down, I've just put United through! Jimmy Greenhof displays the joy of being a footballer on a winning streak as United beat Leeds 2-1 in the 1977

Brian Greenhof was a defender who was often pushed up in emergencies.

Cop that! Steve Coppell's energy was never questioned by manager or fans.

Back in the limelight. United beat Liverpool 2-1 to win the '77 FA Cup.

entre) grabbed the other. Leeds' player Frank Gray is distraught.

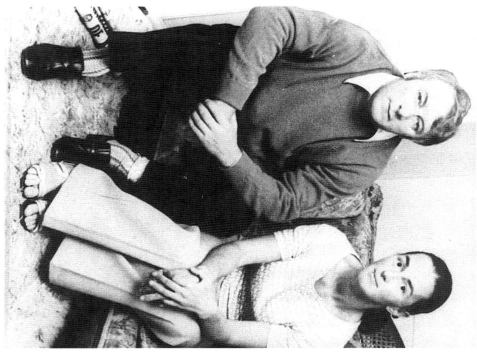

Docherty with Mary Brown in 1977. Their affair would cost him his job.

All at sea. Sexton was dubbed "boring" by the players. He didn't last long.

Dave Sexton had a good football brain, but his style of management was

dition. There were some lighter moments between him and the players, however.

Glenn Hoddle of Spurs turns Mickey Thomas and Ashley Grimes in the 1979 FA Cup sixth round. It was 1–1, but United took the replay 2–0.

Ossie Ardiles gave United fans a taste of what was to come when he faced The Reds. The foreign element at Old Trafford would become crucial.

Nobody messed with Big Joe Jordan, who arrived in 1977 to scare us.

Every mum's pin-up boy. Gordon McQueen rises to a Spurs cross in 1979 and Gary Bailey looks grateful. McQueen was a stout defender for United for eigh

McQueen had two good feet as well. Arsenal's Liam Brady finds out.

On opposite sides. McQueen marshalls Arsenal's Frank Stapleton.

g ability was legendary at Old Trafford.

He was a big man, but Gary Bailey was a great sight in full flight.

One is very amused! The '79 Cup Final team meet The Prince Of Wales.

Mac the knife! Sammy after scoring in the '79 Final against Arsenal.

McQueen leads the celebrations as United fight back at Wembley in 1979.

Oh the ecstasy! Jordan wheels away as United clinch the equaliser against

... but the joy didn't last long.

Alan Sunderland slots home a devastating goal just minutes after United a grabbed an equalizer in the 1979 Final. United fans – and players – just couldn't bel

Graham Rix of Arsenal leaves Steve Coppell floored in the 1979 Final...

lost 3-2

and a dejected Coppell leaves the Wembley pitch after the game which left fans exhausted.

Garry Birtles has borne the unenviable tag of being a big name who couldn't live up to United's expectation of him. He went 30 games without a goal. Atkinso

Mickey Thomas, the Welsh wizard.

Kids' stuff! Ray Wilkins with his wife Jackie and baby Ross in 1981.

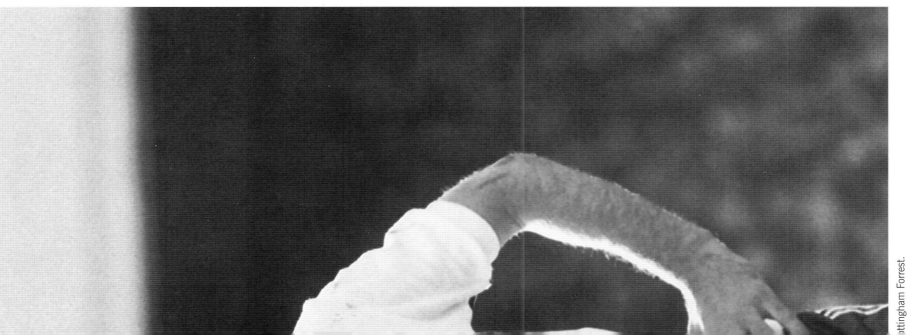

ttingham Forrest.

As one door closes for sacked United manager Dave Sexton in April 1981...

another one opens for "Goldfinger" Ron Atkinson. He transformed the club's fortunes with two FA Cups.

# A Man For All Seasons

U nited fans will forever be grateful to the town of Aberdeen for one very special reason: Alex Ferguson. After the departure of Atkinson, in came a man of down-to-earth steel who would live, eat and breath United under one rule – The Work Ethic. No player, however glamorous, however talented, would survive Fergie's desire for success with the biggest club in Britain unless they gave 110% on the pitch whenever he decided to send them on.

When he arrived at the first training session in 1986 he turned to Bryan Robson and said : "This is a massive club , isn't it?" He was to go on to achieve things that will remain in the minds of United fans to their dying day.

What is it between United and Scotland? The love affair between the two was to become a real marriage with Ferguson, but think of the greats who have come from that country to bring United success over the years – Busby for one, and Docherty, but also Law, Buchan, Jordan, and Strachan to mention but a few. The point is that Manchester built itself into an industrial giant of a city on hard graft, and United as a football team has always relied on the traditional Scottish endeavour among its management and playing staff. Work the hardest and you will succeed.

Ferguson was to prove the master in that department. As manager of Aberdeen he had taken them to honours the club has never repeated since his departure, but when he came to United

it was a case of "no pain, no gain" . Bryan Robson will testify tha even when his legs had been battered and bruised, Ferguson wou give him an alternative training routine to restore his fitness.

His first few seasons, however, were by no means successful an the press was baying for his blood. He was using players like a pac of cards, to distill the squad into the best team in the land but wit little trophy success.

Then Ferguson brought in Viv Anderson and Brian "Chocky McClair to add some meat to the side in 1987. Ferguson also rescue Mark Hughes from his torrid time at Barcelona and secured a de with Norwich for Steve Bruce, one of United's all-time gre defenders .

The title would elude Ferguson and United, but the ninet were to be his decade. He brought on some incredible youth tale in Giggs, Scholes, Beckham and Butt – but his biggest mark w the signing of Eric Cantona, nicked from Leeds for next to nothin at £1 million. Fergie's stage was set. He brought in Andr Kanchelskis, a real flyer of a winger, and Paul Ince shored up th midfield. By 1994, United were awesome with a squad he woul use to tremendous effect to clinch the title, and go on to eve greater heights with five championships in seven seasons.

Little did he know, but Fergie was on the fast track to succe in Europe – and the knighthood that would put him on a par wit the great Sir Matt Busby.

rgie knew it was crucial to
ve a top 'keeper. He was
oved right with Schmeichel.

ABERDEEN

Ferguson cut his managerial teeth at Aberdeen – and then brought his muscle to Old Trafford.

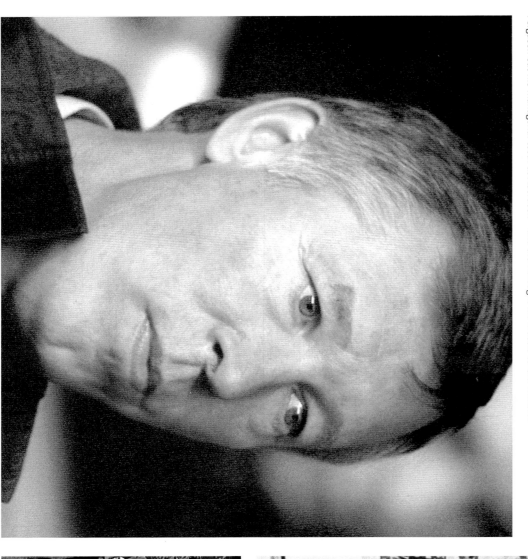

Fergie watches every player on the pitch like a hawk. If they don't perform to his standards, off they come.

The honours start to roll in as Fergu

Great Scots! Busby shares the glory with Ferguson and the Cup Winner's Cup in '91.

...rclay's Manager Of The Year in 1993, gets a hug from Zoe Ball with Sky TV's Personality Of the Year award in 1994, and of course the number one slot

Listen to me... move up Neville.
Get behind 'em Teddy, OK, do it
your own way...

Ferguson and Brian Kidd became a great team at United. Kidd was highly respected by the players as a trainer of real quality and commitment.

MR. MANCHESTER'S

...guson with one-time City favourite and now Sunderland boss Peter Reid. They come from the same managership mould.

"...his team will be the greatest, believe me, it will". Fergie in 1987.

"Believe me, guys. We are going to win the treble!"

## 1980-1981

A succession of injuries began to drag Dave Sexton's team down. The problem forced him to use 16 players during the first three games. Early casualties included key players like Joe Jordan and goalkeeper Gary Bailey. Sexton was forced to call on reserve players like Chris McGrath to plug the gaps. As the nightmare season wore on Buchan and McQueen were added to the list of pain and United were only managing to survive through drawn matches. Desperate to stop the rot, Sexton bought Gary Birtles for a record £1.25m. Despite a late burst of seven United wins in a row, Sexton was a victim of circumstance and was shown the door. The club finished 8th without a hint of Cup glory.

### League (Division 1)

| | | | | |
|---|---|---|---|---|
| Aug 16 | Middlesbrough | H | W | 3-0 |
| Aug 19 | Wolverhampton WA | L | L | 0-1 |
| Aug 23 | Birmingham C | A | D | 0-0 |
| Aug 30 | Sunderland | H | D | 1-1 |
| Sep 6 | Tottenham H | A | D | 0-0 |
| Sep 13 | Leicester C | H | W | 5-0 |
| Sep 20 | Leeds U | A | D | 0-0 |
| Sep 27 | Manchester C | H | D | 2-2 |
| Oct 4 | Nottingham F | A | W | 2-1 |
| Oct 8 | Aston Villa | H | D | 3-3 |
| Oct 11 | Arsenal | H | D | 0-0 |
| Oct 18 | Ipswich T | A | D | 1-1 |
| Oct 22 | Stoke C | A | W | 2-1 |
| Oct 25 | Everton | H | W | 2-0 |
| Nov 1 | Crystal palace | A | L | 0-1 |
| Nov 8 | Coventry C | H | D | 0-0 |
| Nov 12 | Wolverhampton | WH | D | 0-0 |
| Nov 15 | Middlesbrough | A | D | 1-1 |
| Nov 22 | Brighton & HA | A | W | 4-1 |
| Nov 29 | Southampton | H | D | 1-1 |
| Dec 6 | Norwich C | A | D | 2-2 |
| Dec 13 | Stoke C | H | D | 2-2 |
| Dec 20 | Arsenal | A | L | 1-2 |
| Dec 26 | Liverpool | H | D | 0-0 |
| Dec 27 | WBA | A | L | 1-3 |
| Jan 10 | Brighton & HA | H | W | 2-1 |
| Jan 28 | Sunderland | A | L | 0-2 |
| Jan 31 | Birmingham C | H | W | 2-0 |
| Feb 7 | Leicester C | A | L | 0-1 |
| Feb 17 | Tottenham H | H | D | 0-0 |
| Feb 21 | Manchester C | A | L | 0-1 |
| Feb 28 | Leeds U | H | L | 0-1 |
| Mar 7 | Southampton | A | L | 0-1 |
| Mar 14 | Aston Villa | A | D | 3-3 |
| Mar 18 | Nottingham F | H | D | 1-1 |
| Mar 21 | Ipswich T | H | D | 2-1 |
| Mar 28 | Everton | A | W | 1-0 |
| Apr 4 | Crystal Palace | H | W | 1-0 |
| Apr 11 | Coventry C | A | W | 2-0 |
| Apr 14 | Liverpool | A | W | 1-0 |
| Apr 18 | WBA | H | W | 2-1 |
| Apr 25 | Norwich C | H | W | 1-0 |

# The Glory Years

T here has always been a saying among United fans in Manchester that any new manager at the club has one hour and more than anybody else, knew he had to achieve. The side he had assembled was one of the best – Gary Bailey in goal, Duxbury, Albiston, Wilkins, Moran, big Gordon McQueen, Frank Stapleton from Arsenal, Muhren, Whiteside and Manchester-born Alan Davies.

The task of taking over a club of this size – it's the same at Liverpool, Arsenal, Spurs or Chelsea – is immense, but in Atkinson The Reds were in for a real ride as Big Ron set about imposing his own inimitable style on the outfit that had a desperate need to live up to its reputation. He had been a player of quality and, as a manager, had restored the credibility of West Bromwich Albion. He beat the likes of Bobby Robson and Brian Clough to the most coveted job in football.

But he had to succeed. Nothing less was expected and he was in the hot seat. On arriving, he pushed out two-thirds of the backroom staff, including Harry Gregg who was coaching the team and brought in Mick Brown from West Brom as his right-hand man. He then landed a deal that was to be so important to The Reds' future success. In October 1981, he bagged Bryan Robson for £1.5 million from his old team West Brom along with Remi Moses, who went on to become a real United favourite. In addition, he gave youth its chance in the best United tradition by bringing in the young Norman Whiteside who was to go on to score such a memorable last-gasp curling goal to clinch the FA Cup against Everton in 1985.

Third place in his first season in charge was a creditable start, but the fans wanted silverware. United started to chase everything and though they lost to Liverpool in the Milk Cup (the League Cup in effect), they faced Brighton in the FA Cup final of 1983. A gritty 2-2 draw meant another David and Goliath battle back at Wembley. United demolished the south coast side 4-0 with Arnold Muhren slotting home a penalty

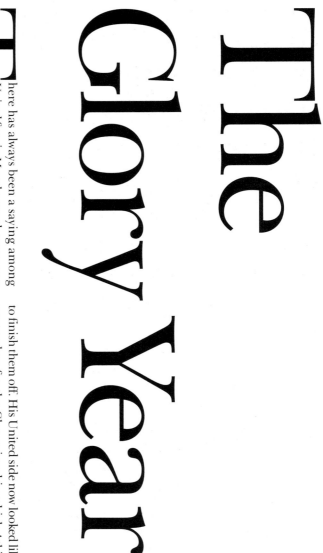

to finish them off. His United side now looked like real contenders for the Championship which Atkinson, more than anybody else, knew he had to achieve. The side he had assembled was one of the best – Gary Bailey in goal, Duxbury, Albiston, Wilkins, Moran, big Gordon McQueen, Frank Stapleton from Arsenal, Muhren, Whiteside and Manchester-born Alan Davies.

But there was more to come from the man with the midas touch. Atkinson realised that in Mark Hughes he had a rare talent – a powerhouse with a deft touch and a knack for scoring. Hughes made his debut for Oxford in the Milk Cup in November 1983. He scored in the 1-1 draw but his performance was impressive enough to start pushing out Norman Whiteside. At the same time, Atkinson shifted Ray Wilkins to AC Milan, a move which shocked many fans but Big Ron had a plan. By the end of the 1983-1984 season, United were playing some of their best football, a flowing, attacking style the fans loved. By 1985 Hughes was on top form scoring a hat-trick when United thrashed Aston Villa 4-0 at Old Trafford and being named Young Footballer Of The Year. He had also brought in some of the best players United have seen in Gordon Strachan and Danish winger Jesper Olsen. The team was pushing Everton for League honours, but Atkinson's love affair with Wembley was on the boil and United progressed to the sixth FA Cup Final in ten years.

T hat day at Wembley in 1985 again Everton was arguably Atkinson's finest moment – the late Whiteside winning brought the Cup back to Manchester and earned him the full respect of the fans. But for United defender Kevin Moran, it was a disaster. A tackle on Everton's Peter Reid saw Moran become the first player ever to be sent off in an FA Cup Final, something he has never been allowed to forget than to pub sports quizzes and media references to the incident

Champs! Mike Phelan, Mark Hughes and Steve Bruce celebrate the 1991 European Cup Winners' Cup in 1991.

# 1981-1982

How does a team lose only eight games all season and still finish third in the League? This was to be United's fate, but it was also a sign of the times. Football was becoming a minefield for managers who did not produce the goods in terms of results. Sexton was out and Ron Atkinson arrived at Old Trafford in June 1981 to start a period of attractive football and flamboyant managership. He had managed West Brom and immediately raided his old club to bring in Bryan Robson. Remi Moses was a part of the deal and in both players Atkinson found two favourites. The young Norman Whiteside was blooded into the senior side and though there were some great results – 4-1 to the home side against Aston Villa and 5-1 away against Sunderland – Liverpool were the team of the day, scoring 21 more goals than United throughout the season. They took the title and began a period of domination United fans would envy.

Championship hopes had disappeared, but at this time United fans were happy with the fact that the team they followed each week was producing some of the most attractive football seen for years. Atkinson kicked of the 1985-1986 season with a running flush of 10 straight victories – a club record for a start to the campaign – and he could reflect with some pleasure at the had put United back on track. The Reds were up winners, back in Europe – though the Heysel disaster would put paid to English participation in European competitions – and flying in the League. But always, fate deals a blow to the over-confident. United were hit by a string of injuries to key players like sen, Strachan – stretchered off after scoring at West om – and then Robson tore a hamstring while playing r England at Wembley. Atkinson brought in Peter arnes to bolster the depleted line-up and he made impressive start. But it was not enough to rescue the anager from the inevitable. The fans grew restless United started a disastrous run of games. The anager, never one to mix his words, retorted with: hey have short memories". He was referring to the ct he had brought two FA Cups to Manchester and eated a team any fan would be proud to support. e thought that would be enough – but not for United. Mark Hughes then left for Barcelona. It was a real ow for the crowds who loved his bullfighting style d his passion in the red shirt, and the clouds were

gathering over the man who put the fizz back into United's champagne. In November 1986, after five and a half years in the hottest seat in football, he turned up for training as normal and was called to see the chairman. A couple of hours later Ron Atkinson emerged to announce his departure from the club because of the string of poor results.

This was a time in football when the phrase "stand by your man" meant nothing. The game was changing into a big-money operation and results were paramount, at whatever cost. Atky left Old Trafford stating that the bore no grudges against the club, had enjoyed his time there and wished his players well.

"I am sure there are good times ahead for this club", he graciously told reporters on leaving, and how right he proved to be. He has gone on to become a house-hold name in football through TV commentary and remains a loyal, though always objective, devotee of United's attacking flair. He brought some great times to Old Trafford when the club needed it the most. Big Ron wrote his name in the history of The Reds and did it his own way.

The irony, of course, is that his departure cleared the way for the arrival of someone United fans now worship almost as much as Busby, the man who would bring to Manchester unprecedented football honours and the biggest prize of them all.

His name was Alex Ferguson.

Final League position: 8th

| | P | W | D | L | F/A | Pts |
|---|---|---|---|---|---|---|
| | 42 | 15 | 18 | 9 | 51/36 | 48 |

**FA Cup**

| | | | | | | | |
|---|---|---|---|---|---|---|---|
| Jan 3 | Brighton & HA (3) | H | D | 2-2 |
| Jan 7 | Brighton & HA (3R) | A | W | 2-0 |
| Jan 24 | Nottingham F | A | L | 0-1 |

**League Cup**

| | | | | | |
|---|---|---|---|---|---|
| Aug 27 | Coventry C (2) | H | L | 0-1 |
| Sep 2 | Coventry C (2) | A | L | 0-1 |

**UEFA Cup**

| | | | | | |
|---|---|---|---|---|---|
| Sep 17 | Widzew Lodz (1) | H | D | 1-1 |
| Oct 1 | Widzew Lodz (1) | A | D | 0-0 |

**League (Division 1)**

| | | | | |
|---|---|---|---|---|
| Aug 29 | Coventry C | A | L | 1-2 |
| Aug 31 | Nottingham F | H | D | 0-0 |
| Sep 5 | Ipswich T | H | L | 1-2 |
| Sep 12 | Aston Villa | A | D | 1-1 |
| Sep 19 | Swansea C | H | W | 1-0 |
| Sep 22 | Middlesbrough | A | W | 2-0 |
| Sep 26 | Arsenal | A | D | 0-0 |
| Sep 30 | Leeds U | H | W | 1-0 |
| Oct 3 | Wolverhampton W | H | W | 5-0 |
| Oct 10 | Manchester C | A | D | 0-0 |
| Oct 17 | Birmingham C | H | D | 1-1 |
| Oct 21 | Middlesbrough | A | W | 2-1 |
| Oct 24 | Liverpool | H | W | 2-0 |
| Oct 31 | Notts County | H | W | 2-1 |
| Nov 7 | Sunderland | A | W | 5-1 |
| Nov 21 | Tottenham H | A | L | 1-3 |

# 1982-1983

Atkinson was beginning to produce results at last. United won their first two games of the season against Birmingham and Nottingham Forest.

Stapleton was on form. Moran was solid at the back and the Robson-Wilkins partnership was a midfield revelation. United made it to the Milk Cup and FA Cup Finals, a golden period for Atkinson. Liverpool ended the honeymoon for Atkinson with a 2-1 defeat at Wembley in the Milk Cup, but then United produced their best form against Brighton to land the FA Cup. Over two games to finish the contest, United put six past Brighton. United's Dutch signing Arnold Muhren finishing the south coast team off with a penalty to lift the trophy in the replay Silverware was back at Old Trafford and Atkinson was on a roll.

## League results

| Date | Opponent | H/A | Result | Score |
|---|---|---|---|---|
| Nov 28 | Brighton & HA | H | W | 2-0 |
| Dec 5 | Southampton | A | L | 2-3 |
| Jan 6 | Everton | H | D | 1-1 |
| Jan 23 | Stoke C | A | W | 3-0 |
| Jan 27 | West Ham U | H | W | 1-0 |
| Jan 30 | Swansea C | A | L | 0-2 |
| Feb 6 | Aston Villa | H | W | 4-1 |
| Feb 13 | Wolverhampton W | A | W | 1-0 |
| Feb 20 | Arsenal | H | D | 0-0 |
| Feb 27 | Manchester C | H | D | 1-1 |
| Mar 6 | Birmingham C | A | W | 1-0 |
| Mar 17 | Coventry C | H | L | 0-1 |
| Mar 20 | Notts C | A | W | 3-1 |
| Mar 27 | Sunderland | H | D | 0-0 |
| Apr 3 | Leeds U | A | D | 0-0 |
| Apr 7 | Liverpool | H | L | 0-1 |
| Apr 10 | Everton | A | D | 3-3 |
| Apr 12 | WBA | H | W | 1-0 |
| Apr 17 | Tottenham H | A | L | 1-2 |
| Apr 20 | Ipswich T | A | W | 1-0 |
| Apr 24 | Brighton & HA | A | W | 1-0 |
| May 1 | Southampton | H | W | 1-0 |
| May 5 | Nottingham F | A | W | 1-0 |
| May 8 | West Ham U | A | D | 1-1 |
| May 12 | WBA | A | W | 3-0 |
| May 15 | Stoke C | H | W | 2-0 |

Final League position: **3rd**

| P | W | D | L | F/A | Pts |
|---|---|---|---|---|---|
| 42 | 22 | 12 | 8 | 59/29 | 78 |

## FA Cup

| Jan 2 | Watford (3) | A | L | 0-1 |
|---|---|---|---|---|

## League Cup

| Oct 7 | Tottenham H (2) | A | L | 0-1 |
|---|---|---|---|---|
| Oct 28 | Tottenham H (2) | H | L | 0-1 |

Frank Stapleton came back to haunt his former team-mates at Arsenal in September 1981.

## League (Division 1)

| Aug 28 | Birmingham C | H | W | 3-0 |
|---|---|---|---|---|
| Sep 1 | Nottingham F | A | W | 3-0 |
| Sep 4 | WBA | A | L | 1-3 |

Atkinson brought steel to the team – in the form of the mighty Joe Jordan.

|  |  | |  |
|---|---|---|---|
| Sep 8 | Everton | H | W 2-1 |
| Sep 11 | Ipswich T | H | W 3-1 |
| Sep 18 | Southampton | A | W 1-0 |
| Sep 25 | Arsenal | H | D 0-0 |
| Oct 2 | Luton T | A | D 1-1 |
| Oct 9 | Stoke C | H | W 1-0 |
| Oct 16 | Liverpool | A | D 0-0 |
| Oct 23 | Manchester City | H | D 2-2 |
| Oct 30 | West Ham U | A | L 1-3 |
| Nov 6 | Brighton & HA | A | L 0-1 |
| Nov 13 | Tottenham H | H | W 1-0 |
| Nov 20 | Aston Villa | A | L 1-2 |
| Nov 27 | Norwich C | H | W 3-0 |
| Dec 4 | Watford | A | W 1-0 |
| Dec 11 | Notts County | H | W 4-0 |
| Dec 18 | Swansea C | A | D 0-0 |
| Dec 27 | Sunderland | H | D 0-0 |
| Dec 28 | Coventry C | A | L 0-3 |
| Jan 1 | Aston Villa | H | D 1-1 |
| Jan 3 | WBA | H | D 0-0 |
| Jan 15 | Birmingham C | A | W 2-1 |
| Jan 22 | Nottingham F | H | W 2-0 |
| Feb 5 | Ipswich T | A | D 1-1 |
| Feb 26 | Liverpool | H | D 1-1 |
| Mar 2 | Stoke C | A | L 0-1 |
| Mar 5 | Manchester C | H | W 2-1 |
| Mar 19 | Brighton & HA | H | D 1-1 |
| Mar 22 | West Ham U | H | W 2-1 |
| Apr 2 | Coventry C | H | W 3-0 |
| Apr 4 | Sunderland | A | D 0-0 |
| Apr 9 | Southampton | H | D 1-1 |
| Apr 19 | Everton | A | L 0-2 |
| Apr 23 | Watford | H | W 2-0 |
| Apr 30 | Norwich C | A | D 1-1 |
| May 2 | Arsenal | A | L 0-3 |
| May 7 | Swansea C | H | W 2-1 |
| May 9 | Luton T | H | W 3-0 |
| May 11 | Tottenham H | A | L 0-2 |
| May 14 | Notts C | A | L 2-3 |

**Final League position: 3rd**

| P | W | D | L | F/A | Pts |
|---|---|---|---|---|---|
| 42 | 19 | 13 | 10 | 56/38 | 70 |

**FA Cup**

| Jan 8 | West Ham U (3) | H | W 2-0 |
|---|---|---|---|
| Jan 29 | Luton T (4) | A | W 2-0 |
| Jan 26 | Derby C (5) | A | W 1-0 |
| Mar 12 | Everton (6) | H | W 1-0 |
| Apr 16 | Arsenal (SF) | N | W 2-1 (at Villa Park) |
| May 21 | Brighton & HA (F) | N | D 2-2 (at Wembley) |
| May 26 | Brighton & HA (FR) | N | W 4-0 (at Wembley) |

**League Cup**

| Oct 6 | Bournemouth (2_ | H | W 2-0 |
|---|---|---|---|
| Oct 26 | Bournemouth (2) | A | D 2-2 |
| Nov 10 | Bradford C (3) | A | D 0-0 |
| Nov 24 | Bradford C (3R) | H | W 4-1 |
| Dec 1 | Southampton (4) | H | W 2-0 |
| Jan 19 | Nottingham F (5) | H | W 4-0 |
| Feb 15 | Arsenal (SF) | A | W 4-2 |
| Feb 23 | Arsenal (SF) | H | W 2-1 |
| Mar 26 | Liverpool | N | L 1-2 (at Wembley) |

**UEFA Cup**

| Sep 15 | Valencia (1) | H | D 0-0 |
|---|---|---|---|
| Sep 29 | Valencia (1) | A | L 1-2 |

# 1983-1984

Atkinson and the team were sitting pretty at the top of Division One by October after eight wins. Could the manager achieve the dream

...kinson loved to mix it with his team on the training field. Seen here in 1983 with his signing Bryan Robson in the background.

of bringing the title back to Old Trafford? The fans certainly thought so. United were an impressive outfit with a mixture of youth and experience needed to survive in an increasingly fierce business. The young Mark Hughes emerged as one of United's best discoveries, demolishing Port Vale with five goals in a 10-0 pre-season friendly. But football is fickle. The team crashed out of the FA Cup in a devastating 2-0 defeat by Bournemouth and the manager was furious. The fans turned on him, but he survived and treated them to a thrilling 3-0 defeat of Barcelona – and the gifted Maradona – in the Cup Winners' Cup. The title, however, was still out of his reach. Liverpool were again Champions, United finishing fourth.

## League (Division 1)

| | | | | |
|---|---|---|---|---|
| Aug 27 | QPR | H | W | 3-1 |
| Aug 29 | Nottingham F | H | L | 1-2 |
| Sep 3 | Stoke C | A | W | 1-0 |
| Sep 6 | Arsenal | A | W | 3-2 |
| Sep 10 | Luton T | H | W | 2-0 |
| Sep 17 | Southampton | A | L | 0-3 |
| Sep 24 | Liverpool | H | W | 1-0 |
| Oct 1 | Norwich C | A | D | 3-3 |
| Oct 15 | WBA | H | W | 3-0 |
| Oct 22 | Sunderland | A | W | 1-0 |
| Oct 29 | Wolverhampton | W H | W | 3-0 |
| Nov 5 | Aston Villa | H | L | 1-2 |
| Nov 12 | Leicester C | A | D | 1-1 |
| Nov 19 | Watford | H | W | 4-1 |
| Nov 27 | West Ham U | A | D | 1-1 |
| Dec 3 | Everton | H | L | 0-1 |
| Dec 10 | Ipswich T | A | W | 2-0 |
| Dec 16 | Tottenham H | H | W | 4-2 |
| Dec 26 | Coventry C | A | D | 1-1 |
| Dec 27 | Notts C | H | D | 3-3 |
| Dec 31 | Stoke C | H | W | 1-0 |
| Jan 2 | Liverpool | A | D | 1-1 |
| Jan 13 | QPR | A | D | 1-1 |
| Jan 21 | Southampton | H | W | 3-2 |
| Feb 4 | Norwich C | H | D | 0-0 |
| Feb 7 | Birmingham C | A | D | 2-2 |
| Feb 12 | Luton T | A | W | 5-0 |
| Feb 18 | Wolverhampton W | A | D | 1-1 |
| Feb 25 | Sunderland | H | W | 2-1 |
| Mar 3 | Aston Villa | A | W | 3-0 |
| Mar 10 | Leicester C | H | W | 2-0 |
| Mar 17 | Arsenal | H | W | 4-0 |
| Mar 31 | WBA | A | L | 0-2 |
| Apr 7 | Birmingham C | H | W | 1-0 |
| Apr 14 | Notts C | A | L | 0-1 |
| Apr 17 | Watford | A | D | 0-0 |
| Apr 21 | Coventry C | H | W | 4-1 |
| Apr 28 | West Ham U | H | D | 0-0 |
| May 5 | Everton | A | D | 1-1 |
| May 7 | Ipswich T | H | L | 1-2 |
| May 12 | Tottenham H | A | D | 1-1 |
| May 16 | Nottingham F | A | L | 0-2 |

Final League position: **4th**

| P | W | D | L | F/A | Pts |
|---|---|---|---|---|---|
| 42 | 20 | 14 | 8 | 71/41 | 74 |

Sir Matt Busby arrives at the funeral of his great pal and fellow Scot Bill Shankly in 1981.

Stroll on! The United squad out for a breather before the 1983 Milk Cup Final.

Sure-shot. Norman Whiteside's FA Cup goal against Everton restored United's pride.

Boy's Own stuff. Brian Robson was

## FA Cup

| | | | | |
|---|---|---|---|---|
| Jan 7 | Bournemouth (3) | A | L | 0-2 |

## League Cup

| | | | | |
|---|---|---|---|---|
| Oct 3 | Port Vale (2) | A | W | 1-0 |
| Oct 26 | Port Vale (2) | H | W | 2-0 |
| Nov 8 | Colchester U (3) | A | W | 2-0 |
| Nov 30 | Oxford U (4) | A | D | 1-1 |
| Dec 7 | Oxford U (4R) | H | D | 1-1 |
| Nov 30 | Oxford U (4R2) | A | L | 1-2 |

## European Cup Winners' Cup

| | | | | |
|---|---|---|---|---|
| Sep 14 | Dukla Prague (1) | H | D | 1-1 |
| Sep 27 | Dukla Prague (1) | A | D | 2-2 |
| Oct 19 | Spartak Varna (2) | A | W | 2-1 |
| Nov 2 | Spartak Varna (2) | H | W | 2-0 |
| Mar 7 | Barcelona (3) | A | L | 0-2 |
| Mar 21 | Barcelona (3) | H | W | 3-0 |
| Apr 11 | Juventus (SF) | H | D | 1-1 |
| Apr 25 | Juventus (SF) | A | L | 1-2 |

## 1984-1985

Fans were shocked when popular Ray Wilkins was sold to AC Milan for £1.4m. The future of Norman Whiteside also looked in doubt as Mark Hughes successfully challenged for a regular place in the squad. Big Ron also bought in class players like Gordon Strachan, Jesper Olsen and Alan Brazil. The stage was set for FA Cup glory. After a memorable semi-final tussle against Liverpool, United took on Everton at Wembley. As usual The Reds gave fans a white-knuckle ride. Down to ten men after Kevin Moran became the first player to be sent off in an FA Cup final, Hughes started a move that ended in extra time that ended with the winner from Whiteside. United ended the season in fourth place.

## League (Division 1)

| | | | | |
|---|---|---|---|---|
| Aug 25 | Watford | H | D | 1-1 |
| Aug 28 | Southampton | A | D | 0-0 |
| Sep 1 | Ipswich T | A | D | 1-1 |
| Sep 5 | Chelsea | H | D | 1-1 |
| Sep 8 | Newcastle U | H | W | 5-0 |
| Sep 15 | Coventry C | A | W | 3-0 |
| Sep 22 | Liverpool | H | D | 1-1 |
| Sep 29 | WBA | A | W | 2-1 |
| Oct 6 | Aston Villa | A | L | 0-3 |
| Oct 13 | West Ham U | H | W | 5-1 |
| Oct 20 | Tottenham H | H | W | 1-0 |
| Oct 27 | Everton | A | L | 0-5 |
| Nov 2 | Arsenal | H | W | 4-2 |
| Nov 10 | Leicester C | A | W | 3-2 |
| Nov 17 | Luton T | H | W | 2-0 |
| Nov 24 | Sunderland | A | L | 2-3 |
| Dec 1 | Norwich C | H | W | 2-0 |
| Dec 8 | Nottingham F | A | L | 2-3 |
| Dec 15 | QPR | H | W | 3-0 |
| Dec 22 | Ipswich T | H | W | 3-0 |
| Dec 26 | Stoke C | A | L | 1-2 |
| Dec 29 | Chelsea | A | w | 3-1 |
| Jan 1 | Sheffield W | H | L | 1-2 |
| Jan 12 | Coventry C | H | L | 0-1 |

United side which won the 1985 Cup Final 1-0 against Everton and boosted Atkinson's reputation with fans and the club bosses.

| | | | | |
|---|---|---|---|---|
| Feb 2 | WBA | H | W | 2-0 |
| Feb 9 | Newcastle U | A | D | 1-1 |
| Feb 23 | Arsenal | A | W | 1-0 |
| Mar 2 | Everton | H | D | 1-1 |
| Mar 12 | Tottenham H | A | W | 2-1 |
| Mar 15 | West Ham U | A | D | 2-2 |
| Mar 23 | Aston Villa | H | W | 4-0 |
| Mar 31 | Liverpool | A | W | 1-0 |
| Apr 3 | Leicester C | H | W | 2-1 |
| Apr 6 | Stoke C | H | W | 5-1 |
| Apr 9 | Sheffield W | A | L | 0-1 |
| Apr 21 | Luton T | A | L | 1-2 |
| Apr 24 | Southampton | H | D | 0-0 |
| Apr 27 | Sunderland | H | D | 2-2 |
| May 4 | Norwich C | A | W | 1-0 |
| May 6 | Nottingham F | H | W | 2-0 |
| May 11 | QPR | A | W | 3-1 |
| May 13 | Watford | A | L | 1-5 |

**Final League position: 4th**

| P | W | D | L | F/A | Pts |
|---|---|---|---|---|---|
| 42 | 22 | 10 | 10 | 77/47 | 76 |

**FA Cup**

| | | | | |
|---|---|---|---|---|
| Jan 5 | Bournemouth (3) | H | W | 3-0 |
| Jan 26 | Coventry C (4) | H | W | 2-1 |
| Feb 15 | Blackburn R (5) | A | W | 2-0 |
| Mar 9 | West Ham U (6) | A | W | 4-2 |
| Apr 13 | Liverpool (SF) (at Goodison Park) | N | D | 2-2 |
| Apr 17 | Liverpool (SFR) (at Maine Road) | N | W | 2-1 |
| May 18 | Everton (at Wembley) | N | W | 1-0 |

**League Cup**

| | | | | |
|---|---|---|---|---|
| Sep 26 | Burnley (2) | H | W | 4-0 |
| Oct 9 | Burnley (2) | A | W | 3-0 |
| Oct 30 | Everton (3) | H | L | 1-2 |

**UEFA Cup**

| | | | | |
|---|---|---|---|---|
| Sep 19 | Raba Vasas (1) | H | W | 3-0 |
| Oct 3 | Raba Vasas (1) | A | D | 2-2 |
| Oct 24 | PSV Eindhoven (2) | A | D | 0-0 |
| Nov 7 | PSV Eindhoven (2) | H | W | 1-0 |
| Nov 28 | Dundee U (3) | H | D | 2-2 |
| Dec 12 | Dundee U (3) | A | W | 3-2 |
| Mar 6 | Videoton (4) | H | W | 1-0 |
| Mar 20 | Videoton (4) | A | L | 0-1 |

# 1985-1986

Ron Atkinson quickly went from hero to zero. Although United got off to a flying start, winning ten League games in a row, the side continued to be dogged by injuries. One of the most notable casualties was Bryan Robson, who ripped a hamstring while playing for England. The team's fortunes dipped in the run-up to Christmas and some fans began to complain about the way Atkinson was running things. United were knocked out of the FA Cup in the fifth round by West Ham and by Liverpool in the fourth round of the Milk Cup. There was no European campaign due to the fall-out from the Heysel Stadium disaster and the club finished fourth. When

Our Cups floweth over. Brian Robson and Arnold Muhren lift the FA Cup after demolishing Brighton 4-0 in the 1983 FA Cup Fina

news got out that Mark Hughes was off to Barcelona, fan discontent became fury.

## League (Division 1)

| Date | Opponent | H/A | Result | Score |
|------|----------|-----|--------|-------|
| Aug 17 | Aston Villa | H | W | 4-0 |
| Aug 20 | Ipswich T | A | W | 1-0 |
| Aug 24 | Arsenal | A | W | 2-1 |
| Aug 26 | West Ham | H | W | 2-0 |
| Aug 31 | Nottingham F | A | W | 3-1 |
| Sep 4 | Newcastle U | H | W | 3-0 |
| Sep 7 | Oxford U | H | W | 3-0 |
| Sep 14 | Manchester C | A | W | 5-1 |
| Sep 21 | WBA | A | W | 3-0 |
| Sep 28 | Southampton | H | W | 1-0 |
| Oct 5 | Luton T | A | D | 1-1 |
| Oct 12 | QPR | H | W | 2-0 |
| Oct 19 | Liverpool | H | D | 1-1 |
| Oct 26 | Chelsea | A | W | 2-1 |
| Nov 2 | Coventry C | H | W | 2-0 |
| Nov 9 | Sheffield W | A | L | 0-1 |
| Nov 16 | Tottenham H | H | D | 0-0 |
| Nov 23 | Leicester C | A | L | 0-3 |
| Nov 30 | Watford | H | D | 1-1 |
| Dec 7 | Ipswich T | H | W | 1-0 |
| Dec 14 | Aston Villa | A | W | 3-1 |
| Dec 21 | Arsenal | H | L | 0-1 |
| Dec 26 | Everton | A | L | 1-3 |
| Jan 1 | Birmingham C | H | W | 1-0 |
| Jan 11 | Oxford U | A | W | 3-1 |
| Jan 18 | Nottingham F | H | L | 2-3 |
| Feb 2 | West Ham U | A | L | 1-2 |
| Feb 9 | Liverpool | A | D | 1-1 |
| Feb 22 | WBA | H | W | 3-0 |
| Mar 1 | Southampton | A | L | 0-1 |
| Mar 15 | QPR | A | L | 0-1 |
| Mar 19 | Luton T | H | W | 2-0 |
| Mar 22 | Manchester C | H | D | 2-2 |
| Mar 29 | Birmingham C | A | D | 1-1 |
| Mar 31 | Everton | H | D | 0-0 |
| Apr 5 | Coventry C | A | W | 3-1 |
| Apr 9 | Chelsea | H | L | 1-2 |
| Apr 13 | Sheffield W | H | L | 0-2 |
| Apr 16 | Newcastle U | H | W | 4-2 |
| Apr 19 | Tottenham H | A | W | 1-0 |
| Apr 26 | Leicester C | H | W | 4-0 |
| May 3 | Watford | A | D | 1-1 |

**Final League position: 4th**

| P | W | D | L | F/A | Pts |
|---|---|---|---|-----|-----|
| 42 | 22 | 10 | 10 | 70/36 | 76 |

## FA Cup

| Date | Opponent | Round | H/A | Result | Score |
|------|----------|-------|-----|--------|-------|
| Jan 9 | Rochdale (3) | | H | W | 2-0 |
| Jan 25 | Sunderland (4) | | A | D | 0-0 |
| Jan 29 | Sunderland (4R) | | H | W | 3-0 |
| Mar 5 | West Ham U (5) | | A | D | 1-1 |
| Mar 9 | West Ham U (5R) | | H | L | 0-2 |

## 1986-1987

United lost the first three games and could only manage one win in the first nine. When the team were knocked out of the FA Cup 4-1 by Southampton in November, Big Ron had to face the board. Shortly after the match he and Mick

## League Cup

| Date | Opponent | Round | H/A | Result | Score |
|------|----------|-------|-----|--------|-------|
| Sep 24 | Crystal Palace (2) | | A | W | 1-0 |
| Oct 9 | Crystal Palace (2) | | H | W | 1-0 |
| Oct 27 | West Ham U (3) | | H | W | 1-0 |
| Nov 26 | Liverpool (4) | | A | L | 1-2 |

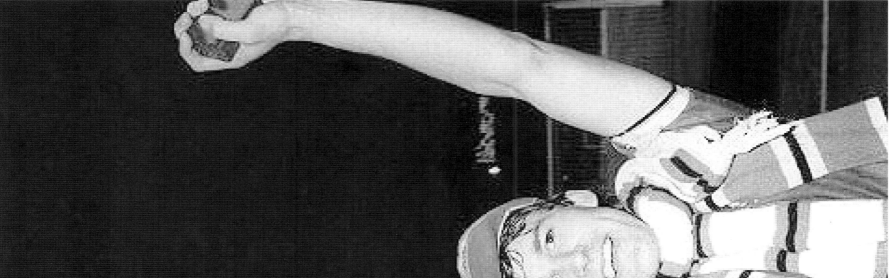

Scenes like this after the '83 Cup Final were treasured.

We're simply the best. Bryan Robson and Norman Whiteside sum up the spirit of the 1983 team.

Brown were sacked. Hours later United chairman Martin Edwards was on his way to talk to Aberdeen's Manager, Alex Ferguson. The Scotsman, who would bring such glory to the club, agreed after talking it over with his family and flew down to start work the next day. There were other departures too. Goalkeeper Gary Bailey retired because of a knee injury, Frank Stapleton went to Ajax in Holland and John Siveback headed for St. Etienne. Although the team finished 11th, hopes were high.

## League (Division 1)

| Date | Opponent | H/A | Result | Score |
|---|---|---|---|---|
| Aug 23 | Arsenal | A | L | 0-1 |
| Aug 25 | West Ham U | H | L | 2-3 |
| Aug 30 | Charlton A | H | L | 0-1 |
| Sep 6 | Leicester C | A | D | 1-1 |
| Sep 13 | Southampton | H | W | 5-1 |
| Sep 16 | Watford | A | W | 1-0 |
| Sep 21 | Everton | A | L | 1-3 |
| Sep 28 | Chelsea | H | L | 0-1 |
| Oct 4 | Nottingham F | A | D | 1-1 |
| Oct 11 | Sheffield W. | H | W | 3-1 |
| Oct 18 | Luton T | A | D | 1-1 |
| Oct 26 | Manchester C | H | D | 1-1 |
| Nov 1 | Coventry C | A | L | 0-2 |
| Nov 8 | Oxford U | A | D | 0-0 |
| Nov 15 | Norwich C | A | D | 0-0 |
| Nov 22 | QPR | H | W | 1-0 |
| Nov 29 | Wimbledon | A | L | 0-1 |
| Dec 7 | Tottenham H | D | | 3-3 |
| Dec 13 | Aston Villa | A | D | 3-3 |
| Dec 20 | Leicester C | H | W | 2-0 |
| Dec 26 | Liverpool | A | W | 1-0 |
| Dec 27 | Norwich C | H | L | 0-1 |
| Jan 1 | Newcastle U | H | W | 4-1 |
| Jan 3 | Southampton | A | d | 1-1 |
| Jan 24 | Arsenal | H | W | 2-0 |
| Feb 7 | Charlton A | H | W | 3-1 |
| Feb 14 | Watford | H | W | 3-1 |
| Feb 21 | Chelsea | A | D | 1-1 |
| Feb 28 | Everton | H | D | 0-0 |
| Mar 7 | Manchester C | A | W | 2-0 |
| Mar 14 | Luton T | H | L | 1-2 |
| Mar 21 | Sheffield W. | A | L | 0-1 |
| Mar 28 | Nottingham F | H | W | 2-0 |
| Apr 4 | Oxford U | H | W | 3-2 |
| Apr 14 | West Ham | A | D | 0-0 |
| Apr 18 | Newcastle U | A | L | 1-2 |
| Apr 20 | Liverpool | H | W | 1-0 |
| Apr 25 | QPR | A | L | 1-1 |
| May 2 | Wimbledon | H | L | 0-1 |
| May 4 | Tottenham H | A | L | 0-4 |
| May 6 | Coventry C | A | D | 1-1 |
| May 9 | Aston Villa | H | W | 3-1 |

**Final League position: 11th**

| P | W | D | L | F/A | Pts |
|---|---|---|---|---|---|
| 42 | 14 | 14 | 14 | 52/45 | 56 |

## FA Cup

| | | | |
|---|---|---|---|
| Jan 10 | Manchester C (3)H | W | 1-0 |
| Jan 31 | Coventry C (4) | H L | 0-1 |

## League Cup

| | | | |
|---|---|---|---|
| Sep 24 | Port Vale (2) | H W | 2-0 |
| Oct 7 | Port Vale (2) | A W | 5-2 |
| Oct 29 | Southampton (3)H | D | 0-0 |
| Nov 4 | Southampton (3R)A | L | 1-4 |

Atkinson brought Gordon Strachan from Aberdeen, managed then by Alex Ferguson!

Paul McGrath was a feared defender who ran his socks off for United. Skilled on the ball and a deadly tackler, not much got past The Big Mac.

Dane Jesper Olsen started with Atkinson, then blossomed under Alex Ferguson.

By 1989, Whiteside was fighting for his place against the likes of Alan Brazil.

Alan Brazil never quite clicked at United. The team was filling up with stars.

# 1987-1988

Alex Ferguson moved quickly to strengthen United. In July 1987 he signed Viv Anderson and Brian McClair for bargain prices. The new manager made it clear to them and the rest of his squad that nobody had an automatic right to be in the team. Anybody who wanted to play would have to prove their worth through hard work. Other new arrivals were Steve Bruce and goalkeeper Jim Leighton. Arthur Albiston was given a free transfer after 11 years at the club and fans were ecstatic when Mark Hughes returned to the United fold from Barcelona. The club finished the season in second place with 81 points. Behind the scenes Ferguson had been busy boosting United's youth system, strengthening the ground staff and improving the scouting system.

## League (Division 1)

| | | | |
|---|---|---|---|
| Aug 15 | Southampton | A | D 2-2 |
| Aug 19 | Arsenal | H | D 0-0 |
| Aug 22 | Watford | H | W 2-0 |
| Aug 29 | Charlton | A | W 3-1 |
| Aug 31 | Chelsea | H | W 3-1 |
| Sep 5 | Coventry C | A | D 0-0 |
| Sep 12 | Newcastle U | H | D 2-2 |
| Sep 19 | Everton | A | L 1-2 |
| Sep 26 | Tottenham | H | W 1-0 |
| Oct 3 | Luton T | A | D 1-1 |
| Oct 10 | Sheffield W | A | W 4-2 |
| Oct 17 | Norwich c | H | W 2-1 |
| oct 25 | West Ham U | A | D 1-1 |
| Oct 31 | Nottingham F | H | D 2-2 |
| Nov 15 | Liverpool | H | D 1-1 |
| Nov 21 | Wimbledon | A | L 1-2 |
| Dec 5 | QPR | A | W 2-0 |
| Dec 12 | Oxford U | H | W 3-1 |
| Dec 19 | Portsmouth | A | W 2-1 |
| Dec 26 | Newcastle U | A | L 0-1 |
| Dec 28 | Everton | H | W 2-1 |
| Jan 1 | Charlton A | H | D 0-0 |
| Jan 2 | Watford | A | W 1-0 |
| Jan 16 | Southampton | H | L 0-2 |
| Jan 24 | Arsenal | A | W 2-1 |
| Feb 6 | Coventry C | H | W 1-0 |
| Feb 10 | Derby C | H | W 2-1 |
| Feb 13 | Chelsea | A | W 2-1 |
| Feb 23 | Tottenham | H | D 1-1 |
| Mar 5 | Norwich C | A | L 0-1 |
| Mar 12 | Sheffield W | H | w 4-1 |
| Mar 19 | Nottingham F | A | D 0-0 |
| Mar 26 | West Ham U | H | W 3-1 |
| Apr 2 | Derby C | A | W 4-1 |
| Apr 4 | Liverpool | A | D 3-3 |
| Apr 12 | Luton T | H | W 3-0 |
| Apr 30 | QPR | H | W 2-1 |
| May 2 | Oxford U | A | W 2-0 |
| May 7 | Portsmouth | H | W 4-1 |
| May 9 | Wimbledon | H | W 2-1 |

Mark "Sparky" Hughes was one of the best-loved players at United. Built like a bull, he terrified defenders. A class act all round.

## 1988-1989

Alex Ferguson's attempts to move United forward were dogged by the bane of managers before him – injuries. One of the worst examples was Viv Anderson, who needed a back operation. Ferguson was forced to try 23 players in 24 games and drew heavily on young talent. Lee Sharpe, aged 17, was signed from Torquay and fledglings like Russell Beardsmore, Deiniol Graham and David Wilson were given a chance to shine in the first team. Gordon Strachan left the club to excel at Leeds as The Reds struggled through a difficult season. Their FA Cup run ended in the sixth round when they met Nottingham Forest and lost 1-0. When the club finished 11th in the League, Ferguson had to face criticism from fans and the media. He told them to keep the faith.

### Final League position: 2nd

| P | W | D | L | F/A | Pts |
|---|---|---|---|---|---|
| 40 | 23 | 12 | 5 | 71/38 | 81 |

### FA Cup

| | | | |
|---|---|---|---|
| Jan 10 | Ipswich T (3) | A | w 2-1 |
| Jan 30 | Chelsea (4) | H | W 2-0 |
| Feb 20 | Arsenal (5) | A | L 1-2 |

### League Cup

| | | | |
|---|---|---|---|
| Sep 23 | Hull City (2) | H | W 5-0 |
| Oct 7 | Hull City (2) | A | w 1-0 |
| Oct 28 | Crystal Palace (3) | H | W 2-1 |
| Nov 18 | Bury (4) | H | W 2-1 |
| Jan 20 | Oxford U (5) | A | L 0-2 |

### League (Division 1)

| | | | |
|---|---|---|---|
| Aug 27 | QPR | H | D 0-0 |
| Sep 3 | Liverpool | A | L 0-1 |
| Sep 10 | Middlesbrough | H | W 1-0 |
| Sep 27 | Luton T | A | W 2-0 |
| Sep 24 | West Ham United | H | W 2-0 |
| Oct 1 | Tottenham H | A | D 2-2 |
| Oct 22 | Wimbledon | A | D 1-1 |
| Oct 26 | Norwich C | H | L 1-2 |
| Oct 30 | Everton | A | D 1-1 |
| Nov 5 | Aston Villa | H | d 1-1 |
| Nov 12 | Derby C | A | D 2-2 |
| Nov 19 | Southampton | H | D 2-2 |
| Nov 23 | Sheffield W | H | D 1-1 |
| Nov 27 | Newcastle U | A | D 0-0 |
| Dec 3 | Charlton A | H | W 3-0 |
| Dec 10 | Coventry C | A | L 0-1 |
| Dec 17 | Arsenal | A | L 1-2 |
| Dec 26 | Nottingham F | H | W 2-0 |
| Jan 1 | Liverpool | H | W 3-1 |
| Jan 2 | Middlesbrough | A | L 0-1 |
| Jan 14 | Millwall | H | W 3-0 |
| Jan 21 | West Ham U | A | W 3-1 |
| Feb 5 | Tottenham H | H | W 1-0 |
| Feb 11 | Sheffield W | A | W 2-0 |

The United bench goes wild as Whiteside scores a beautiful goal against Everton in the 1985 Cup Final. Kevin Moran (second f

| | | | | |
|---|---|---|---|---|
| Feb 25 | Norwich C | A | L | 1-2 |
| Mar 12 | Aston Villa | A | D | 0-0 |
| Mar 25 | Luton T | H | W | 2-0 |
| Mar 27 | Nottingham F | A | L | 0-2 |
| Apr 2 | Arsenal | H | D | 1-1 |
| Apr 8 | Millwall | A | D | 0-0 |
| Apr 15 | Derby C | H | L | 0-2 |
| Apr 22 | Charlton A | A | I | 0-1 |
| Apr 29 | Coventry C | H | L | 0-1 |
| May 2 | Wimbledon | H | W | 1-0 |
| May 6 | Southampton | A | L | 1-2 |
| May 8 | QPR | A | L | 2-3 |
| May 10 | Everton | H | L | 1-2 |
| May 13 | Newcastle U | H | W | 2-0 |

**Final League position: 11th**

| P | W | D | L | F/A | Pts |
|---|---|---|---|---|---|
| 38 | 13 | 12 | 13 | 45/35 | 51 |

**FA Cup**

| | | | | |
|---|---|---|---|---|
| Jan 7 | QPR (3) | H | D | 0-0 |
| Jan 11 | QPR (3R) | H | D | 2-2 |
| Jan 23 | QPR (3R2) | H | W | 3-0 |
| Jan 28 | Oxford U (4) | H | W | 4-0 |
| Feb 18 | Bournemouth (5) | A | D | 1-1 |
| Feb 22 | Bournemouth (5R) | H | W | 1-0 |
| Mar 18 | Nottingham F (6) | H | L | 0-1 |

**League Cup**

| | | | | |
|---|---|---|---|---|
| Sep 28 | Rotherham U (2) | A | W | 1-0 |
| Oct 12 | Rotherham (2) | H | W | 5-0 |
| Nov 2 | Wimbledon (3) | A | L | 1-2 |

# 1989-1990

While businessman Michael Knighton's failed bid to takeover the club dominated proceedings off the pitch, an FA Cup win, plus the arrival of £2m midfield ace Paul Ince from West Ham and £2.3m Gary Pallister from Middlesbrough were the main causes of excitement on it. Alex Ferguson also sought to find a winning formula by recruiting Michael Phelan from Norwich City, Neil Webb from Nottingham Forest and Danny Wallace from Southampton. The team was without Norman Whiteside, who went to Everton and Paul McGrath, who left to join Aston Villa. Despite ending up a dismal 13th in Division One, they won the FA Cup after two thrilling matches against Crystal Palace.

**League (Division 1)**

| | | | | |
|---|---|---|---|---|
| Aug 19 | Arsenal | H | W | 4-1 |
| Aug 22 | Crystal Palace | A | D | 1-1 |
| Aug 26 | Derby C | A | L | 0-2 |
| Aug 30 | Norwich C | H | L | 0-2 |
| Sep 9 | Everton | A | L | 2-3 |
| Sep 16 | Millwall | H | W | 5-1 |
| Sep 23 | Manchester C | A | L | 1-5 |
| Oct 14 | Sheffield W | H | D | 0-0 |
| Oct 21 | Coventry C | H | W | 4-1 |
| Oct 28 | Southampton | H | W | 2-1 |
| Nov 4 | Charlton A | A | L | 0-2 |

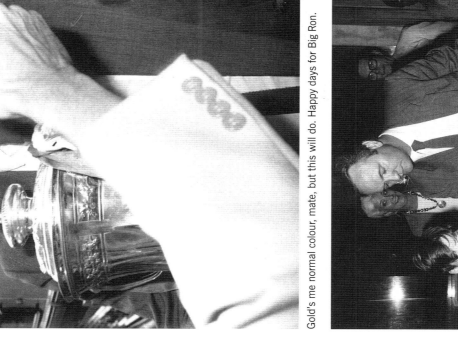

Gold's me normal colour, mate, but this will do. Happy days for Big Ron.

Atkinson won't let go of the 1985 FA Cup. Quite right.

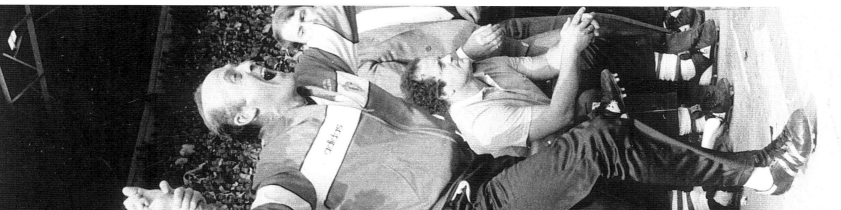

sent off and made history of his own.

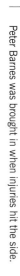

| | | | |
|---|---|---|---|
| Nov 12 | Nottingham F | H | W 1-0 |
| Nov 18 | Luton T | A | W 3-1 |
| Nov 25 | Chelsea | H | D 0-0 |
| Dec 3 | Arsenal | A | L 0-1 |
| Dec 9 | Crystal Palace | H | L 1-2 |
| Dec 16 | Tottenham H | A | L 0-1 |
| Dec 23 | Liverpool | A | D 0-0 |
| Dec 26 | Aston Villa | A | L 0-3 |
| Dec 30 | Wimbledon | A | D 2-2 |
| Jan 1 | QPR | H | D 0-0 |
| Jan 13 | Derby C | H | L 1-2 |
| Jan 21 | Norwich C | A | L 0-2 |
| Feb 3 | Manchester C | H | D 1-1 |
| Feb 10 | Millwall | H | W 2-1 |
| Feb 24 | Chelsea | A | L 0-1 |
| Mar 3 | Luton T | H | W 4-1 |
| Mar 14 | Everton | H | D 0-0 |
| Mar 18 | Liverpool | h | L 1-2 |
| Mar 21 | Sheffield W | A | L 0-1 |
| Mar 24 | Southampton | A | W 2-0 |
| Mar 31 | Coventry C | H | W 3-0 |
| Apr 14 | QPR | A | W 2-1 |
| Apr 17 | Aston Villa | H | w 2-0 |
| Apr 21 | Tottenham H | A | L 1-2 |
| Apr 30 | Wimbledon | H | D 0-0 |
| May 2 | Nottingham F | A | L 0-4 |
| May 5 | Charlton A | H | W 1-0 |

**Final League position: 13th**

| P | W | D | L | F/A | Pts |
|---|---|---|---|---|---|
| 38 | 13 | 9 | 16 | 46/47 | 48 |

## FA Cup

| | | | |
|---|---|---|---|
| Jan 7 | Nottingham F (3) | A | W 1-0 |
| Jab 28 | Hereford U (4) | A | W 1-0 |
| Feb 18 | Newcastle U (5) | A | W 3-2 |
| Mar 11 | Sheffield U (6) | A | W 1-0 |
| Apr 8 | Oldham A (SF) | N | D 3-3 (at Maine Road) |
| Apr 11 | Oldham A (SFR) | N | W 2-1 (at Maine Road) |
| May 12 | Crystal Palace (F) | N | D 3-3 (at Wembley) |
| May 17 | Crystal Palace (FR) | N | W 1-0 (at Wembley) |

## League Cup

| | | | |
|---|---|---|---|
| Sep 20 | Portsmouth (2) | A | W 3-2 |
| Oct 3 | Portsmouth (2) | H | D 0-0 |
| Oct 25 | Tottenham H (3) | H | L 0-3 |

## 1990-1991

Mark Hughes became the hero of the season by scoring both goals for United when they beat Barcelona 2-1 in the final of the European Cup Winner's Cup in Rotterdam. The team also mounted strong challenges in the Rumbelows Cup, where they were beaten in the final by Sheffield Wednesday, and the FA Cup, where they reached the fifth round, before being knocked out by Norwich. A lucky winner off the pitch was club chairman Martin Edwards. He netted millions when United was floated on the stock market. The move also meant money for a new Stretford End at Old Trafford.

Gordon Strachan is stretchered off against West Brom in 1985. Atkinson's injury headaches piled up.

Peter Barnes was brought in when injuries hit the side.

After the joy of Cup victories, Ron suffers the agony of a slum

## League (Division 1)

| Aug 25 | Coventry C | A | W | 2-0 |
|---|---|---|---|---|
| Aug 28 | Leeds U | A | D | 0-0 |
| Sep 1 | Sunderland | A | L | 1-2 |
| Sep 4 | Luton T | A | W | 1-0 |
| Sep 8 | QPR | H | W | 3-1 |
| Sep 16 | Liverpool | A | L | 0-4 |
| Sep 22 | Southampton | H | W | 3-2 |
| Sep 29 | Nottingham F | H | L | 0-1 |
| Oct 20 | Arsenal | H | L | 0-1 |
| Oct 27 | Manchester C | A | D | 3-3 |
| Nov 3 | Crystal Palace | H | W | 2-0 |
| Nov 10 | Derby C | A | D | 0-0 |
| Nov 17 | Sheffield U | H | W | 2-0 |
| Nov 25 | Chelsea | H | L | 2-3 |
| Dec 1 | Everton | A | W | 1-0 |
| Dec 8 | Leeds U | H | D | 1-1 |
| Dec 15 | Coventry C | A | D | 2-2 |
| Dec 22 | Wimbledon | A | W | 3-1 |
| Dec 26 | Norwich C | H | W | 3-0 |
| Dec 29 | Aston Villa | H | D | 1-1 |
| Jan 1 | Tottenham H | A | W | 2-1 |
| Jan 12 | Sunderland | H | W | 3-0 |
| Jan 19 | QPR | A | D | 1-1 |
| Feb 3 | Liverpool | H | D | 1-1 |
| Feb 26 | Sheffield U | A | L | 1-2 |
| Mar 2 | Everton | H | L | 0-2 |
| Mar 9 | Chelsea | A | L | 2-3 |
| Mar 13 | Southampton | A | D | 1-1 |
| Mar 16 | Nottingham F | H | D | 1-1 |
| Mar 23 | Luton T | H | W | 4-1 |
| Mar 30 | Norwich C | A | W | 3-0 |
| Apr 2 | Wimbledon | H | W | 2-1 |
| Apr 6 | Aston Villa | A | D | 1-1 |
| Apr 16 | Derby C | H | W | 3-1 |
| May 4 | Manchester C | H | W | 1-0 |
| May 6 | Arsenal | A | L | 1-3 |
| May 11 | Crystal Palace | A | L | 0-3 |
| May 20 | Tottenham H | H | D | 1-1 |

### Final League position: 6th

| P | W | D | L | F/A | Pts |
|---|---|---|---|---|---|
| 38 | 16 | 12 | 10 | 58/45 | 59 |

## FA Cup

| Jan 7 | QPR (3) | H | W | 2-1 |
|---|---|---|---|---|
| Jan 26 | Bolton W (4) | H | W | 1-0 |
| Feb 18 | Norwich C (5) | A | L | 1-2 |

## League Cup

| Sep 26 | Halifax T (2) | A | W | 3-1 |
|---|---|---|---|---|
| Oct 10 | Halifax T (2) | H | W | 2-1 |
| Oct 31 | Liverpool (3) | H | W | 3-1 |
| Nov 28 | Arsenal (4) | A | W | 6-2 |
| Jan 16 | Southampton (5) | A | D | 1-1 |
| Jan 23 | Southampton (5) | H | W | 3-2 |
| Feb 10 | Leeds U (SF) | H | W | 2-1 |
| Feb 24 | Leeds U (SF) | A | W | 1-0 |
| Apr 21 | Sheffield W (F) | N | L | 0-1 |

(at Wembley)

## European Cup Winners' Cup

| Sep 19 | Pecsi Muncas (1) | H | W | 2-0 |
|---|---|---|---|---|
| Oct 3 | Pecsi Muncas (1) | A | W | 1-0 |
| Oct 23 | Wrexham (2) | H | W | 3-0 |
| Nov 7 | Wrexham (2) | A | W | 2-0 |
| Mar 6 | Montpelier (3) | H | D | 1-1 |
| Mar 19 | Montpelier (3) | A | W | 2-0 |
| Apr 10 | Legia Warsaw (SF) | A | W | 3-1 |
| Apr 24 | Legia Warsaw (SF) | H | D | 1-1 |
| May 15 | Barcelona (F) | N | W | 2-1 |

(at Stadion Feijenoord)

...ay I state my case! Alex Ferguson joined United in November 1987. He would go on to incredible success at the club.

## 1991-1992

More names were added to Alex Ferguson's squad. The Danish goalkeeper, Peter

Schmeichel joined the club along with Andrei Kanchelskis and Paul Parker. Brian McClair became Man Of The Match when he scored against Nottingham Forest at Wembley to win United the Rumbelows Cup. The team performed well in the League too, losing only six out of the 42 matches they played. Good results, including a 5-0 hammering of Luton Town and a 4-0 drubbing of Coventry, ensured they finished in second place behind Leeds United. Overall it was a good season for Ferguson who seemed to be getting his team right at last.

## League (Division 1)

| | | | |
|---|---|---|---|
| Aug 17 | Notts County | H | W 2-0 |
| Aug 21 | Aston Villa | A | W 1-0 |
| Aug 24 | Everton | A | D 0-0 |
| Aug 28 | Oldham A | H | W 1-0 |
| Aug 31 | Leeds u | H | D 1-1 |
| Sep 3 | Wimbledon | A | W 2-1 |
| Sep 7 | Norwich C | H | W 3-0 |
| Sep 14 | Southampton | A | W 1-0 |
| Sep 21 | Luton T | H | W 5-0 |
| Sep 28 | Tottenham H | A | W 2-1 |
| Oct 6 | Liverpool | H | D 0-0 |
| Oct 19 | Arsenal | H | D 1-1 |
| Oct 26 | Sheffield W | A | L 2-3 |
| Nov 2 | Sheffield U | H | W 2-0 |
| Nov 16 | Manchester C | A | D 0-0 |
| Nov 23 | West Ham U | H | W 2-1 |
| Nov 30 | Crystal Palace | A | W 3-1 |
| Dec 7 | Coventry C | H | W 4-0 |
| Dec 15 | Chelsea | A | W 3-1 |
| Dec 26 | Oldham A | A | W 6-3 |
| Dec 29 | Leeds U | A | D 1-1 |
| Jan 1 | QPR | H | L 1-4 |
| Jan 11 | Everton | H | W 1-0 |
| Jan 18 | Notts C | H | W 1-0 |
| Jan 22 | Aston Villa | H | W 1-0 |
| Feb 1 | Arsenal | A | D 1-1 |
| Feb 8 | Sheffield W | H | D 1-1 |
| Feb 22 | Crystal Palace | H | W 2-0 |
| Feb 26 | Chelsea | H | D 1-1 |
| Feb 29 | Coventry C | A | D 0-0 |
| Mar 14 | Sheffield U | A | W 2-1 |
| Mar 18 | Nottingham F | A | L 0-1 |
| Mar 21 | Wimbledon | H | D 0-0 |
| Mar 28 | QPR | A | D 0-0 |
| Mar 31 | Norwich C | A | W 3-1 |
| Apr 7 | Manchester C | H | D 1-1 |
| Apr 16 | Southampton | H | W 1-0 |
| Apr 18 | Luton T | A | D 1-1 |
| Apr 20 | Nottingham F | H | L 1-2 |
| Apr 22 | West Ham U | A | L 0-1 |
| Apr 26 | Liverpool | A | L 0-2 |
| May 2 | Tottenham H | H | W 3-1 |

### Final League position: 2nd

| P | W | D | L | F/A | Pts |
|---|---|---|---|---|---|
| 42 | 21 | 15 | 6 | 63/33 | 78 |

## FA Cup

| | | | |
|---|---|---|---|
| Jan 15 | Leeds U (3) | A | W 1-0 |
| Jan 27 | Southampton (4) | A | D 0-0 |
| Feb 5 | Southampton (4R)H | D 2-2 |
| | (lost on pens) | | |

Ferguson started to inject some backbone in the side. Roy Keane in 1993.

Garry Pallister formed a great team with Bruce.

Hennig Berg would find life tough at Old Trafford.

Mike Phelan and Neil Webb arrive in 1989.

Hughes returns from Barcelona to the relief of the fans in 1988.

Denis Irwin joins in 1990. Thank the Lord.

## League Cup

| | | | | | |
|---|---|---|---|---|---|
| Sep 25 | Cambridge U (2) | H | W | 3-0 | |
| Oct 9 | Cambridge U (2) | A | D | 1-1 | |
| Oct 30 | Portsmouth (3) | H | W | 3-1 | |
| Dec 4 | Oldham A (4) | H | W | 2-0 | |
| Jan 8 | Leeds U (5) | A | W | 3-1 | |
| Mar 4 | Middlesbrough (SF) | A | D | 0-0 | |
| 11 Mar | Middlesbrough (SF) | H | W | 2-1 | |
| Apr 12 | Nottingham F (F) | N | W | 1-0 | |
| | (at Wembley) | | | | |

## European Cup Winners' Cup

| | | | | |
|---|---|---|---|---|
| Sep 18 | Athinaikos (1) | A | D | 0-0 |
| Oct 2 | Athinaikos (1) | H | W | 2-0 |
| Oct 23 | Atletico Madrid (2) | A | L | 0-3 |
| Nov 6 | Atletico Madrid (2) | H | D | 1-1 |

## 1992-1993

A momentous season for United. When the club was offered Denis Irwin by Leeds, Alex Ferguson said "No." However, he used the opportunity to make a bid for controversial French star Eric Cantona. His cheek paid off and the charismatic figure was soon on his way from Leeds to United to take his place in the club's hall of eternal fame. Thanks to his goal-making skills he was soon crowned the new "King" of Old Trafford, a title previously reserved only for the legendary marksman Denis Law. Cantona had the kind of power and flair United needed to succeed in the tough new Premier League. They lost only six games all season and finished top. It was United's first Championship win in 26 years.

## Premier League

| | | | | |
|---|---|---|---|---|
| Aug 15 | Sheffield U | A | L | 1-2 |
| Aug 19 | Everton | H | L | 0-3 |
| Aug 22 | Ipswich T | H | D | 1-1 |
| Aug 24 | Southampton | A | W | 1-0 |
| Aug 29 | Nottingham F | A | W | 2-0 |
| Sep 2 | Crystal Palace | H | W | 1-0 |
| Sep 6 | Leeds U | H | W | 2-0 |
| Sep 12 | Everton | A | W | 2-0 |
| Sep 19 | Tottenham H | A | D | 1-1 |
| Sep 26 | QPR | H | D | 0-0 |
| Oct 3 | Middlesbrough | A | D | 1-1 |
| Oct 18 | Liverpool | H | D | 2-2 |
| Oct 24 | Blackburn R | A | D | 0-0 |
| Oct 31 | Wimbledon | H | L | 0-1 |
| Nov 7 | Aston Villa | A | L | 0-1 |
| Nov 21 | Oldham A | H | W | 3-0 |
| Nov 28 | Arsenal | A | W | 1-0 |
| Dec 6 | Manchester C | H | W | 2-1 |
| Dec 12 | Norwich C | H | W | 1-0 |
| Dec 19 | Chelsea | A | D | 1-1 |
| Dec 26 | Sheffield W | H | D | 3-3 |
| Dec 28 | Coventry C | H | W | 5-0 |
| Jan 9 | Tottenham H | H | W | 4-1 |
| Jan 18 | QPR | A | W | 3-1 |
| Jan 27 | Nottingham F | H | W | 2-0 |
| Jan 30 | Ipswich T | A | L | 1-2 |
| Feb 6 | Sheffield U | H | W | 2-1 |
| Feb 8 | Leeds U | A | D | 0-0 |

...rgie with three crackers – Paul Parker, Andrei Kanchelskis and Peter Schmeichel. They all served United so well.

...erguson's greatest transfer coup. Cole's arrival from Newcastle stunned everyone, not least the Newcastle fans.

## 1993-1994

United completed the double for the first time, winning the League and FA Cups. Irish midfielder Roy Keane made his debut in the Charity Shield victory against Arsenal at Wembley, after being bought by Alex Ferguson from Nottingham Forest for £4m. Although United didn't get past the second round of the European Cup, they dominated the Premier League, losing only four games all season. There was trouble on the pitch. Peter Schmeichel was sent off for handling the ball outside his area and Eric Cantona was dismissed twice. Although the club retained the Championship, it was plunged into mourning following the death on January 20, 1994 of Sir Matt Busby, aged 84.

### Final League position: 1st

| P | W | D | L | F/A | Pts |
|---|---|---|---|-----|-----|
| 42 | 24 | 12 | 6 | 67/31 | 84 |

### FA Cup

| Jan 5 | Bury (3) | H | W | 2-0 |
|---|---|---|---|---|
| Jan 23 | Brighton & HA (4)H | W | 1-0 |  |
| Feb 14 | Sheffield U (5) | A | L | 1-2 |

### League Cup

| Sep 23 | Brighton & HA (2) A | D | 1-1 |
|---|---|---|---|
| Oct 7 | Brighton & HA (2) H | W | 1-0 |
| Oct 28 | Aston Villa (3) | A | L | 0-1 |

### UEFA Cup

| Sep 16 | Torpedo Moscow(1) H | D | 0-0 |
|---|---|---|---|
| Sep 29 | Torpedo Moscow(1) A | D | 0-0 |

### Premiership

| Aug 15 | Norwich City | A | W | 2-0 |
|---|---|---|---|---|
| Aug 18 | Sheffield U | H | W | 3-0 |
| Aug 21 | Newcastle U | H | D | 1-1 |
| Aug 23 | Aston Villa | H | D | 1-1 |
| Aug 28 | Southampton | A | W | 3-1 |
| Sep 1 | West Ham U | H | W | 3-0 |
| Sep 11 | Chelsea | A | L | 0-1 |
| Sep 19 | Arsenal | H | W | 1-0 |
| Sep 25 | Swindon T | H | w | 4-2 |
| Oct 2 | Sheffield w | A | W | 3-2 |
| Oct 16 | Tottenham H | H | W | 2-1 |
| Oct 23 | Everton | A | W | 1-0 |
| Feb 20 | Southampton | H | W | 2-1 |
| Feb 27 | Middlesbrough | H | W | 3-0 |
| Mar 6 | Liverpool | A | W | 2-1 |
| Mar 9 | Oldham A | A | L | 0-1 |
| Mar 14 | Aston Villa | H | D | 1-1 |
| Mar 20 | Manchester C | A | D | 1-1 |
| Mar 24 | Arsenal | H | d | 0-0 |
| Apr 5 | Norwich C | A | W | 3-1 |
| Apr 10 | Sheffield W | H | W | 2-1 |
| Apr 12 | Coventry C | A | W | 1-0 |
| Apr 17 | Chelsea | H | W | 3-0 |
| Apr 21 | Crystal Palace | A | w | 2-0 |
| May 3 | Blackburn | H | W | 3-1 |
| May 9 | Wimbledon | A | W | 2-1 |

The Neville brothers were a real find for United. Club glory and England honours beckoned soon.

A tower of strength at work and at home. Many believe Steve Bruce will return to United one day.

Pensive. Andy Cole fe

| | | | | |
|---|---|---|---|---|
| Oct 30 | QPR | H | W | 2-1 |
| Nov 7 | Manchester C | A | W | 3-2 |
| Nov 20 | Wimbledon | H | w | 3-1 |
| Nov 24 | Ipswich T | H | D | 0-0 |
| Nov 27 | Coventry C | A | W | 1-0 |
| Dec 4 | Norwich C | H | D | 2-2 |
| Dec 7 | Sheffield U | A | W | 3-0 |
| Dec 11 | Newcastle U | A | D | 1-1 |
| Dec 19 | Aston Villa | H | W | 3-1 |
| Dec 26 | Blackburn R | H | D | 1-1 |
| Dec 29 | Oldham A | H | W | 5-2 |
| Jan 1 | Leeds U | H | D | 0-0 |
| Jan 4 | Liverpool | A | D | 3-3 |
| Jan 15 | Tottenham H | A | W | 1-0 |
| Jan 22 | Everton | H | W | 1-0 |
| Feb 5 | QPR | A | W | 3-2 |
| Feb 26 | West Ham | A | D | 2-2 |
| Mar 5 | Chelsea | H | L | 0-1 |
| Mar 16 | Sheffield W | H | W | 5-0 |
| Mar 19 | Swindon t | A | D | 2-2 |
| Mar 22 | Arsenal | A | D | 2-2 |
| Mar 30 | Liverpool | H | W | 1-0 |
| Apr 2 | Blackburn R | A | L | 0-2 |
| Apr 4 | Oldham A | H | W | 3-2 |
| Apr 16 | Wimbledon | A | L | 0-1 |
| Apr 23 | Manchester City | H | W | 2-0 |
| Apr 27 | Leeds U | A | W | 2-0 |
| May 1 | Ipswich T | A | W | 2-1 |
| May 4 | Southampton | H | W | 2-0 |
| MAy 8 | Coventry C | H | D | 0-0 |

**Final League position: 1st**

| P | W | D | L | F/A | Pts |
|---|---|---|---|---|---|
| 42 | 27 | 11 | 4 | 80/38 | 92 |

**FA Cup**

| | | | | |
|---|---|---|---|---|
| Jan 9 | Sheffield U (3) | A | W | 1-0 |
| Jan 30 | Norwich C (4) | A | W | 2-0 |
| Feb 20 | Wimbledon (5) | A | W | 3-0 |
| Mar 12 | Charlton A (6) | H | W | 3-1 |
| Apr 10 | Oldham A (SF) | N | D | 1-1 (at Wembley) |
| Apr 13 | Oldham A (SFR) | N | W | 4-1 (at Maine Road) |
| May 14 | Chelsea | N | W | 4-0 (at Wembley) |

**League Cup**

| | | | | |
|---|---|---|---|---|
| Sep 22 | Stoke C (2) | A | L | 1-2 |
| Oct 6 | Stoke C (2) | H | W | 2-0 |
| Oct 27 | Leicester C (3) | A | W | 5-1 |
| Nov 30 | Everton (4) | A | W | 2-0 |
| Jan 12 | Portsmouth (5) | H | D | 2-2 |
| Jan 26 | Portsmouth (R) | A | W | 1-0 |
| Feb 13 | Sheffield W (SF) | H | W | 1-0 |
| Mar 2 | Sheffield W (SF) | A | W | 4-1 |
| Mar 27 | Aston Villa | N | L | 1-3 (at Wembley) |

**European Cup**

| | | | | |
|---|---|---|---|---|
| Sep 15 | Kispest Honved (1) | A | W | 3-2 |
| Sep 29 | Kispest Honved (1) | H | W | 2-1 |
| Oct 20 | Galatasaray (2) | H | D | 3-3 |
| Nov 3 | Galatasaray (2) | A | D | 0-0 |
| | (lost on away goals rule) | | | |

# 1994-1995

Volatile Eric Cantona brought shame on the club with his infamous kung-fu kick against an abusive Crystal Palace supporter. The Frenchman leapt into the crowd after being sent off during a game against the London side on January 25, 1995. He was charged

Paul Ince lifts the Premiership trophy in 1994. The Reds were flying high.

expectations at Old Trafford and handled it.

with assault and given 150
hours community service.
United suspended Cantona
until the end of the season
and fined him two weeks
wages, £20,000. The
Football Association
extended his ban until
September 30, 1995 and
ordered him to pay a further
£10,000. Alex Ferguson
added Andy Cole, David
May and Keith Gillespie.
Despite their problems
United beat Ipswich 9-0,
finished second and won
the Charity Shield.

## Premiership

| | | | | |
|---|---|---|---|---|
| Aug 20 | QRP | H | W | 2-0 |
| Aug 22 | Nottingham F | A | D | 1-1 |
| Aug 27 | Tottenham H | A | W | 1-0 |
| Aug 31 | Wimbledon | H | W | 3-0 |
| Sep 11 | Leeds U | A | L | 1-2 |
| Sep 17 | Liverpool | H | W | 2-0 |
| Sep 24 | Ipswich T | A | L | 2-3 |
| Oct 1 | Everton | H | W | 2-0 |
| Oct 8 | Sheffield W | A | L | 0-1 |
| Oct 15 | West Ham U | H | W | 1-0 |
| Oct 23 | Blackburn R | A | W | 4-2 |
| Oct 29 | Newcastle U | H | W | 2-0 |
| Nov 6 | Aston Villa | A | W | 2-1 |
| Nov 10 | Manchester C | H | W | 5-0 |
| Nov 19 | Crystal place | H | W | 3-0 |
| Nov 26 | Arsenal | A | D | 0-0 |
| Dec 3 | Norwich C | H | W | 1-0 |
| Dec 10 | QPR | A | W | 3-2 |
| Dec 17 | Nottingham F | H | L | 1-2 |
| Dec 26 | Chelsea | H | W | 3-2 |
| Dec 28 | Leicester C | H | D | 1-1 |
| Dec 31 | Southampton | A | D | 2-2 |
| Jan 3 | Coventry c | H | W | 2-0 |
| Jan 15 | Newcastle U | A | D | 1-1 |
| Jan 22 | Blackburn R | H | W | 1-0 |
| Jan 25 | Crystal Palace | A | D | 1-1 |
| Feb 4 | Aston Villa | H | W | 1-0 |
| Feb 11 | Manchester C | A | W | 3-0 |
| Feb 22 | Norwich C | A | W | 2-0 |
| Feb 25 | Everton | A | L | 0-1 |
| Mar 4 | Ipswich T | H | W | 9-0 |
| Mar 7 | Wimbledon | A | W | 1-0 |
| Mar 15 | Tottenham H | H | D | 0-0 |
| Mar 19 | Liverpool | A | L | 0-2 |
| Mar 22 | Arsenal | H | W | 3-0 |
| Apr 2 | Leeds U | H | D | 0-0 |
| Apr 15 | Leicester City | A | W | 4-0 |
| Apr 17 | Chelsea | H | D | 0-0 |
| May 1 | Coventry C | A | W | 3-2 |
| May 7 | Sheffield w | H | W | 1-0 |
| May 10 | Southampton | H | W | 2-1 |
| May 14 | West Ham U | A | D | 1-1 |

**Final League position: 2nd**

| P | W | D | L | F/A | Pts |
|---|---|---|---|---|---|
| 42 | 26 | 10 | 6 | 77/28 | 88 |

## FA Cup

| | | | | |
|---|---|---|---|---|
| Jan 9 | Sheffield U (3) | A | W | 2-0 |
| Jan 28 | Wrexham (4) | H | W | 5-2 |
| Feb 18 | Leeds U (5) | H | W | 3-1 |
| Mar 12 | QPR (6) | H | W | 2-0 |
| Apr 9 | Crystal Palace (SF) | N | D | 2-0 |
| | (at Villa Park) | | | |
| Apr 12 | Crystal Palace (SFR) | N | W | 2-0 |
| | (at Villa Park) | | | |
| May 20 | Everton (F) | N | L | 0-1 |
| | (at Wembley) | | | |

Schmeichel provided an amazing sight when he rushed up field as United pressed for a goal against Rotor Volgograd 1995 – an

## League Cup

| | | | | |
|---|---|---|---|---|
| Sep 21 | Port Vale (0) | A | W | 2-1 |
| Oct 5 | Port Vale (0) | H | W | 2-0 |
| Oct 26 | Newcastle U (0) | A | L | 0-2 |

## European Cup

| | | | | |
|---|---|---|---|---|
| Sep 14 | IFK Gothenburg (0) | H | W | 4-2 |
| Sep 28 | Galatasaray (0) | A | D | 0-0 |
| Oct 19 | Barcelona (0) | H | D | 2-2 |
| Nov 2 | Barcelona (0) | A | L | 0-4 |
| Nov 23 | IFK Gothenburg (0) | A | L | 1-3 |
| Dec 7 | Galatasaray (0) | H | W | 4-0 |

# 1995-1996

Le King, Eric Cantona, returned to help United achieve their record-breaking second double in three years. He was captain of the team when he scored the only goal in the FA Cup Final against Liverpool. It was the perfect answer to critics who had predicted little glory for him or United at the beginning of the season. Although the club were knocked out of the UEFA Cup by Rotor Volgograd, goalkeeper Peter Schmeichel delighted fans by heading a goal during the match. While David Beckham, Paul Scholes and the Neville brothers began to shine, Paul Ince, Mark Hughes and Andrei Kanchelskis all left the club.

## Premiership

| | | | | |
|---|---|---|---|---|
| Aug 19 | Aston Villa | A | L | 1-3 |
| Aug 23 | West Ham U | H | w | 2-1 |
| Aug 26 | Wimbledon | H | w | 3-1 |
| Aug 28 | Blackburn R | A | W | 2-1 |
| Sep 9 | Everton | A | W | 3-2 |
| Sep 16 | Bolton W | H | W | 3-0 |
| Sep 23 | Sheffield W | A | D | 0-0 |
| Oct 1 | Liverpool | H | D | 2-2 |
| Oct 14 | Manchester C | H | W | 1-0 |
| Oct 21 | Chelsea | A | W | 4-1 |
| Oct 28 | Middlesbrough | H | W | 2-0 |
| Nov 4 | Arsenal | A | L | 0-1 |
| Nov 18 | Southampton | H | W | 2-1 |
| Nov 22 | Coventry City | A | W | 4-0 |
| Nov 27 | Nottingham F | A | D | 1-1 |
| Dec 2 | Chelsea | H | D | 1-1 |
| Dec 9 | Sheffield W | H | D | 2-2 |
| Dec 17 | Liverpool | A | L | 0-2 |
| Dec 24 | Leeds U | A | L | 1-3 |
| Dec 27 | Newcastle U | H | W | 2-0 |
| Dec 30 | QPR | H | W | 2-1 |
| Jan 1 | Tottenham H | A | L | 1-4 |
| Jan 13 | Aston Villa | H | D | 0-0 |
| Jan 22 | West Ham U | A | W | 1-0 |
| Feb 3 | Wimbledon | A | W | 4-2 |
| Feb 10 | Blackburn R | H | W | 1-0 |
| Feb 21 | Everton | H | W | 2-0 |
| Feb 25 | Bolton W | A | W | 6-0 |
| Mar 4 | Newcastle U | A | W | 1-0 |
| Mar 16 | QPR | A | D | 1-1 |
| Mar 20 | Arsenal | H | W | 1-0 |

Success is so sweet, and Peter Schmeichel gave his all for United. He left great memories at the club.

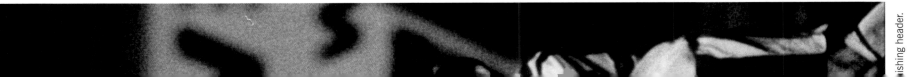

...ishing header.

# 1996-1997

David Beckham kicked off the season with his amazing 75-yard shot from inside United's own half during a game against Wimbledon. Eric Cantona stunned fans by retiring from football and Teddy Sheringham left Tottenham to join United for £3.5m. Alex Ferguson bought in more foreign players, notably Ole Gunnar Solskjaer from Molde, Johan Cruyff's son Jordi from Barcelona and Karel Poborsky from Slavia Prague. There was controversy on the pitch when Ian Wright accused Peter Schmeichel of making racist comments. The allegation was strongly denied by the Dane. United were crowned champions for the fourth time in five seasons.

**Final League position: 1st**

| P | W | D | L | F/A | Pts |
|---|---|---|---|-----|-----|
| 38 | 25 | 7 | 6 | 73/35 | 82 |

**FA Cup**

| Jan 6 | Sunderland (3) | H | D | 2-2 |
|---|---|---|---|---|
| Jan 16 | Sunderland (3R) | A | W | 2-1 |
| Jan 27 | Reading (4) | A | W | 3-0 |
| Feb 18 | Manchester C (5) | H | W | 2-1 |
| Mar 11 | Southampton (6) | H | W | 2-0 |
| Mar 31 | Chelsea (SF) (at Villa Park) | N | W | 2-1 |
| May 11 | Liverpool (F) (at Wembley) | N | W | 1-0 |

**League Cup**

| Sep 20 | York City (0) | H | L | 0-3 |
|---|---|---|---|---|
| Oct 3 | York City (0) | A | W | 3-1 |

**UEFA Cup**

| Sep 12 | Rotor Volgograd (0) | A | D | 0-0 |
|---|---|---|---|---|
| Sep 26 | Rotor Volgograd (0) | H | D | 2-2 |

**Premiership**

| Aug 17 | Wimbledon | A | W | 3-0 |
|---|---|---|---|---|
| Aug 21 | Everton | H | D | 2-2 |
| Aug 25 | Blackburn R | H | D | 2-2 |
| Sep 4 | Derby C | A | D | 1-1 |
| Sep 7 | Leeds U | A | W | 4-0 |
| Sep 14 | Nottingham F | H | W | 4-1 |
| Sep 21 | Aston Villa | A | D | 0-0 |
| Sep 29 | Tottenham H | H | W | 2-0 |
| Oct 12 | Liverpool | H | W | 1-1 |
| Oct 20 | Newcastle U | A | L | 0-5 |
| Oct 26 | Southampton | A | L | 3-6 |
| Nov 2 | Chelsea | H | L | 1-2 |
| Mar 24 | Tottenham H | H | W | 1-0 |
| Apr 6 | Manchester C | A | W | 3-2 |
| Apr 8 | Coventry C | H | W | 1-0 |
| Apr 13 | Southampton | A | L | 1-2 |
| Apr 17 | Leeds U | H | W | 1-0 |
| Apr 28 | Nottingham F | H | W | 5-0 |
| May 5 | Middlesbrough | A | W | 3-0 |

Playtime for a genius. Ryan Giggs was protected by Ferguson but he's matured into his own man now and a diehard Red.

Hello girls, remember my goal against Arsenal? No? Let me tell you about it. Right: Giggs and Lee Sharpe with adoring fans.

Streetwise. Giggs has had fame and fortune thrust on him at an early age, but taken it all in his stride. A real United star.

| Date | Opponent | H/A | Result | Score |
|---|---|---|---|---|
| Nov 16 | Arsenal | H | W | 1-0 |
| Nov 23 | Middlesbrough | A | D | 2-2 |
| Nov 30 | Leicester C | H | W | 3-1 |
| Dec 8 | West Ham U | H | D | 2-2 |
| Dec 18 | Sheffield W | A | D | 1-1 |
| Dec 21 | Sunderland | A | W | 5-0 |
| Dec 26 | Nottingham F | H | W | 4-0 |
| Dec 28 | Leeds U | H | W | 1-0 |
| Jan 1 | Aston Villa | H | D | 0-0 |
| Jan 12 | Tottenham H | A | W | 2-1 |
| Jan 18 | Coventry C | A | W | 2-0 |
| Feb 1 | Southampton | H | W | 2-1 |
| Feb 19 | Arsenal | A | D | 1-1 |
| Feb 22 | Chelsea | H | W | 3-1 |
| Mar 1 | Coventry C | A | L | 1-2 |
| Mar 8 | Sunderland | H | W | 2-0 |
| Mar 15 | Sheffield W | H | W | 2-0 |
| Mar 22 | Everton | A | W | 2-0 |
| Apr 5 | Derby C | H | L | 2-3 |
| Apr 9 | Chelsea | H | L | 1-2 |
| Apr 12 | Blackburn R | A | W | 3-2 |
| Apr 19 | Liverpool | H | W | 3-1 |
| May 3 | Leicester C | A | D | 2-2 |
| May 5 | Middlesbrough | H | D | 3-3 |
| May 8 | Newcastle U | H | D | 0-0 |
| May 11 | West Ham U | A | W | 3-1 |

Final League position: **1st**

| P | W | D | L | F/A | Pts |
|---|---|---|---|---|---|
| 38 | 21 | 12 | 5 | 76/44 | 75 |

**FA Cup**

| Date | Opponent | H/A | Result | Score |
|---|---|---|---|---|
| Jan 5 | Tottenham H (3) | H | W | 2-0 |
| Jan 25 | Wimbledon (4) | H | D | 1-1 |
| Feb 4 | Wimbledon (4R) | A | L | 0-1 |

**League Cup**

| Date | Opponent | H/A | Result | Score |
|---|---|---|---|---|
| Oct 23 | Swindon T (0) | H | W | 2-1 |
| Nov 27 | Leicester C (0) | A | L | 0-2 |

**European Cup**

| Date | Opponent | H/A | Result | Score |
|---|---|---|---|---|
| Sep 11 | Juventus (0) | A | L | 0-1 |
| Sep 25 | Rapid Vienna (0) | H | W | 2-0 |
| Oct 16 | Fenerbahce (0) | A | W | 2-0 |
| Oct 30 | Fenerbahce (0) | H | L | 0-1 |
| Nov 20 | Juventus (0) | H | W | 3-2 |
| Dec 4 | Rapid Vienna (0) | A | W | 2-0 |
| Mar 5 | Porto (0) | H | W | 4-0 |
| Mar 19 | Porto (0) | A | D | 0-0 |
| Apr 9 | B Dortmund (0) | A | L | 0-1 |
| Apr 23 | B Dortmund (0) | H | L | 0-1 |

Schmeichel's attempt to repeat his goal against Volgograd in 1995 during a clash with Arsenal resulted in a hamstring injury that put paid to title hopes. However United did win the Charity Shield at Wembley. They beat Chelsea 4-2 after a penalty shoot out. Ronnie Johnsen scored his first goal for The Reds.

**Premiership**

| Date | Opponent | H/A | Result | Score |
|---|---|---|---|---|
| Aug 10 | Tottenham H | A | W | 2-0 |
| Aug 13 | Southampton | H | W | 1-0 |
| Aug 23 | Leicester C | A | L | 0-1 |
| Aug 27 | Everton | A | W | 2-0 |
| Aug 30 | Coventry C | H | W | 3-0 |
| Sep 13 | West Ham U | H | W | 2-1 |
| Sep 20 | Bolton W | A | D | 0-0 |
| Sep 24 | Chelsea | H | D | 2-2 |
| Sep 27 | Leeds U | A | L | 0-1 |
| Oct 4 | Crystal Palace | A | D | 2-2 |
| Oct 18 | Derby C | A | D | 2-2 |
| Oct 25 | Barnsley | H | W | 7-0 |
| Nov 1 | Sheffield W | H | W | 6-1 |
| Nov 9 | Arsenal | A | L | 2-3 |
| Nov 22 | Wimbledon | H | W | 5-2 |
| Nov 30 | Blackburn R | A | W | 4-0 |
| Dec 6 | Liverpool | A | W | 3-1 |
| Dec 15 | Aston Villa | H | W | 1-0 |
| Dec 21 | Newcastle U | A | W | 4-1 |
| Dec 26 | Everton | H | W | 2-0 |
| Dec 28 | Coventry C | A | L | 2-3 |
| Jan 10 | Tottenham H | H | W | 2-0 |
| Jan 19 | Southampton | A | L | 0-1 |
| Jan 31 | Leicester C | H | L | 0-1 |
| Feb 7 | Bolton W | H | D | 1-1 |
| Feb 18 | Aston Villa | A | W | 2-0 |
| Feb 21 | Derby C | A | W | 2-0 |
| Feb 28 | Chelsea | A | W | 1-0 |
| Mar 7 | Sheffield W | H | L | 0-2 |
| Mar 11 | West Ham U | A | D | 1-1 |
| Mar 14 | Arsenal | H | L | 0-1 |
| Mar 28 | Wimbledon | H | W | 2-0 |
| Apr 6 | Blackburn R | A | W | 3-1 |
| Apr 10 | Liverpool | H | D | 1-1 |
| Apr 18 | Newcastle U | H | D | 1-1 |
| Apr 27 | Crystal Palace | A | W | 3-0 |
| May 4 | Leeds U | H | W | 3-0 |
| May 10 | Barnsley | A | W | 2-0 |

# 1997-1998

United suffered a bad blow as Cantona's replacement as captain Roy Keane damaged cruciate ligaments during a game against Leeds and needed surgery. Despite other injury woes, the team had some convincing wins, particularly 7-0 against Barnsley and 6-1 against Sheffield Wednesday. United only lost seven games and came second with 77 points. The 40th anniversary of the Munich Air Disaster was marked by a memorial service at Manchester Cathedral attended by survivors and their families. Peter

Final League position: **2nd**

| P | W | D | L | F/A | Pts |
|---|---|---|---|---|---|
| 38 | 23 | 8 | 7 | 73/26 | 77 |

**FA Cup**

| Date | Opponent | H/A | Result | Score |
|---|---|---|---|---|
| Jan 4 | Chelsea (3) | A | W | 5-3 |
| Jan 24 | Walsall (4) | H | W | 5-1 |
| 15 Feb | Barnsley (5) | H | D | 1-1 |
| Feb 25 | Barnsley (5R) | A | L | 2-3 |

**League Cup**

| Date | Opponent | H/A | Result | Score |
|---|---|---|---|---|
| Oct 14 | Ipswich T (3) | A | L | 0-2 |

**European Cup**

| Date | Opponent | H/A | Result | Score |
|---|---|---|---|---|
| Sep 17 | Kosice (G) | A | W | 3-0 |
| Oct 1 | Juventus (G) | H | W | 3-2 |
| Oct 22 | Feyenoord (G) | H | W | 2-1 |
| Nov 5 | Feyenoord (G) | A | W | 3-1 |
| Nov 27 | Kosice (G) | H | W | 3-0 |
| Dec 10 | Juventus (G) | A | L | 0-1 |
| Mar 4 | Monaco (G) | A | D | 0-0 |
| Mar 18 | Monaco (G) | H | D | 1-1 |

...e shy kid turns heart-throb. Giggs is followed everywhere by the cameras.

# Le King

A few years ago, a massive advertising hoarding suddenly appeared in streets all over Britain. Alongside a picture of a fierce-looking Frenchman were the words: "1966 was a great year for English football. Eric was born." Since then, there have been many occasions when United fans have indeed thanked heaven for the very existence of Eric Cantona, a footballer who arrived at Old Trafford in 1992 with a fearsome reputation as being one of the most difficult players in the world and a man who would walk away from a club at the merest hint of criticism.

Prior to his donning the Red shirt, the tag was seemingly justified. He had been banned from international football for a year after a stand up row with the French national coach and then compounded the crime in 1991 by branding members of a disciplinary committee "idiots". After a fiery career with the likes of Auxerre, Montpellier and Marseille, Cantona had had enough. He announced he was retiring from football and the bad-boy tag was well and truly stapled to his name. But the French loss was the English game's gain. He decided to move to England, first for a trial with Sheffield Wednesday, then a full squad place with Leeds United under Howard Wilkinson. Mention the name Cantona to any Leeds supporter today – should they actually want to talk to you as a Red – and the subject will be changed immediately. He was the darling of the Elland Road faithful, helping the team to the title and a Charity Shield victory with a hat-trick in 1992, but the mix of Gallic fire and Yorkshire grit was like oil and water. Alex Ferguson says that Cantona was the best signing of his career, but stories differ as to who exactly signed him. United chairman Martin Edwards claims that Fergie was on holiday when the call came

through from Wilkinson enquiring about the possibility of signing Denis Irwin and mentioned that Eric might be up for grabs. Edward businessman through and through, says he turned down the b for Irwin flat but then followed up with: "We'll have Canto though." At £1 million it was the best deal United had done decades, and much to the dismay of Leeds fans Eric The Ma became Eric The Red.

It changed United's fortunes dramatically for the next five yea and brought to the club success they had lived, breathed and dream of for 26 years. When he took to the field against Tottenham January 1993, United fans flocked to the match, along with hord of press and TV cameras, eager to see what all the fuss was abo Who was this strutting, silent Frenchman who could barely utt word of English but who somehow attracted all the attention? Th soon found out. In a 4-1 win, Cantona scored a stunning head and then set up Denis Irwin to ram home another goal. The pape were full of his prowess, the crowds took up the chant of "Oo ahh Cantona" while rival fans and jealous pundits muttered dark about his "arrogance" and predicted that Ferguson would nev handle him. How wrong they proved to be.

Cantona strutted and strolled like the French national cocker back upright and collar upturned, leading the marauding Re in some devastating performances. He had been at United f just six months and, glory of glories, they were Champions. B the best was yet to come. The following season saw United rom to the Double with Cantona scoring 18 goals and yet more prai being heaped upon his broad shoulders. The Frenchman took all in his stride, as if it was obvious that United would hit the heig The philosopher/footballer was supremely confident of his, a

s team-mates' abilities. But those critics who had been forced to t their words suddenly came into their own in 1995 when Cantona w more than red and launched himself with a Kung-Fu style ck at a fan at Selhurst Park who had hurled abuse at his nationality. ough never condoning his actions, Ferguson stood by him and rtured Cantona through an eight-month ban and a two-week ntence, reduced to 120 hours of community service. He served s "time" in exemplary fashion, turning out to teach youngsters s skills every day and becoming the role model few had given him edit for in the past.

e returned to the game in October 1995 and continued where he left off, leading United to a string of stylish victories which had even the most hardened sports pundits purring at his talent.

His relationship with Ferguson grew into genuine endship as the team prospered, especially in the Cup Final against verpool when he broke the deadlock of a hard-fought match d gave United a great victory with a late goal that pierced a owded Liverpool goalmouth like an arrow. After captaining the eds to a fourth championship in 1997 Le King decided to quit the top, and though United fans were stunned by the news, the ow was softened with the thought that no other team would be tting the benefit of Cantona's sublime skills. He left Old Trafford emotional scenes and moved to Barcelona to take up writing and ting, appearing in recent years in several movies, to critical claim. For the millions who followed his every move on the ch he will always be known as simply King Eric. He came, he w, he conquered, and they will never forget what he did for United.

Cantona hails his new followers.

Le King arrives and the legend begins.

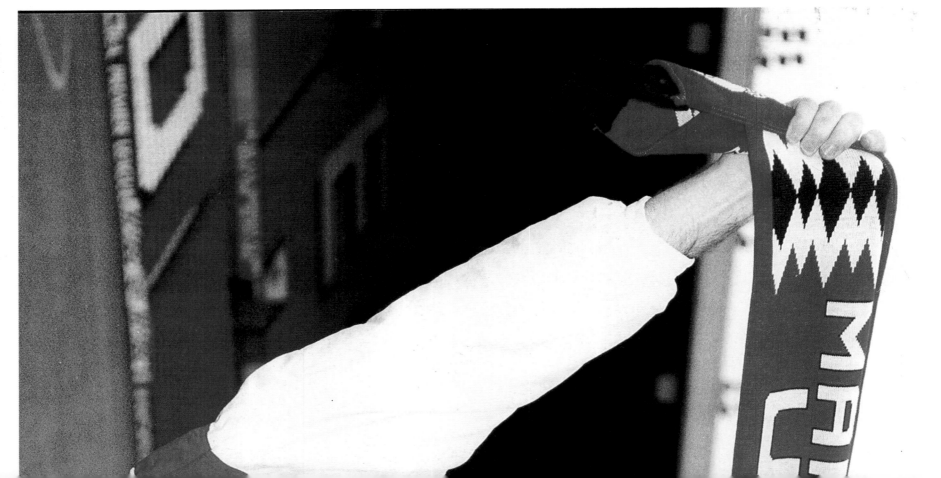

Surveying his domain at the Theatre Of Dreams. Old Trafford was to be the stage on which he proved his right to rule.

The unmistakable style of Eric Cantona in a match against Leeds. Some called it arrogance, the fans responded with their own assessment –"Ooh ahh Canto...

Head and shoulders above the opposition as Irwin looks on in admiration.

Come on, take it off me if you can. Cantona was a master at holding the ball in play.

May I make a couple of points, ref! Cantona disputes a decision in the 1997 FA Cup game against Wimbledon but was booked for his trouble. He made referees as

Where'd he go? The power and the passion of Cantona.

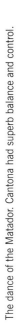

The dance of the Matador. Cantona had superb balance and control.

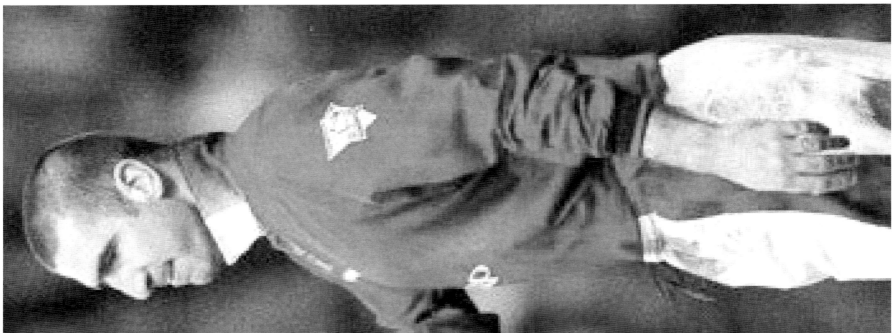

defenders.

Eric and his son Raphael line up with Bryan Robson at the Munich Testimonial in 1998.

My ball. Cantona with team-mate Andy Cole.

Brothers in arms. Despite his reputation as a

...he forged a genuine friendship with Alex Ferguson built on mutual respect.

Cantona had a stunning array of weapons in his armoury, and there were many celebrations for the fantastic Frenchman as a result. Above: Cantona climbed another rung on the ladder of his fame.

After signing for United in 1992, the fans clamour for his signature and he always obliged. It was one of the reasons supporters loved Eric Cantona.

He even spent time with fans in the dugout...

...and gave youngsters moments they would treasure.

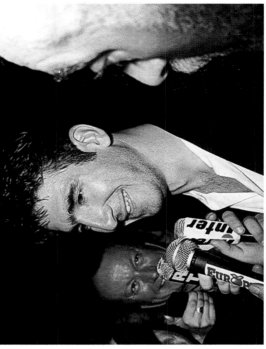

The press couldn't get enough of Cantona's views on the game.

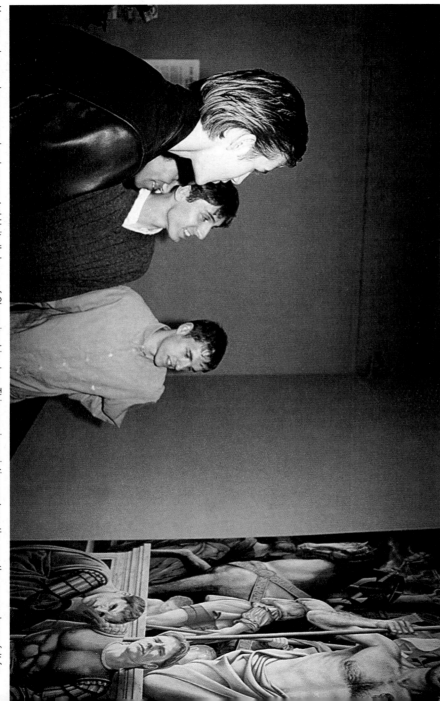

He came, he saw, he conquered and resurrected United's hopes of Championship glory. This amazing painting captures the awe the young players felt for Cantona. Beckham and the Neville Brothers, seen here with the artist, readily admit they learned a huge amount from their French colleague.

**UNITED LEGENDS** ERIC CANTONA

Proclaim his name from the rooftops! A fan makes a reference to Cantona's famous speech about seagulls following the trawler expecting sardines to be thrown to them. It was a comparison with his own relationship with media which hung on his every word.

The style man. Cantona arrives to collect his Player Of The Year Award.

Cantona off-duty after a training session.

Sacre bleu! TV's Spitting Image lampooned Eric mercilessly.

Bring me my Shield. Cantona lifts the Charity Shield in 1995.

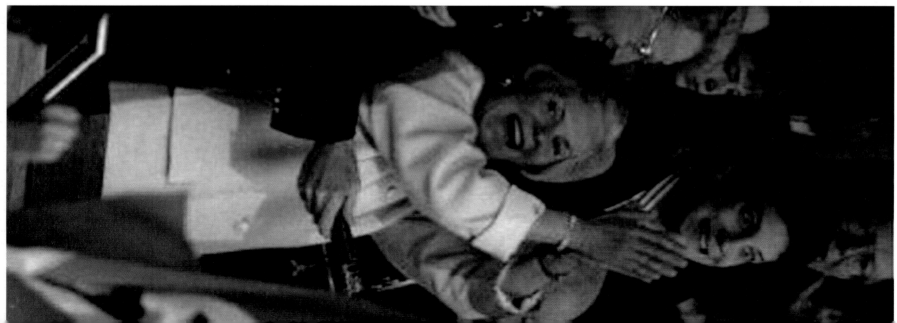

Even The Duchess Of Kent is a fan as Cantona hoists the FA Cup in 199

er brought Liverpool to their knees.

I did it my way. Cantona bids the fans and the club a fond farewell after his decision to turn his back on football in 1997. United followers couldn't believe it, but he was going out at the top and there was only one thing they wanted to say to Le King – "so long, it was good to know you".

# Man And Boy

P icture the scene. Beckham pauses for a moment on the half-way line, he looks up, sees the Wimbledon keeper Sullivan off his line and blasts a shot straight into the history books. Fans gasped as the ball hit the back of the net 75 yards away. It's the kind of moment you usually read about in soccer comics, but with that incredible kick in the closing moments of the opening game of the 1996-97 season between United and Wimbledon, David Beckham gave notice to the world he was a talent to be reckoned with in the mould of greats like Best and Law.

Now picture another scene, 18 months later. Beckham, clad in England strip, lies on the pitch after being floored during the second-round World Cup match against Argentina. Amazingly, with the referee only feet away, he lashes out with a boot at the player who brought him down. Beckham's petulance earned him the red card and the scorn of England fans as his team, now down to ten men, England lost the crucial game on penalties and were knocked out of the competition. United's young golden wonder had gone from hero to zero in an instant, as adoration turned to hatred. Instead of caving in under the pressure he took the advice of his mentor and boss at United, Alex Ferguson. Beckham picked himself up, dusted off his battered ego, put his head down and got on with the job. The boy had become a man. He was now truly ready for superstardom.

Born on May 2, 1975 in the East End of London, Beckham started playing the beautiful game a soon as he could fit into a pair of boots. A United fanatic, his dad bought him a new replica strip every Christmas. There was never any doubt where the boy's true loyalties lay – he once arrived for a trial at Tottenham wearing United kit. By the age of 11 his talents were obvious. He beat everyone hollow in a Bobby Charlton skills competition and was snapped up by the club. United's youth coach, Eric Harrison, summed up the teenager's potential when he said his skills had to be "seen to be believed." Fans got a chance to see their new boy wonder in action when he made his first-team debut in September 1992. He came on as a substitute at Brighton and, due to his good looks and mop of blond hair, became an instant hit with the girls. The fellas warmed to him too when he scored against Galatasaray during a European Cup game in December 1994. However, it

wasn't until the 1995-96 season that Beckham really began to shine. With Ince and Kanchelskis out of the way he was able to make the midfield his own. In 32 appearances he scored eight times, notably the winner in the FA Cup semi-final against Chelsea. Beckham had become the best crosser of a ball in Europe (he destroyed Inter Milan in the Champions' league semi-final in Turin with crosses so accurate no defender could touch them). The following season produced his wonder goal, the longest successful shot since the Premiership started in 1992. It sparked a string of dead-ball crackers from outside the area – now regarded as his speciality. Nobody was surprised when he was voted the PFA's Young Player of the Year. In 1997-98 he was the club's number one midfield goal scorer. He netted 11 and set-up 22.

T he blond bombshell was obviously good enough to play for his country and became the only player to appear in all of the qualifying matches for the 1998 World Cup Finals. As well as dazzling fans with his skills on the pitch, the young heart-throb scored sensationally off it as well. His love match with Victoria Adam better known as Posh Spice from the Spice Girls, made headlin news around the world. They now have a son called Brooklyn. doting dad, Beckham even went so far as to have his boy's nam tattooed across his back. United fans are now waiting to see Brooklyn is going to follow in his father's stud marks. Fame h brought the lad from Leytonstone riches beyond the dreams of ordinary young men. As well as a bumper pay packet from Unite he also earns millions a year for advertising soccer gear, so drinks and cosmetics. His vast income, estimated at £8 million year, has enabled Beckham to live the millionaire lifestyle, comple with fast cars, a luxury home, exotic holidays and designer outfit However, his love of expensive clothes has left him open to ridicul by some critics, who have labelled the trend-setter a bit of a "fashio victim." They smirked when he was pictured strolling along wit his arm round Victoria wearing a skirt-like sarong. Such barbs ar unlikely to trouble Beckham too much and anyway, United fans ar quite prepared to excuse his little eccentricities, provided h keeps performing like a hero on the pitch. With Beckham now more mature, family man, they know the best is yet to come.

Star in the making: Beckham's talent was obvious even at the age of 12.

He meets his hero Bobby Charlton – now they're both European Cup winners.

He's quiet off the pitch, but when he scores he sure lets you know how it feels.

The best crosser of a ball in the world. But the dead-ball skill of Beckham con

practice every day with that sweet right foot.

You should be in movies! Becks is blessed with good looks as well as talent

Heading for the heights. Becks gives his all again on the pitch.

Just like George Best before him, flooring the boy wonder is the only way defenders can stop him. He used to react, but he's matured greatly now.

we ever forget that amazing lob of the Wimbledon 'keeper in 1998? No. Here he takes them on again in the return match.

Superstars. Becks with Posh Spice Victoria Adams. The couple have a lifestyle the envy of millions.

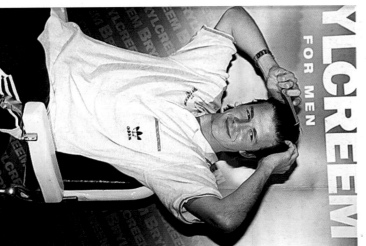

Smooth operator. Beckham promotes Brylcreem.

Lucky boy indeed, to be playing for the biggest club in the world with Fergie as your boss!

## 1998/99

A glorious season. United won the treble. Alex Ferguson was hailed as the greatest manager the club has ever seen – even surpassing Sir Matt Busby's legendary achievements. Supersubs Teddy Sheringham and Ole Gunnar Solksjaer were the heroes, coming on to score breathtaking goals in the heartstopping European Cup Final against Bayern Munich in Barcelona. Towering defender Jaap Stam hardened United's defence and captain Roy Keane was hit by terrible luck. An injury flared up again at the start of the FA Cup Final, forcing him to watch Sheringham ensure glory. Two bookings in the European Cup competition also ruled him out of the final. The scenes when United brought the trophies home to Manchester echoed the glory of 1968.

### Premier League

| | | | | | | F/A | |
|---|---|---|---|---|---|---|---|
| Aug 15 | Leicester C | H | D | 2-2 | | | |
| Aug 22 | West Ham U | A | D | 0-0 | | | |
| Sep 9 | Charlton A | H | W | 4-1 | | | |
| Sep 12 | Coventry C | H | W | 2-0 | | | |
| Sep 20 | Arsenal | A | L | 3-0 | | | |
| Sep 24 | Liverpool | H | W | 2-0 | | | |
| Oct 3 | Southampton | A | W | 3-0 | | | |
| Oct 17 | Wimbledon | H | W | 5-1 | | | |
| Oct 24 | Derby Co | A | D | 1-1 | | | |
| Oct 31 | Everton | A | W | 4-1 | | | |
| Nov 8 | Newcastle U | H | D | 0-0 | | | |
| Nov 14 | Blackburn R | H | W | 3-2 | | | |
| Nov 21 | Sheffield W | A | L | 1-3 | | | |
| Nov 29 | Leeds U | H | W | 3-2 | | | |
| Dec 5 | Aston Villa | A | D | 1-1 | | | |
| Dec 12 | Tottenham H | A | D | 2-2 | | | |
| Dec 16 | Chelsea | H | D | 1-1 | | | |
| Dec 19 | Middlesbrough | H | L | 2-3 | | | |
| Dec 26 | Nottingham F | H | W | 3-0 | | | |
| Dec 29 | Chelsea | A | D | 0-0 | | | |
| Jan 10 | West Ham U | H | W | 4-1 | | | |
| Jan 16 | Leicester C | A | W | 6-2 | | | |
| Jan 31 | Charlton A | A | W | 1-0 | | | |
| Feb 3 | Derby Co | H | W | 1-0 | | | |
| Feb 6 | Nottingham F | A | W | 8-1 | | | |
| Feb 17 | Arsenal | H | D | 1-1 | | | |
| Feb 20 | Coventry C | A | W | 1-0 | | | |
| Feb 27 | Southampton | H | W | 2-1 | | | |
| Mar 13 | Newcastle U | A | W | 2-1 | | | |
| Mar 21 | Everton | H | W | 3-1 | | | |
| April 3 | Wimbledon | A | D | 1-1 | | | |
| April 17 | Sheffield W | H | W | 3-0 | | | |
| April 25 | Leeds U | A | D | 1-1 | | | |
| May 1 | Aston Villa | H | W | 2-1 | | | |
| May 5 | Liverpool | A | D | 2-2 | | | |
| May 9 | Middlesbrough | A | W | 1-0 | | | |
| May 12 | Blackburn R | A | D | 0-0 | | | |
| May 15 | Tottenham H | H | W | 2-1 | | | |

Final League position: **1st**

| P | W | D | L | F/A | Pts |
|---|---|---|---|---|---|
| 38 | 22 | 13 | 3 | 83/34 | 79 |

# Three Steps To Heaven

A ugust 15, 1998. Manchester United are playing badly against Leicester at Old Trafford in the first match of the season. The team is labouring 2-0 down when David Beckham, still smarting from his World Cup exit, curls a stunning 25-yard free kick into the corner of the net. Then Alex Ferguson plays his final card. He sends on a certain Edward Sheringham and United start an amazing fightback to salvage a point from the jaws of imminent defeat.

Now where did we see this again?

May 26, 1999 is where. At the Nou Camp Stadium in Barcelona the United team – average age an incredible 24 – scaled unparalleled heights of sporting achievement and finished nine months in the most gruelling League in the world with the ultimate success. They made history as the only English club to achieve the treble of the Premiership, the FA Cup and the European Cup, but the way they did it was typical. We started this story of Manchester United with the words The Agony and The Ecstasy. That night in Barcelona was to prove just how true this is with The Reds. United were not to have it all their own way though

in a season which tested not only the resolve of manage Alex Ferguson and his young squad, but the very nerv endings of the fans. Arsenal had a powerful side c French stars buoyed up by World Cup success, Chelsea glamour-boys were a threat and the talented young sters at Leeds under David O'Leary were alway expected to come good and mount a late challenge John Gregory's Aston Villa got off to a flying start a the beginning of the season, clinching a string c swaggering victories with former Manchester Unite striker Dion Dublin seemingly unable to miss the bac of the net with his eyes shut. They were top, but th midlands side was to fade as the real pace of life in the fast lane took its toll.

Ferguson, however, had built a squad to prevent such a collapse at United. Dwight Yorke and Andy Co were beginning to purr as a front force, the home grown young guns of Beckham, Giggs, the Nevil brothers, Paul Scholes and Nicky Butt were hung Roy Keane was making the midfield his own domain and the back line of Stam, Johnsen, and the unfailin Dennis Irwin were starting to gel as a defensive uni On the bench, the manager could rely on world-cla

ack-up men in Teddy Sheringham, Ole Gunnar
olskjaer, Jordi Cruyff and the recently signed Jesper
lomqvist should injuries threaten the team's progress.
How he would need them as an astonishing year
rogressed. Solskjaer proved the point by coming off
he bench and scoring four times in the last 10 minutes
n United's stunning 8-1 destruction of a hapless
ottingham Forest on February 6. Critics of the
modern game say that United bought the success that
ame the club's way, but this is not borne out by history.
lackburn spent a vast fortune and were consigned to
vision One, Arsenal, Chelsea and Newcastle all went
or the chequebook and won nothing.

September saw United in 9th position with a
4-1 victory over Charlton—three goals coming
in 10 minutes – and though they slipped up
badly at Arsenal, losing 3-0, the defeat seemed
to shake them up. In October, they tested
he patience of the Saints at Southampton who felt
he full force of the revival, dispatched 3-0 at The Dell
hich is always a tricky day out for United. Wimbledon
ere slaughtered 5-1 and Everton put to the sword 4-

1 at Goodison. The Reds soared to second position and
never left the top three for the rest of the season.

The European campaign was also looking good.
United had beaten LKS Lodz 2-0 on aggregate, drawn
3-3 in a thrilling match with Barcelona and 2-2 with
Bayern Munich before demolishing Brondby 6-2 in
Denmark and 5-0 at home. Ferguson was developing
his squad rotation system with great effect, resting key
players and relying on the bench to help the team
maintain the challenge. There were risks in this of
course. Over the past ten years, the League Cup has
traditionally been sacrificed for the greater prizes, but
the FA Cup is a different matter. A day out to Wembley
in May is always a romantic affair and one that has a
special significance in the hearts of fans and players
alike, so Ferguson's team selection was to prove vital.
There would be many times during the season when
he would cause a few raised eyebrows among United's
followers with his selections.

There had been no thoughts of a treble at this time
– such ponderings were a mere distraction and
dangerous – but a repeat of the Double was certainly
looking a possibility as United went into cruise control

## FA Cup

| Jan 3 | Middlesbrough(3) | H | W | 3-1 |
| Jan 24 | Liverpool(4) | H | W | 2-1 |
| Feb 14 | Fulham(5) | H | W | 1-0 |
| Mar 7 | Chelsea(6) | H | D | 0-0 |
| Mar 10 | Chelsea(6R) | A | W | 2-0 |
| Apr 11 | Arsenal(SF) (at Villa Park) | N | D | 0-0 |
| Apr 14 | Arsenal(SFR) (at Villa Park) | N | W | 2-1 |
| May 22 | Newcastle(F) (at Wembley) | N | W | 2-0 |

## European Cup

| Aug 12 | LKS Lodz (Q) | H | W | 2-0 |
| Aug 26 | LKS Lodz (Q) | A | D | 0-0 |
| Sep 16 | Barcelona | H | D | 3-3 |
| Sep 30 | Bayern Munich | A | D | 2-2 |
| Oct 21 | Brondby | A | W | 6-2 |
| Nov 4 | Brondby | H | W | 5-0 |
| Nov 25 | Barcelona | A | D | 3-3 |
| Dec 9 | Bayern Munich | H | D | 1-1 |
| Mar 3 | Inter Milan (QF) | H | W | 2-0 |
| Mar 17 | Inter Milan (QF) | A | D | 1-1 |
| Apr 7 | Juventus (SF) | H | D | 1-1 |
| Apr 21 | Juventus (SF) | A | W | 3-2 |
| May 26 | Bayern Munich (F) (at Nou Camp) | N | W | 2-1 |

in the initial rounds. Home advantage was a help, and Bryan Robson's Middlesbrough took the first beating 3-1 with goals from Cole, Irwin and Giggs. Another unthinkable comeback against Liverpool to win 2-1 at Old Trafford followed, and then Fulham succumbed to an Andy Cole goal in the fifth round. United were through to the sixth to face Chelsea, a team which had flourished into an attractive attacking outfit under Gianluca Vialli, but one the Manchester club had got the measure of the previous season when they spanked the Londoners 5-3 at Stamford Bridge. A 0-0 draw in the first game forced United to travel south for the replay. Two goals from Yorke put paid to Vialli's hopes of a giantkilling and a titanic clash with Arsenal beckoned United in the semi-final.

In the League, Ferguson's tactics were tested but proved to be sound. United were winning crucial matches such as the March 13 victory against Newcastle 2-1. The Magpies' boss Ruud Gullit summed up the opposition that day as: "The best team we have faced all season." Praise indeed from the guru of "sexy football". On April 17, Teddy Sheringham and Solskjaer replaced the rested Yorke and Cole on the front-line and Sherry proceeded to bang one home against Sheffield Wednesday, then set up two more for the Norwegian and Scholes. United were at the top and fighting for every point.

Roy Keane was now proving to be one of the best investments United had ever made. He was the natural captain and displayed a passion which filtered through the team and down to the crowds that packed Old Trafford every week. He was the pivotal force on which United drove forward. As he said at the time: "We never go on to the pitch with worries about losing, only winning."

By March, the team was facing the real prospect of a treble. Top of the League, two games away from Wembley in the FA Cup and a massive Champions League Cup quarter-final against Inter Milan at Old Trafford. Yorke won that one with two goals and a trip to Italy clinched it 3-1 on aggregate.

Now United supporters knew something special was on, though they still only whispered the word "Treble". United's battle with Arsenal in the semi-final was monumental. The Gunners held United to a 0-0 draw at Villa Park and the north-south struggle had to continue. United took it after Beckham's astonishing 30-yard curling shot which left Arsenal 'keeper Seaman for dead and then a wonder-goal from Ryan Giggs - a piece of football magic which leaves nothing more to be said about how Ferguson's kids were growing into a force which could take on any team.

What followed for the team, the club, and the millions of fans who support The Reds was astonishing. The Championship was won on May 15. The Reds took

on Spurs at Old Trafford needing a win to destroy Arsenal's challenge. Goals by David Beckham and Andy Cole brought the trophy back to Manchester. Round one was sorted.

Round two. United faced Newcastle at Wembley in the FA Cup Final on May 22. Despite the loss of midfield maestro Roy Keane through injury after eight minutes, Ferguson brought on Teddy Sheringham. The striker proved his worth by scoring almost as soon as he walked on the pitch. The Reds took the game 2-0. It wasn't a classic match, but two out of the treasured three titles were in the bag. Manchester had to wait though for the Big One - the clash with Bayern Munich. It came on Wednesday May 26.

United were the underdogs and as the game got underway it was clear The Reds were suffering. A goal conceded early on was a disaster, and though the team had most of the possession, The Reds seemed to be fighting a lost cause. Chances came and went for Cole. United looked out of it, stifled by the German resilience.

Then the Ferguson factor kicked in - he sent on Teddy Sheringham and Solskjaer as a desperate attempt to second guess the Germans. It worked. Sheringham lashed home an equaliser in injury time and United fans were looking forward to taking the opposition in the "golden goal" extra time period.

It was an amazing night for every English football fan, but one man who was there sums up the experience for us. Sports journalist and lifelong United fan John Evans had travelled to Barcelona on a wing and a prayer with his brothers to watch the biggest game of their lives. This is his report: "It was awesome. United certainly like to take you through the mill, but if they do what they did tonight, who cares?

"I'd never been so convinced in my life that we were losing the game. We weren't in it. To score one when we did was joy on a level I've never known. We didn't even have time to celebrate Teddy's cracker before we got the corner. I turned to my brother Mark and said: "Marky, this one's going in as well."

"He looked at me as if I was mad. The next thing I knew he had his arms around me, crying like a baby. To be honest, I was doing the same. Every time I think of it, I just smile - I can't help it. And if I'm not smiling I'm filling up. Truly stupendous.

"We've all known what it's like to sit back and watch Liverpool win things, go down to the Second Division, struggle to ever mount a challenge in the League, let alone the big one. And this was the biggest of the big ones. What must Sir Matt have made of that - I'm sure he had something to do with it."

Whether he did or didn't, Sir Matt would have been as proud of his players as Alex Ferguson was. His first words to the world after the final whistle were a little crude, but they said it all: "Football - b***** hell!" The next thing he said was: "I'm so proud of my boys." Alex, so are we.

Stam leads the players across the pitch in the earlier match against Bayern Munich in December.

A dream team – Paul Scholes...

...'Denis Irwin

...'Ryan Giggs

...'David Beckham

...'Andy Cole

...'Peter Schmeichel

...'Jesper Blomqvist

...'Roy Keane

...'Dwight Yorke

'Jaap Stam applauds the fans for their support.

The war zone. In the heat of the battle against Liverpool in September, 1998, Keane was a majestic figure and crucial to United's title challenge.

Midfield dynamo Paul Scholes faces up to a Charlton attack in 1998.

United faced the might of Inter Milan in March in Italy and the passion shows.

It's in the bag. Schmeichel's celebrations were legendary.

David Beckham kept his cool against Bayern in the biggest game of his life.

Photo: Action Press

Jaap Stam's resilience at the back against Bayern Munich was a masterful display.

Photo: Action Press

Ole,Ole,Ole! Solksjaer stamped himself in the hist

with his amazing comeback goal in injury time to win The European Cup. What a moment to cherish for him and the fans!

Unconfined joy as United clinch the European Cup.

Photo: Action Press

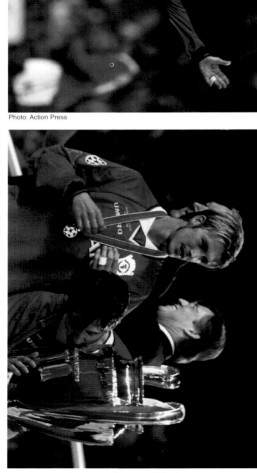

A kiss for the Cup, the Treble, and a priceless medal to boot.

Bayern Munich players are devastated after United snatched the Cup.

Now you're gonna believe us – we went and won the lot!

The deadly duo, Yorke and Cole, lift the biggest trophy of their careers.

Stop for The Reds. These youngsters will never forget that night.

Teddy went to Man U and he won it all...

Reaching for the stars... fans say thanks for everything.

He's a main man! Dwight Yorke is on cloud nine as United bring home the goodies.

Ole Solskjaer and David Beckham salute the fans on their return.

This is for you. Alex Ferguson hangs on to the biggest prize.

# Dreamland

From a bombed-out shell when Busby took over in 1946, Old Trafford has been redeveloped steadily into a super-modern stadium, now known universally as The Theatre Of Dreams. This picture was taken in 1969. Some great names were to follow in the footsteps of that European Cup winning team.

The old Scoreboard End of Old Trafford was a favourite haunt of the United faithful.

United's ground staff sprucing up Old Trafford for the 1966 World Cup.

The Munich clock will always be there, but the development of Old Trafford became a serious business.

The new cantilevered stand started the modern transformation of Old Trafford in 1967.

# On The Move...

Success at United brought huge rewards off the pitch, but the cars the players chose reflected each personality at the club – from Best's top of the range sports models to the more humble choice of Nobby Stiles. Here we take a journey with the stars and their cars.

On a roll. United boss Matt Busby leaves Old Trafford in his Rolls Royce after learning he had been granted a place on the Board in 1971.

Midfield dynamo Nobby Stiles tinkers under the bonnet of his Austin 1100.

## STYLE WATCH CARS, CARS, CARS

Best shows off his latest supercar, a Jaguar XJ6 in 1976 after he joined Fulham. The star could still cut a dash on and off the field despite his previous problems at Old Trafford.

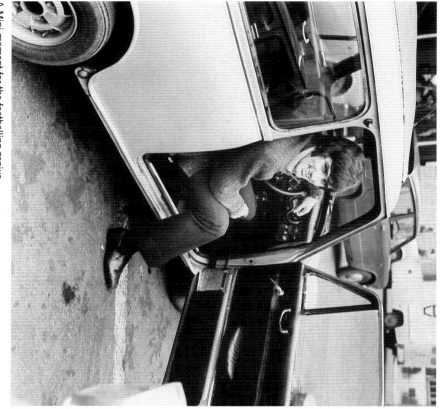

A Mini moment for the footballing genius.

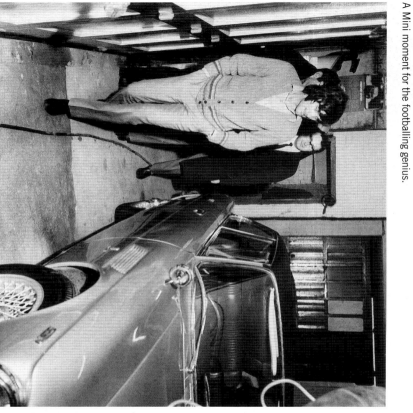

Eyeing up his latest acquisition in '69 – a beautiful Iso Rivolta.

Best's Lotus Europa always caused a stir in Manchester in 196

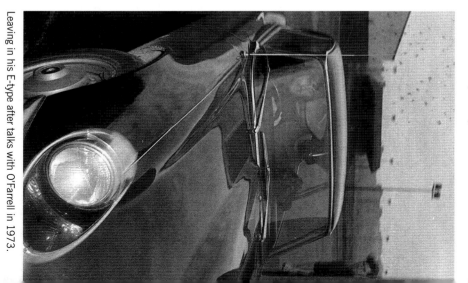

Leaving in his E-type after talks with O'Farrell in 1973.

Sitting pretty – David Herd and his MG in 1968.

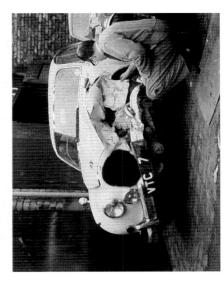

Brian Kidd sits it out in his Triumph Herald in 1970.

Best's jag under repair after a crash in 1967.

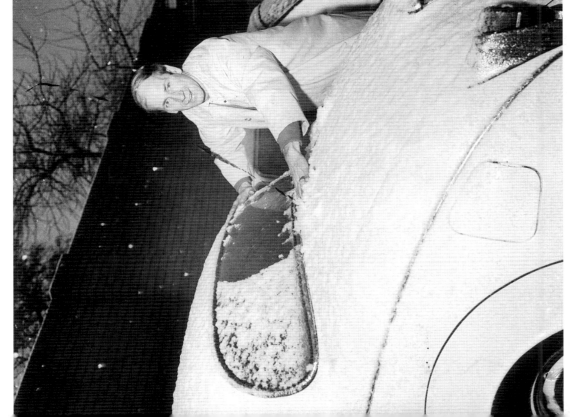

Bobby beats the big freeze with his Jaguar in 1970.

Fit for The King. Law arrives home in 1970 – the year he was transfer listed.

Top of the range – Willie Morgan arrives at the ground for training with his new Daimler Sovereign in 1979.

Striker Sammy McIlroy with his new Vauxhall in 1973.

Gordon Hill with his wife Jackie and their vintage Rolls Royce in 1976.

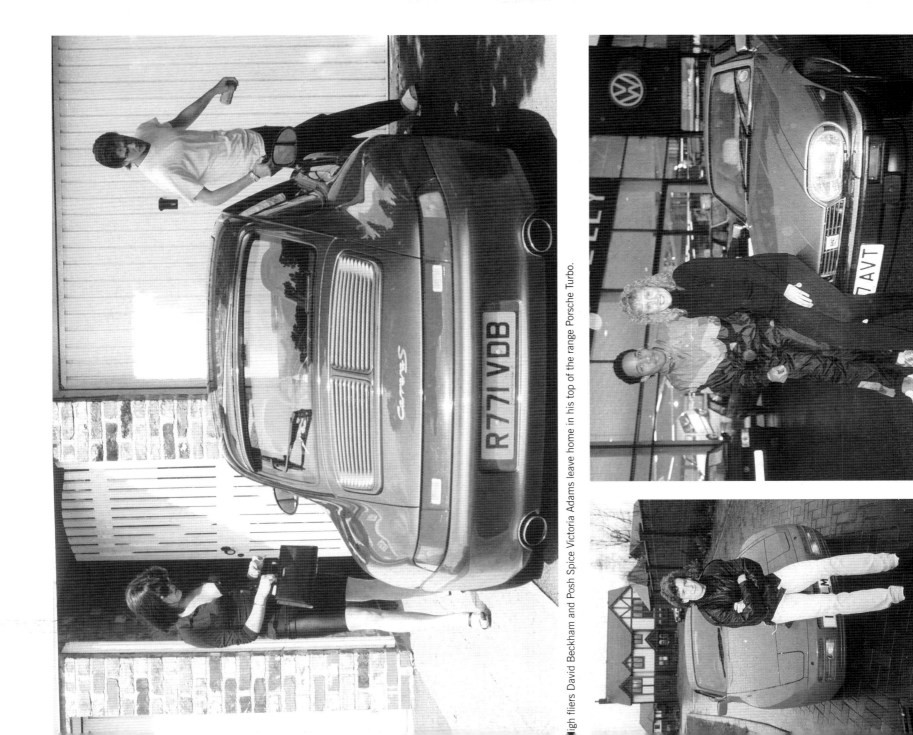

High fliers David Beckham and Posh Spice Victoria Adams leave home in his top of the range Porsche Turbo.

Paul Ince tries a new Jaguar XJS for size with his girlfriend in 1991.

"Sparky" Hughes and his new Porsche.

# Friends In High Places…

The power, the glamour and the success of Manchester United meant that the players became stars in their own right, mixing with the rich and famous from politics and showbusiness. They all wanted to be associated with the best club in the land.

The team was feted by Prime Minister Harold Wilson at Downing Street in 1970.

Charlton meets youngsters during Boys Club Week in 1967.

The PM hosted a reception for Matt Busby in 1967.

United fan Marlene Dietrich met with Busby and Coronation Street star Violet Carson in 1965

George Best with pop star Sting and actress Francesca Annis at the 1985 premiere of the movie Dune.

American singer Andy Williams dropped into Old Trafford by helicopter to meet the team and their families in 1974.

You've a long way to go, son. Busby is unimpressed as pint-sized comedy star Jimmy Clitheroe "joins" The Reds 1965.

Kneesy does it. Busby with Ken Dodd and Joe Mercer during the 1966 election.

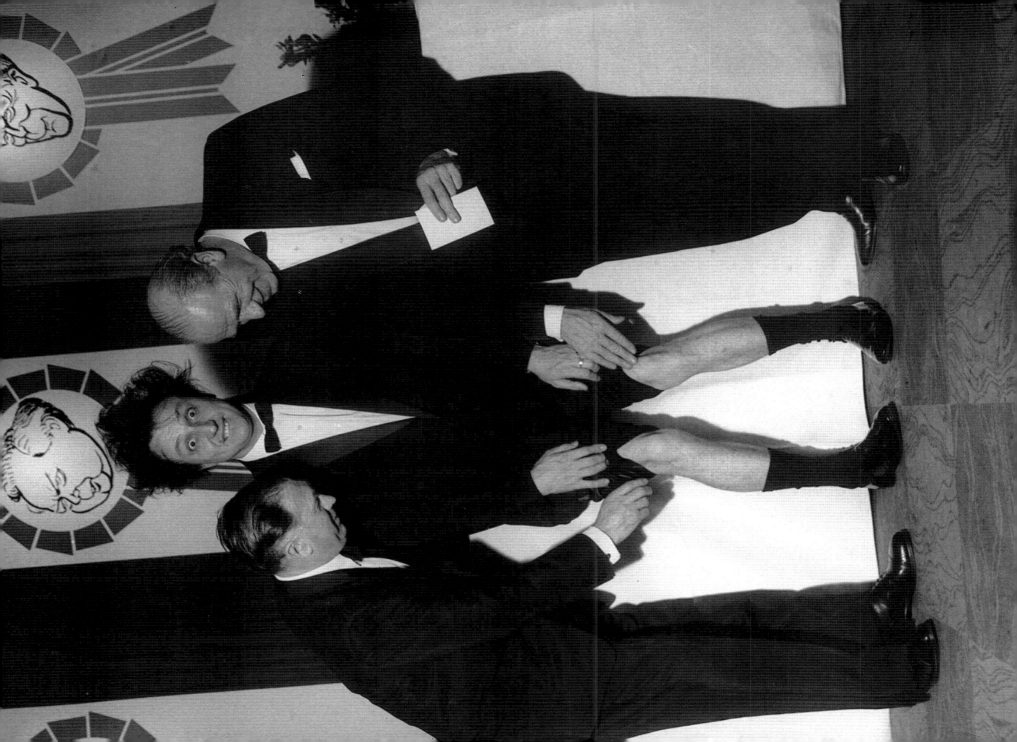

# "We'll Support You Ever More"

Millions follow United worldwide these days, but the club has always had a fanatical following at home as well. During the Seventies crowd trouble blighted football and United didn't escape the problem. The fans now just enjoy the superb playing skills.

Police hold back the crowds after United's victory over Leicester City in 1963 and left, triumphant supporters return to Manchester

"We've won the Cup!". Jubilant fans pour out of Manchester's Central Station after watching United at Wembley in 1963

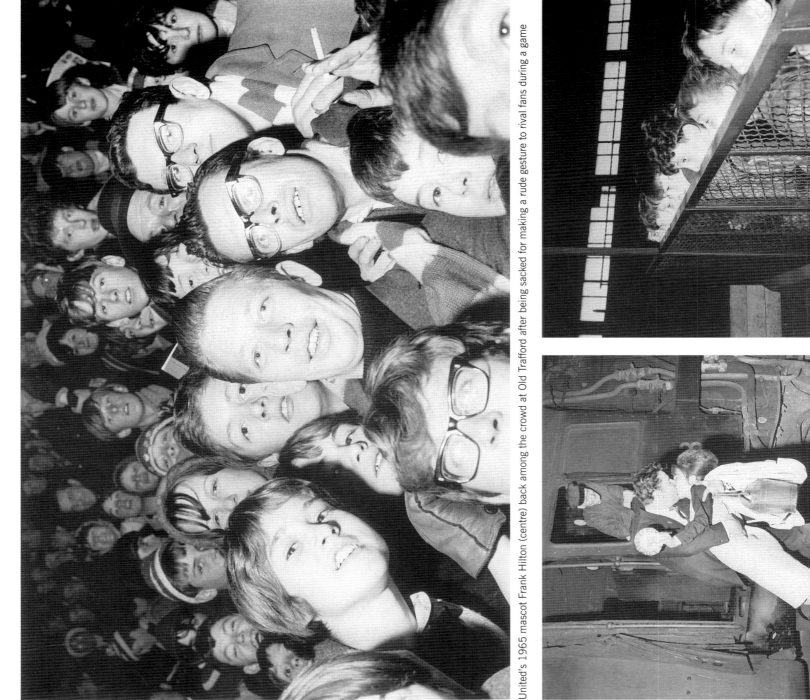

United's 1965 mascot Frank Hilton (centre) back among the crowd at Old Trafford after being sacked for making a rude gesture to rival fans during a game

Adoring schoolboy United fans watch their heroes train at Old Trafford

Sealed with a kiss. Two United fans celebrate the '63 Cup win.

Even United officials signed autographs.

It's all a bit too much for one young fan at Old Trafford.

Girls scream for George as the team return from playing Benfica in Lisbon in 1966.

We did it! United fans pour off the tra

ester after United's historic European Cup victory over Benfica in 1968. Now, 31 years later, we know how they felt.

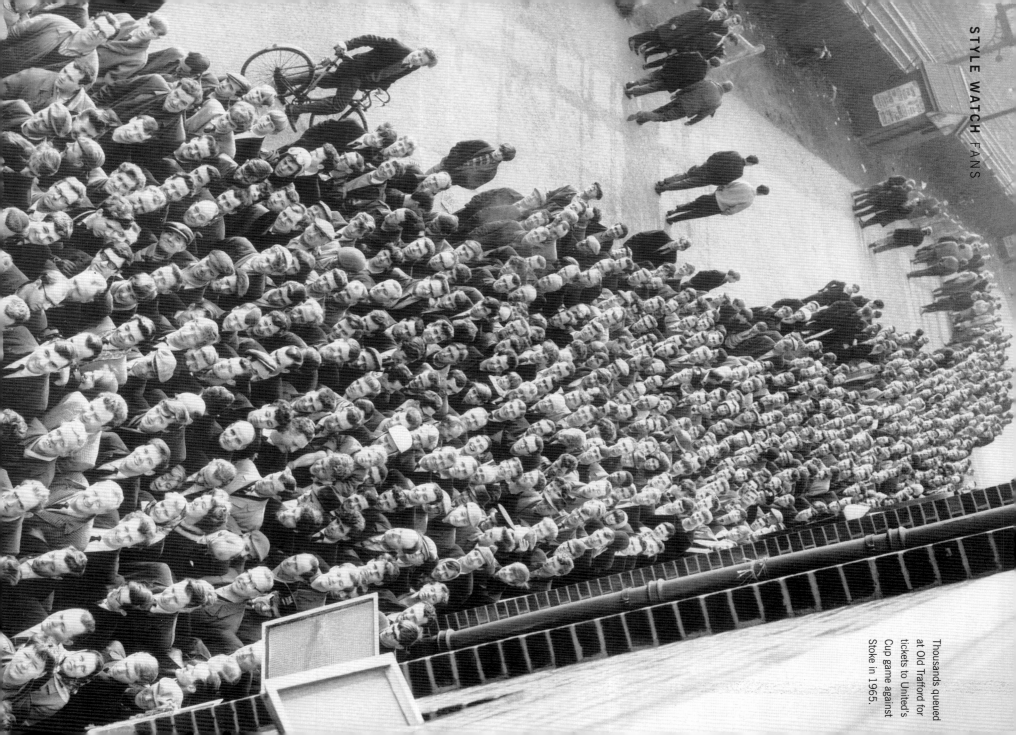

Thousands queued at Old Trafford for tickets to United's Cup game against Stoke in 1965.

A fan jumps for joy after getting her ticket to the '68 European Cup final

You're never too young to follow The Reds. These two got a Cup ticket in 1965.

A youngster got on his bike to grab a ticket to see The Reds in 1962.

Fans wait patiently for European Cup Final tickets at Old Trafford

Trouble flares between fans during United's match against Arsenal at Highbury in 1981.

A fan is ejected from Old Trafford at the height of the crowd troubles in 1974.

Fans invade the pitch, a re

The police check the mis

...rence at matches, during United's game against Southampton in 1977.

...n by the crowd while more fans are collared and United players try to calm the tense situation.

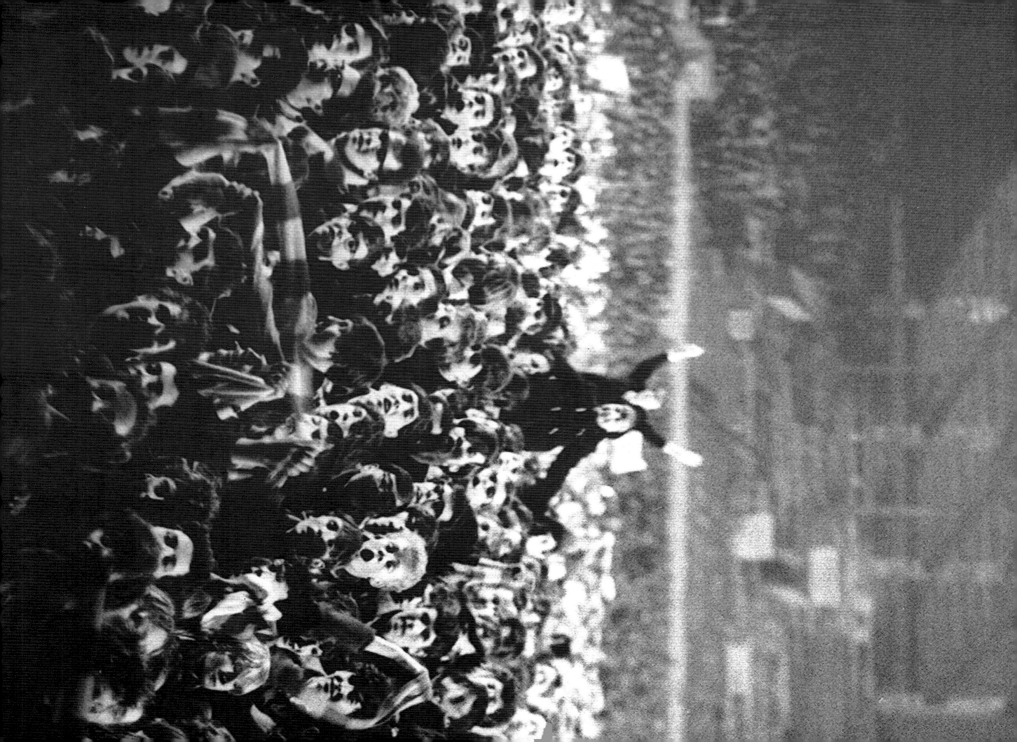

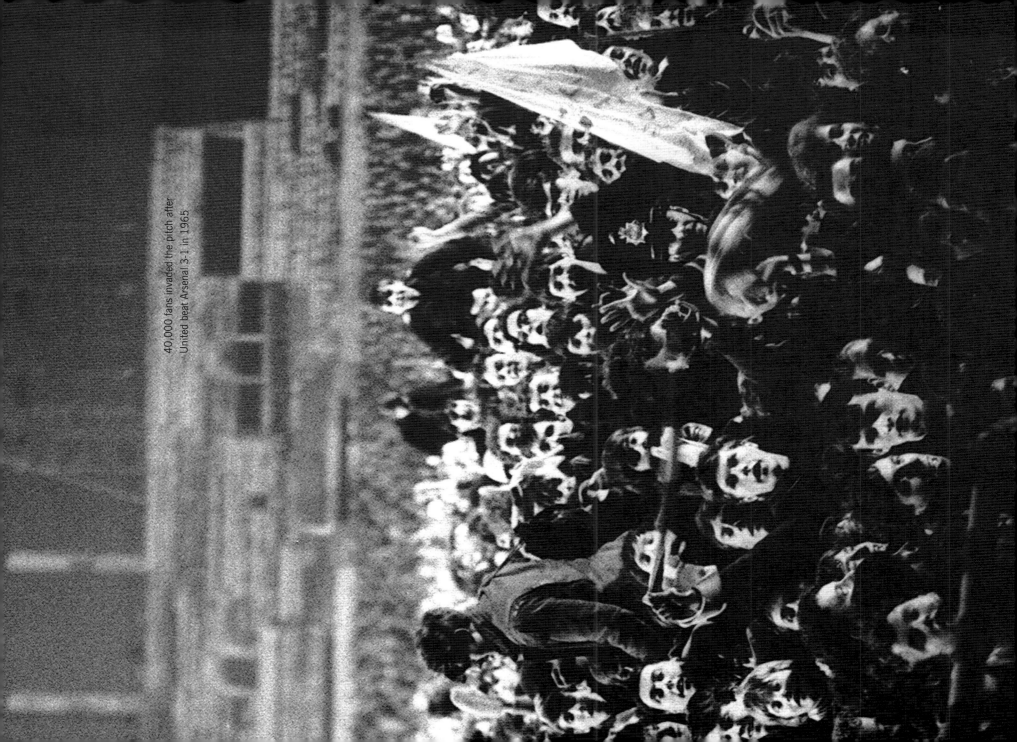

40,000 fans invaded the pitch after
United beat Arsenal 3-1 in 1965

Ryan Giggs introduces young fans to Fred The Red at the souvenir shop.

Peter Schmeichel and the team meet fans to sign autographs.

It's agony and ecstasy for United fans again...

The feeling's mutual...as United players pay tribute to the fans and their loyal

...onship between the club and its supporters has always been crucial to the team's success on the pitch.